DR. KRITSICK'S

TENDER LOVING CAT CARE

The Concerned Owner's Guide
to the Growth, Nurturance,
and Day-to-Day Care
of a Cat

Stephen M. Kritsick, D.V.M.

Introduction by John F. Kullberg, President, ASPCA

Linden Press/Simon & Schuster
New York 1986

Published by Linden Press/Simon & Schuster
A Division of Simon & Schuster, Inc.
Simon & Schuster Building
Rockefeller Center
1230 Avenue of the Americas
New York, New York 10020
LINDEN PRESS/SIMON & SCHUSTER and colophon are trademarks of
Simon & Schuster, Inc.

ILLUSTRATIONS BY WENDY FROST

Designed by Levavi & Levavi
Manufactured in the United States of America

10 9 8 7 6 5 4 3 2

Library of Congress Cataloging in Publication Data
Kritsick, Stephen.
  Dr. Kritsick's Tender loving cat care.

  Includes index.
  1. Cats. II. Cats—Diseases. I. Title. II. Title:
Doctor Kritsick's Tender loving cat care.
SF447.K75   1986   636.8   85-23996
ISBN: 0-671-46725-5

This book is not meant to be a substitute for the medical advice of your veterinarian. Your pet should receive regular checkups, and you should consult your veterinarian if you notice any symptoms that may require medical diagnosis and treatment.

To my great-aunt Lillian
and my niece Allison Kate

ACKNOWLEDGMENTS

Throughout the years I've been in practice, I have been fortunate to work closely with many fine colleagues and on many wonderful pets. All of these have contributed to the circumstances in my life and career that have led to this book's publication. But special acknowledgment is due to Drs. Florence Barton and Jean Holzworth, whose love of cats was inspirational early on, and to Drs. Gordon Robinson, Susan Cotter, William Hardy, Jerry Williams and Peter Borchelt for their help in the preparation of this book.

Thanks to everyone at Linden Press, and to Mindy Werner.

Finally, I thank my family for their continued support and love.

INTRODUCTION

Perhaps because they are more adaptable to the peripatetic life-
style of most of us, cats have dramatically come into their own as
the pet of choice for most Americans. Today more than 40 million
of these marvelous and complex creatures are very much in need
of our tender loving care.

Many books on cat care are currently available, but Dr. Kritsick's eminently readable, carefully researched, intelligently organized and warmly personal achievement has resulted in a long
overdue volume that is for felines what Dr. Spock provided several decades ago for babies.

Those of us who have been fortunate to know Steve Kritsick
through his professional career as a veterinary clinician and na-
tionally renowned animal advocate are well aware of the depth
of veterinary experience and compassionate care behind *Tender
Loving Cat Care.* He has served on the veterinary staffs of three of
the largest animal hospitals in the world: the Angell Memorial
Animal Hospital of the Massachusetts Society for the Prevention

of Cruelty to Animals in Boston, and New York City's two largest veterinary hospitals, the Animal Medical Center and the Henry Bergh Memorial Animal Hospital of the American Society for the Prevention of Cruelty to Animals. Not only has he cared for literally tens of thousands of cats, dogs and other animals from every strata and substrata of society, but he has also had the good input of professional advice and friendship from some of the most brilliant animal care practitioners in the world. We and our feline companions are the fortunate recipients of Dr. Kritsick's experience and insight so thoughtfully and readably shared with us in the pages of this important compendium of tender loving cat care.

If you care about cats, and particularly if for the first time you are thinking about sharing your life with a cat, read *Tender Loving Cat Care* through from cover to cover. Whether you are a new caretaker of cats or one who has known the special pleasures and responsibilities of cat care for many years, this book will provide many insights. And then keep it handy: I believe you will find it your most useful reference when responding to any cat that requires your intelligent protection and understanding.

JOHN F. KULLBERG
President
The American Society for the
Prevention of Cruelty to Animals

CONTENTS

PREFACE

As an aspiring animal doctor, I apprenticed when in high school at a veterinary clinic where all the cats were kept in a separate room. Frankly, I dreaded my encounters with those creatures. When I cleaned their cages, they set up a nightmarish clamor with their yowling and, on top of that, I got swiped numerous times by their claws. I also had some dopey notion that men— real men—weren't *supposed* to like cats. So when the cats acted up, my distaste was reinforced—and my plans were made clear: when I became a veterinarian, my practice would be limited to treating dogs and horses, which, in my adolescent mind, went with maleness as did the Marlboro Man and his cigarette. I went through school accordingly, determined to stick to dogs, horses and "manhood" à la John Wayne.

Then I began my internship at the Angell Memorial Animal Hospital in Boston. In no time I was under the benign spell of Dr. Jean Holzworth, a devoted advocate of cats as well as one of the foremost feline experts in the world. She awakened in me an understanding of the feline species. She demonstrated the details of their physical beauty, pointing out in many cases the astonishing symmetry of their markings. She trained me to watch for their sensitivity, to admire their agile movements and luxurious softness. I learned that cats come in an endless variety, from the feisty to the marvelously sweet.

Today, though I see as many dogs as cats, I actually prefer treating felines. Since I've been in practice, a cat is the only pet I've owned. I enjoy getting to know the feline—each with its unique personality. It takes time to build trust with a cat, but as millions of cat owners can attest, it is time well spent. As strongly as I recommend cats, however, it behooves you to know the pros and cons of sharing your home with a feline.

A man I know—the proud father of two young girls—swears that the decision to acquire and rear a pet is, altogether, a more serious matter than choosing to have a child. I'm not sure I would go quite as far as *that*. Yet my friend makes a point that is well taken. Far too many people have taken animals into their homes on a moment's notice (this seems, for some reason, to apply especially to cats), later—perhaps at the first broken vase—to turn them out on the streets or over to the local pound. But whether the expulsion is ruthlessly done or the product of grief doesn't matter in the least to the discarded and forlorn cat.

Let's get this straight: the joys of owning a member of the feline species are just about infinite and the obligations worth every bit of time, tumult and trouble. But no *domestic* animal, not even the so-called "independent," resourceful cat, which is the focus of these pages, can get along without concerted, loving care from its owners. When you adopt that little fluff of fur, you had better have a heartfelt commitment to its future life, its happiness and its welfare. As you take it into your home right now, the creature is probably small, maybe tiny. In many ways, it's totally at your mercy; in any event, you want its love. You can get it. But just like a child, the animal must receive affection or it's not very likely to give it back. Just like a child, the animal must have care. And care—the love and care of cats—is what this book is about.

Please do not use this book in place of your veterinarian. It is meant to increase your awareness of the feline with which you live and to guide you in aiding a sick or injured animal in an emergency situation. In using this book I hope you will become more safety-conscious, and I believe that you and your pet will be rewarded with a happy and healthy lifetime together.

STEPHEN M. KRITSICK, D.V.M.
Senior Staff Clinician,
Henry Bergh Memorial Hospital,
American Society for the Prevention
   of Cruelty to Animals (ASPCA)
New York City, 1985

PART ONE

IN THE BEGINNING

DO YOU REALLY WANT
A CAT?

*U*ntil perhaps the last decade, the dog—bless its bountiful canine soul—reigned supreme as the most favored of household pets. After all, the dog is "man's best friend." (And to this day I haven't known a single cat that would mind relinquishing the title—though I'll have considerably more to say in these pages about the sometimes quixotic but always interesting nature of feline affections.)

Yet now, at least in the United States, cats are becoming the most popular of all domestic animals. Consider the bestsellerdom of the Garfield book series, the immense appeal of "Morris," the whopping success of *Cats,* the Broadway show. We have cat cards at every turn, cat calendars, a plethora of books about cats. Each and every one of these has both sparked and reflected the boom in cat popularity, though which really came first, chicken or egg (or cat, as it were), is impossible to say. Undoubtedly, the frenzy of contemporary American life has some bearing on the phenomenon. We look for a haven from the whirlwind, and pets provide us with love, solace and comfort that are just about unconditional. For dispelling loneliness, the human connection can never be matched, but it is nonetheless true that in comparison with people, pets—be they of the canine or feline variety—can hardly be called demanding. Give an animal shelter, food, water, plus doses of relaxed affection and you'll get a loyal companion to the death. For people who live alone—and we know that their numbers are increasing—a pet can fill the blackest void; its presence, too, can strengthen the ties that bind together the closest and warmest of families. None of this is mere speculation: medically, it's been proven that animals are assets to our health, that they enrich and prolong our lives. Still, except in rural areas, people just don't seem to have the time they once had to devote to a pet.

That the cat doesn't have to be walked surely makes it the easiest of all pets to care for. (I refer, of course, only to mammals of high intelligence who present a full range of emotional response. Turtles don't count here.) The procedure of "housebreaking," often arduous in the case of the dog, is virtually unnecessary with a cat, which, after its first introduction or two, is drawn to a box full of litter as easily as metal to magnet. Not only are its toilet habits fastidious, it is scrupulously clean in general. In fact, grooming itself is part of its very instinctual life: if you have to bathe a cat—and some people never do—it certainly isn't often. Needless to say, no possibility exists of leaving a dog alone for a weekend while you scoot off on a trip. Yet, a cat *can* fend for itself if it's only for a couple of days, providing that an ample supply of food and water is there for its consumption. As for an animal's need for a bit of the outdoor life, you're stuck in the case of the dog—not only with its toilet habits, but with a definite requirement for regular extensive exercise. With the exception of an unneutered "tomcat" (about which more later), any cat can live its entire life, happily and well, confined within the walls of your house, your apartment, your room. And at least in the urban setting, a cat is far less annoying to neighbors.

These then are the physical basics that add up to easy care. But this placid picture has another side. Litter, for instance—whether it be in the form of small clay pebbles, sawdust or whatever— must be changed often and the feline is prone to kick it all over the place and trek it everywhere. Cats shed their hair, some more heavily than others, but nonetheless, it's a nuisance to clean up, and for those with allergies or respiratory difficulties, it can be a serious problem. There is the cost of food, which is minimal but at the same time an extra expense that must be considered, surely by anyone on a budget. Money is obviously involved in trips to the veterinarian as well, which, never mind illness or injury, are a requisite part of raising a cat. Finally, the scenario becomes more muddled still when one starts to take into account the feline personality.

To this day, the cat is an animal that, no matter how well ensconced in the household, how genuinely loving a member of the family, is still attuned to the call of the wild. Its ancestors (and distant cousins) were and are carnivorous hunters that, in their natural habitat—the lion excepted—go about their daily business alone. In the wild, the feline species is almost never part of a pack, which is to say that, the lion and its pride aside, it forms no alliances with its kind. In the face of such roots, it is astonishing that cats are capable of forming bonds of affection with human beings. Yet, wonder of wonders, they repeatedly do.

Anyone who is not prepared, however, to accept the fundamentals of cathood had best steer clear. You cannot wish away
the wild solitary heritage of the feline and its primitive role as
hunter. Take it or leave it, that is the crux of its most conspicuous
characteristics, whether amusing, lovable or a pain in the neck.
In the truest light, those characteristics—baffling and provocative
though they may be—are nothing more than the remnants of
behavior patterns that were once part of nature's awesome design
for feline survival.

If you have any familiarity with cats whatsoever, you already
know that each is a born eccentric, an unalloyed nonconformist
who marches (or to be more accurate, quietly creeps) to the beat
of a different drummer; and you'll be doing terrifically as an
owner if you can be sure that, most of the time, that drummer is
you. Be patient enough and you can teach the feline to fetch and
retrieve small objects, for instance; an occasional cat will even
"sit." Yet, more often than not—exactly when you want to show
off to your friends its repertoire of adorable tricks—the cat will
turn its back and stubbornly refuse. It didn't do that yesterday!
Well then, is the feline stupid?

No. Cats are simply inconsistent. The cat discriminates to the
extreme. With the best disposition in the world, the most gentle,
responsive cat of them all may select one person for affection and
coldly shun another. (Beyond human ken is the uncanny attraction of some cats toward people who absolutely loathe them.)
Even in relationship to its owner, the cat remains mercurial, com-
plying all right with its owner's wishes—if it happens to be in the
mood. Perhaps having survived so long by its wits in the wild
without help from so much as fellow beast, the feline species,
over the years, developed a kind of accompaniment to its understandable independence, that which we invariably see in today's
domestic cat as a powerful streak of the perverse. Never mistake
that for a lack of intelligence. It's just that a cat is . . . well . . .
an animal of another color.

Naturally enough, in the manner of people, some cats are just
plain dull. But speaking in general, the domestic cat—to one
degree or another—has a fabulous flair for fun. In a dizzying
blur, the cat whips across the room driven by a burst of maniacal
energy. It whirls, it pounces, it dances about, it hops like a
drunken kangaroo. And it *climbs*. The problem is that the endear-

ing behavior that can have you in stitches one minute can get totally out of hand the next. Is the cat inquisitive? Don't underestimate the negative potential of that extremely amusing trait (shades once more of the primeval search for food). And always understand that the independence of the feline decidedly has its limits. Left by itself too long, allowed to get lonely, piqued and bored, many a cat will go on a binge of curiosity, and while climbing about, looking to entertain itself, will wreak havoc. Time and again I've seen it happen: when the blitz hits the living room, the laughs—if not always the lovable cat, though I've known that to happen too—go straight out the window.

Some cats are simply more needy than others, and more energetic as well. Combine those two qualities with a large quotient of curiosity and you *could* have a lot of trouble. Moreover, cats have uncommonly regular habits. If accustomed to frequent human company, the feline can become highly upset should the attention be suddenly withdrawn. It can then show that upset with considerable destructive vigor aided by—as if you hadn't already guessed—its intractable need to sharpen its claws and also, through scratching, to express its territoriality. That's what it's doing when it rubs against the furniture too. Apparently the cat, in its very own animal way, wants to leave its mark.

These tendencies—to sharpen its claws and to mark its territory—can be handled well enough (short of declawing the cat, a procedure, by the way, that I almost always oppose); they can also be handled badly, which is something I've usually seen occur when an individual tries to force a cat to go against its feline grain. In my section on training (see page 82), you'll find some detailed suggestions in regard to what I like to refer to as "managing" feline behavior. You can modify those methods or follow them to the letter. But, especially for the novice owner, I can't stress enough that without a grasp of the central concept, just about all you can do is *manage* feline behavior; nothing you can do is going to change its stripes. You can't "break" a cat as you can a horse or make it comply as you can a dog—not to the same degree. And furthermore, in my opinion, words like "bad" are unfairly applied to behavior so deeply connected to biological imperatives. There is no possible way that the impulse to scratch can be made to disappear (as can, for instance, inappropriate barking in the case of the dog). But you can condition the cat to a scratching post instead of to your antique credenza. The point is that when there's a feline will, there's bound to be a determined feline way. Get that will and way to correspond with your own and both you and the cat can emerge from what could turn into a terrible battle as contented, satisfied winners.

Having said all this, I must add that as long as there are cats, there are going to be exceptions. For every amiable feline that stays off the furniture, obediently eats its food and never, in an act of petulance, so much as soils the rug, there is another that persists in misbehaving. Almost always, however, there is an explanation and a way of correcting, through proper conditioning, what the cat is doing. Obviously, were these potential problems truly formidable, there wouldn't be such a wave of cat popularity or so many happy owners. To be sure, owning a cat calls for some sacrifice; you might ask yourself if there's anything worth having that doesn't. Besides, I never meant to promise the proverbial rose garden, only warm good feelings and love.

Can the feline actually feel love? We can speak of feline affections and intense attachments to people without being particularly fanciful, and there's simply no doubt that anyone watching a cat raise its paw and tenderly touch its owner's face has got plenty of cause to wonder.

Leave the cosmic import of "love" in the province of the human species or transfer the emotion to the cat if you will. But if the animal has a need to be "parented," which it clearly does, and the owner a need to "parent," that ought to be enough. It ought to be enough, moreover, if *you* are able to love the cat and let the feline's feelings go with all the rest that makes up feline mystery. I don't know anyone who has ever lost by knowing that it's better to give than to receive.

The Responsible Cat Owner: Some Questions to Consider

Before you take the plunge, I ask you to indulge in some serious self-inquiry. For your own sake and the sake of the animal, *do not* acquire a cat without pondering answers to the following questions:

1. First question: Do you have enough space? Cramped living quarters are hard on *any* animal, the cat included. There are

no clear guidelines to follow—just use common sense. If your apartment gives you claustrophobia, it will do the same to the cat. While there are many happy, healthy cats living in small spaces, a younger animal will adapt more easily to its surroundings. So if you do live in a studio or small apartment, consider getting a kitten instead of an adult cat.

2. Are you the only one in the house who wants this animal? If so, forget it.

3. Do you have one of those jobs that are all consuming, that make for eighteen-hour days? The cat simply cannot abide seemingly unending solitude.

4. Does your job require a lot of traveling? No matter how much you want a cat, take a deep breath and pass.

5. How stable is your job and living situation in geographical terms? To say that a cat's home is its castle is putting it mildly. Sure, the cat can survive a move. But if you expect frequent upheavals, you can expect a discontented cat as well.

6. Can you afford a cat? To be sure, the cost of food and litter isn't very much, but add on medical care and you'll see that expenses can pile up. You could end up resenting the cat for cutting into your budget.

7. Do cats make good gifts? This is a corker, having to do with preserving friendship as well as bearing on the welfare of the cat. *Never* give a pet to someone unless he or she has given you the go sign.

Children and Pets

Anyone who is about to get a cat should also consider the presence of young children in the household. They can frighten a cat that may, under other circumstances, respond very well to humans. In cherubic innocence, a youngster can advance toward a cat very quickly in what might be taken for a threatening movement; it can pull the cat's tail, stick objects in its ears, embrace it too strongly, poke it, do anything that strikes the child's fancy. To the untutored child this is fun; to the cat it is not, and the most gentle, docile animal may respond with a bite or scratch.

And yet, having young children in the house is not a reason to reject the idea of getting a cat. On the contrary, the experience of owning a pet can be one of the unforgettable wonders of growing up, an unsurpassable way of learning about love, responsibility and general respect for life. Just be sure that the young child understands that he must be gentle with the pet. Then you can proceed to get a cat with confidence that you are providing your child with a special opportunity.

Having worked for many years on the television program "Romper Room," I've had the chance to observe very closely the interaction of children and animals and how this affects a child's relationships with other children. There is no doubt that relationships of all kinds are enhanced by contact between children and pets. Take just the simple process of sharing in the care and feeding of the cat. That alone stirs nurturing instincts in children which then extend to an overall kindness toward people. So please: once you know you want a cat, don't let unnecessary concerns override the value of the lessons about humanity that are there for your child to absorb.

Owning a cat can be instructive to children on so many other educational fronts. Encourage children to keep a daily log or diary about the cat and describe its activities and habits. Certainly, let the child participate in training and cleaning up after the pet, as well as feeding.

Just a few words of caution, however: if a child is under six years of age, never leave it alone with a pet. You don't want injuries to occur. Children should also be advised to practice good hygiene around cats. To be sure, warn them about scratches and bites, but do so with tact and sensitivity: you hardly want to instill unwarranted fears in the child.

WHERE TO GET A CAT

*M*ost of your doubts are resolved and your heart is set on getting a cat. Now where are you going to go? Be careful. The business of selecting a cat can—if you let it—become a touchy subject. Your best friend who owns an exquisite Russian Blue, your neighbor who has a worldly-wise Seal Point Siamese, will undoubtedly swear by the breeder, the pet shop, what have you, where they picked out their own animals.

I have no intention of quarreling with the virtues of purebred cats or the merits of dealing with a good honest breeder. Nonetheless, when people ask *my* opinion—and by reading this book you more or less have—I tell them to pay a visit to their local animal shelter, ASPCA or Humane Society. Millions of endearing, beautiful animals end up in these facilities. Just have a look. You'll find that the biggest problem is selecting only one pet, so great is the variety of cats and kittens waiting for a home. Yes, most of the felines are of mixed breeds. What of it? When it comes to affection and loyalty, it hardly makes a difference. And a mixed-breed cat can be beautiful.

If, however, you're seriously toying with the prospect of getting a purebred cat—possibly for show—I advise you to do some sound research. Find out about the different breeds. One excellent source of information is:

The Cat Fanciers Association
1309 Allaire Avenue
Ocean, New Jersey 07712
(201) 531-2390

There you can get specific breed information and official standards for show. Then proceed to do some thorough investigation into breeders. That will be your most reliable route when picking a purebred cat.

Cat magazines can be a source of information, too. Three of these are:

Cat Fancy Magazine
P.O. Box 6050
Mission Viejo, California 92690
(714) 240-6001

Cats Magazine
P.O. Box 37
Port Orange, Florida 32029
(904) 788-2770

Cat Fanciers Almanac
(C.F.A.)
1309 Allaire Avenue
Ocean, New Jersey 07712
(201) 531-2390

Now, far be it from me to tell you that if you're wandering by a pet shop and fall in love with the adorable cat in the window you should grit your teeth and walk on by. Just be advised that some pet stores are simply not reputable. The animals can be unhealthy. You won't notice it at first and the store owner surely won't tell you. As often as not, moreover, pet stores will sell "less desirable" purebred animals for a higher price than a breeder would charge. I'm not saying the animal wouldn't be lovable, but for the money you're putting out, the feline you choose ought to be show quality. The pet shop purebred usually isn't. So if what you want is a show quality cat, your best bet is to deal with an established breeder.

It's a rare occurrence, but because of "inbreeding," some pure-bred cats are predisposed to medical and behavior problems. Thus, *if you want a purebred cat, be sure to select a conscientious breeder.*

But I can't stress enough how lucky so many owners are in adopting felines from animal shelters. For some, the cost alone is advantage enough; most shelters charge a nominal fee for a pet which usually includes an initial vaccination and free spaying or neutering when the time is right. You can save $200 to $400 on the purchase price alone. (That's the cost of a purebred, all right!) Surely, that's money in the bank, which you can use to cover the pet's routine medical care expenses.

As you can tell, I'm prejudiced. I'm not so prejudiced, how-ever, that I won't tell the truth. Purebred cats can be glorious to look at and can make exceptionally affectionate pets. Yet it's also true that the personality characteristics of various feline breeds are not nearly so easy to identify as they are with the various breeds of dogs. In truth, there are all kinds of personalities among the cats in any given breed. Some of my favorite patients have been purebreds and never will I hold a feline's pedigree against the animal or its owner. But if it's a matter of niceness, cuteness or sheer lovability, it's not the breed that will make the difference.

And keep in mind that mixed breeds might have better disposi-
tions than purebreds, and may be healthier too.

Should you visit a shelter to adopt a cat, don't be surprised if
you get quite a bit of scrutiny. The ASPCA, for example, will
screen you to make sure that only responsible owners acquire
their pets. The situation of the unwanted animal is sad enough;
the screening process is to lessen the chances that a cat will be
returned after it has finally been given what it has every reason
to feel is love and shelter.

The classified section of your local newspaper, bulletin boards
in supermarkets and notices in veterinarians' offices are other fine
sources for pets. The Yellow Pages may carry ads as well. These
sources, in fact, may have one special advantage, particularly if
you're looking for a kitten: you can sometimes see the parents.
(Most breeders will have the parents there for viewing, too.) The
parents should look healthy, well treated and well fed. Talk with
their owner. You should feel satisfied that he or she is conscientious about proper sanitation, routine medical care and vaccinations. This will give you an indication of how the kitten has been
treated since birth, which will have a lot of bearing on the animal's personality. Also observe the behavior of your prospective
pet: the kitten should be affectionate and outgoing, and if kept
with its litter mates, should be sociable and compatible with the
others. Knowing the parents and/or the former owner can weight
the dice in your favor.

There is one more reason to raise the flag for the domestic
short- or long-haired cat. More purebred animals are bound,
eventually, to get a home. Mixed-breed animals simply aren't that
fortunate. Multitudes that end up in shelters are going to be
euthanatized (i.e., humanely put to sleep). Keep that in mind
when you make your decision.

Lost Cats

Our streets and countrysides are filled with stray animals trying
to survive on their own. A large percentage of these strays are
cats. Some have been heartlessly dumped by their owners and
left to fend for themselves; others have wandered away from
home. All are lost, lonely, usually hungry and bereaved. These
cats need help.

Should you notice a strange cat hanging out on your doorstep or in your backyard, first look to see if it is wearing a collar with an attached identification tag. The likelihood is that such a cat is lost rather than abandoned, and reuniting the pet with its owner will be a relatively simple task.

Observe the cat's overall condition. The healthier the cat appears to be, the more recently it can be assumed to have left its home. If you have your own cat(s), do not bring the animal into your house, especially if the stray appears unhealthy. It could transmit an infection or parasite infestation to your cat.

Should you decide to shelter the cat temporarily, provide the local animal organizations with as vivid a description of the stray as possible. You should notify the police too. You might also place an ad in a local newspaper, as well as put a notice on the bulletin boards of your veterinarian's office and supermarket. People who have lost a pet usually check with the local pound, the police and in the newspaper in the hope that someone has found their pet. Naturally, you should check the lost and found section of your local paper. If the cat is not wearing any identification and you are unable to locate the owner, call your local animal control officer or the ASPCA or pound to report the location of the stray and ask if the cat can be picked up. Otherwise you can bring the cat to the animal shelter yourself.

These steps may seem obvious. But I'm trying to stress that should you find a stray cat, you'd be doing the animal a great disservice to leave it on the street. There are well-meaning people —just like you and probably cat owners already—who are reluctant to turn a stray over to a shelter for fear that the animal will be euthanatized. However, at most shelters, the animals are kept for a reasonable amount of time, in the hopes that they'll be adopted. If and when euthanasia is carried out, it will be done humanely. This is by far kinder than allowing the cat to be abused and to die in the streets where it's not very likely it will have a chance.

Some people have had a wonderful stroke of good fortune in being adopted by such strays. Before you give the cat to a shelter, consider that the lost purring creature sitting on your doorstep might be your best bit of luck in an age.

KITTEN OR CAT?
MALE OR FEMALE?
OTHER COMMON
DILEMMAS

*P*robably nothing in the world—certainly nothing in the animal kindgom—is as thoroughly adorable as a soft baby kitten. Even some people who are prone to shun cats can be seduced by the enormous innocent eyes of the very young kitten, its roly-poly body and, heaven knows, by its sweet and playful antics. But whether you finally go for kitten or cat has to come down to personal preference, since there are drawbacks and assets to both.

Watching a kitten develop, of course, is the most fascinating of experiences; the sheer *fun* of it is undeniable. Along with giving you many hours of very special pleasure, raising a kitten gives you a chance to affect its personality; because it will grow up in your surroundings, it's more likely to adapt to your habits and household than is an older cat. Start out with a mature cat and you'll miss the joys of kitten play, and the whole adventure of rearing. You're also liable to miss some taxing craziness, since a kitten can be rambunctious, unbelievably daring and often unstoppable in whatever it's up to. An older cat will have established habits and manners; for some people, that's a negative factor, for others, a benefit.

Weigh the pluses and minuses and after that, go on instinct. If, for example, you have a house full of expensive antiques, think over your choice. Yes, you can get that cute little kitten you're dying for, but you might have to hide your priceless Ming vase until the animal is older. In the final analysis, if you listen to your heart, you're not very likely to make a wrong decision.

There's one special circumstance, however, in which I always advocate a kitten; that's when the household already has a resident cat. Full-grown dogs do very well with new full-grown dogs around. Cats do not; introducing a kitten to a mature cat works out much better. The older animal's powerful sense of territory is less threatened by the smaller creature.

As far as gender is concerned, unless you're planning on breeding your cat, you needn't let the sex of the animal determine your choice. A female in heat can be a terrible nuisance; the male cat "sprays" urine that has a noxious odor and is unremovable. These things must be considered if you do, in fact, plan on breeding your pet. Otherwise, you'll proceed—as I strongly advise—at the cat's appropriate age to have it neutered (see pages 72–74 and 97–100). Then, except in a rare instance,* neither of these feline tendencies will matter. The individual cat will have its individual traits, but in the general sense, male and female are equally affectionate, equally obstinate animals. Let your attraction to a particular feline be your guide.

If you see a long-haired cat that strikes your fancy, go ahead and get it *unless* you have an aversion to shedded hair. Any cat is going to shed its hair, expecially in warm weather, but the longer the hair, the more of it there's bound to be. For obvious reasons, you have to groom a long-haired cat with unwavering regularity. Also, if you have children about, a long-haired cat can pose a problem: do you want to spend hours getting bubble gum out of the cat's long hair?

HOW TO CHOOSE A HEALTHY, HAPPY CAT

*W*e all know that a sick person is not likely to be especially happy. Why should we expect a sick animal to be very different? The health of the cat you want to adopt should be the highest priority. Lest you feel guilty about passing up the lonely feline who is ragged-looking and failing, try to remember that the strikes against the animal are certainly not your fault. Having been a veterinarian for many years, I know about rescue fantasies. I sympathize with your kindness—and you can select that unhealthy cat if you insist. But you must be aware that should you choose a cat that is not well, you may have to put consider-

---

* Some male cats will continue to spray after being neutered. This phenomenon has been known to occur when an animal has begun the spraying before the operation. Some observers believe it can also be caused by exceptional stress.

able effort into nursing it back to health and, in the end, your effort may not succeed. Furthermore, there are so many healthy kittens in need of homes who, unless they are adopted, will eventually be euthanatized. I ask you to keep that in mind if you are committed to saving a life.

Many animal shelters and reputable breeders utilize the services of a veterinarian. When you go to such a facility to adopt a kitten or cat, it may already have been examined to determine the state of its health. Nonetheless, it is your responsibility to observe the prospective pet for signs of physical well-being, basically seen in the condition of the eyes, ears, nose, mouth and hair coat. I know, for example, the effect of those large beseeching eyes. But they should also be luminous, clear and free of irritation or discharge. No nasal discharge should be present either, and the kitten or cat should not be sneezing. Look inside its ears; if there is an accumulation of waxy debris and/or odor in the ears, there could be ear mites or an infection. Examine the gums and the inside of the mouth. You want to see a nice, healthy pink color and no signs of irritation. Pay attention to the skin and the coat. The skin should be free of irritation or sores, and the coat should be even and shining. And though a little potbelly might be cute, it could also indicate intestinal parasites. When you observe such a condition, you should see to it that a stool sample is submitted to a veterinarian for examination.

As for personality, I know that the shy little kitten can grab your heart and, as it scurries away, it may even seem to challenge you to coax it into responding to your warmth, comfort and love. Some animals like that *can* change with lots of nurturing. Nonetheless, and for reasons we don't quite understand, the normal kitten is absolutely fearless—even magnetized by the lovingness of people. To be sure, you can't ever be positive about the transformation of kitten to cat. But here is a special tip: try to see if the kitten will follow you when encouraged. The kitten that does so is bright, alert, playful and curious. With a lively baby kitten you're at least two steps ahead.

It will help considerably, too, if you can observe the litter mates or other cats living closely to the kitten you plan to select. It's a good sign if they all interact well with one another. Knowing that the mother has really been "mothering" the kitten will also help assure you of a good-natured pet. Of equal importance: has the cat been handled by people and—need I add?—handled with lots of love?

I advise that you adopt a kitten when it is 6 to 8 weeks old. Any younger, it may not have been properly weaned away from its mother onto solid foods. On the other hand, a kitten that has lived more than 3 to 4 months without being handled by people a lot has missed out on a critical period of socialization with human beings. Bad habits in such a cat can easily have developed. They will be hard to break.

EXOTIC CATS

*U*nfortunately, many people still have the mistaken notion that an exotic cat would make a unique and wonderful pet. While a lion cub, an ocelot or bobcat may seem agreeably docile, be aware that these species will *always* remain wild; they can never be tamed. Fortunately, many cities and counties throughout the country have introduced ordinances which prohibit such ownership. Yet, these laws are not sufficient to discourage all people, and since a number of breeds of exotic cats are readily available—and some surprisingly inexpensive, especially through the black market—many animals end up in houses, which are poorly equipped to handle them.

I love cats, and the larger exotics are no exception. They are truly amazing animals—beautiful and sensitive creatures. Yet, they are wild animals, even when raised in captivity, and once they reach sexual maturity, with its natural hormonal changes, their behavior becomes inconsistent, the love they exhibit erratic. Adorable kittens grow up to be powerful cats, and even in play, the swipe of a paw or bite of the jaw may inflict serious and possibly fatal injuries. If you really love exotic cats, you will want to do what is best for them. *Do not* attempt to bring one into your home to be raised as a pet. Most people have no idea of what they are getting into, and once these animals outgrow the kitten stage, they are no longer desired. Then what does one do with the cat? When such a cat is raised in a home environment, one cannot simply re-introduce it into the wild; the cat would die. In many cases these animals have been mutilated by having their canine teeth filed down or removed and by being declawed. In these cases, zoological parks, which get stuck with the cast-offs, have difficulty keeping them and adapting them to a natural habitat. In addition, since many breeds are plentiful, the zoos are unable to accept all these unwanted animals.

Here are some important points to ponder:

1. Most people who attempt to raise an exotic cat in a home environment are eventually hurt by them.
2. Even knowledgeable animal trainers and zoo keepers have been injured (or even killed) when working with and caring for captive animals because of an error in judgment or invasion of the animal's territory.
3. Exotic animal food is very expensive, and exotic cats need a balanced, high-protein, feline diet which is very costly.
4. It is almost impossible to create an environment that simulates the natural setting in a home situation. The simulated situation is important to avoid stress because excessive stress can lower the animal's immune system, thereby making it more susceptible to illnesses.
5. The amounts of urine and stool these animals void are relatively large, and the odor can be extremely objectionable. Zoos and wildlife parks can accommodate this situation and are able to disinfect large areas.

It is possible to maintain dominance over some wild animals, such as the elephant, because scientific data exists regarding "patterned behavior." There is no way, however, with exotic cats because dominant behavior is not understood in these animals.

Exotic animals—even those such as birds and reptiles, which can be kept as household pets—require very specialized care. Most people who acquire exotics to raise as pets *do not* have the proper knowledge of their requirements. Unfortunately, many pet owners are unaware of many things regarding the proper care of domestic pets such as the dog and cat!

Please consider the exotic cat first and place your own desire to own one aside. Domestic cats do make great pets, and you can visit zoological parks all around the country to learn about and see many species of exotic cats.

PART TWO

BASIC CAT CARE

*T*his section of the book introduces the fundamentals of cat care—from selecting the proper veterinarian to feeding, household safety and grooming. Armed with this basic information, you're sure to provide for all the primary needs of your feline.

STARTING OFF
ON THE RIGHT PAW

*N*o one is quite as generous as a novice owner in giving security and tenderness to the feline pet, and such attentiveness has my encouragement. But some novice owners are suckers too. All too often, they neglect to set what might be called "a structured tone" in their homes. The cat is quick to take advantage. Saucy, devilish, seductively *cute*, it wants a happy household too and, just like you, it wants the home to be indivisible—but of the cat, by the cat and for the cat. Don't let it happen. Unless you exert a touch of discipline right from the start, all your efforts toward establishing a mutually pleasurable relationship with your cat will boomerang. Some of the following suggestions for helping you make your cat feel at home are strictly routine tips regarding basic matters. A few, however, are meant to aid you in easing your pet into a situation wherein *you* are the loving authority.

1. Obviously, the kitten or cat will need dishes for its food and water. Shallow dishes and bowls are best, and I recommend that they be made of stainless steel which is sturdy and easily cleaned. Ceramic or glass can break; and an occasional cat may be allergic to plastic, which also, because of its lightness, can easily be flipped over. Where you put the dishes is up to you. Most people choose the kitchen for sheer convenience. Just make sure that you always put them in the same place. Switching things around does not sit well with cats.

2. There was a time when a manufactured litter box was a shallow open pan and that was that. As a result, the cat owner was stuck daily with having to sweep up what looked like tons of litter scattered around the area of the box. Thanks to man's ingenuity, there are many better types of litter boxes available today. If you decide to stick with an open pan, be sure its sides are not too low or you'll constantly be using a broom. For the sake of the little cat in particular, the sides of the pan should also not be too high. I myself tend to favor the type of box that is covered and has a small entry hole in the front. Cats are not exhibitionists and prefer to use the litter box unobserved; therefore, a bathroom is

generally a good spot for the box. Remember, it should never be placed near the pet's food and water. There's one other matter: it's understandable that an owner would want a litter box not to be conspicuous. Be sure, however, that you don't keep it *too* much out of sight. Your guests may not see it, but the cat may not either!

3. Of the types of litter used to fill the box, clay, sawdust and wood shavings are the most common. Clay litter most resembles the dirt or sand that a cat would use outside in a natural environment. Many brands of litter are scented, too, although sometimes the scent is so strong it can repel the cat. You'll have to test them out. The litter should be placed evenly in the box and should be at least 2 inches deep. Try to select a litter that has a minimal amount of dust because dust residue in the box can provoke respiratory disorders in some cats. (You'll know the dust is heavy if it rises in a cloud when you put the litter in the box.) For odor control, sprinkle a small amount of baking soda into the litter every time you change it and, for the best odor control of all, change the litter frequently—as often as every other day. What is referred to as "a cat smell" can almost always be traced to a dirty litter box. Furthermore, the cat itself cannot abide an unclean toilet area, and changing the litter two or three times a week will help to avoid toilet problems. Also, remove fecal material daily. When you change the litter, clean out the box with soap and water or a mild disinfectant. People who have more than one cat would be wise to have a couple of litter boxes around the house. The same would apply to people with very large homes. A couple of litter boxes here and there will better ensure that the cat doesn't take to anything but the box to "do its business."

4. A good, sturdy cat carrier is also a necessity, not only for travel but for trips to the veterinarian as well. There are several types of carriers available at any good pet supply store. Just get one that is large enough for the cat to move around in a bit and stretch, and be sure that it has holes so the animal can breathe.

5. Who doesn't like a nice comfortable bed? All types of fancy beds are available for cats, and if you want to spend the money to buy some plush velvet affair, feel free to do it. Such an expenditure isn't necessary, though. No cat will care about the fanciness of its bed. Mainly, it wants to sleep in a dry, draft-free, warm and quiet location. You could make a bed from an empty fruit or

milk crate (with nails removed, please). Just place a folded towel
or blanket on the bottom and change or clean this periodically
just as you would the sheets on your bed.

Or, you could let the cat sleep with *you*. Cat owners who live
in one-room apartments may have no choice. Just be aware that
your little squirt of a cat might start walking on your face at five
in the morning! It may want food; it may want attention; it may
have an urge to play. Whatever it's about, the impulse to rouse
the owner seems to seize the cat at dawn. This is a typical discipline problem and if you let the cat sleep with you, you may find
the problem unsolvable. The cat that knows it can get you up will
have you forever at its command in this arena and you will never
get a good night's sleep—at least not while that cat is young. You
might try sticking to your guns (or dreams, if you can) when the
cat gets active in the morning. But talk is cheap: who can ignore
a paw in the mouth? The only way to really ensure uninterrupted
sleep is to put the cat in another room with its very own bed.

6. The owner who fails to get a good solid scratching post for
his or her cat is headed for the worst kind of trouble. On page 84
you will find a detailed discussion of posts and how to train the
cat to use one. If you have a cat, you must have a scratching post.
It will give the animal exercise and allow it to sharpen its claws
without damaging your furniture. *Scratching, if not properly handled, is the most problematic drawback to having a cat.* This does *not*
need to be. I am repeatedly amazed by people who, having been
told to get a scratching post when they get a cat, delay in taking
this uncomplicated but necessary step. By the time they do it, the
cat is entrenched in bad habits that are often impossible to break.
Similarly, should you discover that your cat is an avid climber
(some are, some aren't), you can purchase or build a cat "tree-
house" solely for this purpose. The cat will be delighted and you
won't have to concern yourself with breakage of objects around
the house.

7. For exercise, for fun, for distracting the cat from making
mischief, there's nothing like a toy. Any good pet supply store
will have a variety to choose from. But you don't have to spend a
lot of money to keep your feline entertained. A Ping-Pong ball
makes a terrific toy, as does a wad of paper or a clump of aluminum foil. Light from the sun reflected on a mirror, then flashed
on the wall will give the cat a great old time. You may drop from

exhaustion, but the cat will never tire of chasing the light. There's just one thing you must be careful of with toys: don't give your cat any plaything that has parts that might come loose and be swallowed. Also, there's catnip. A soft toy filled with catnip will put the cat in a state of ecstasy. Judging from the antics displayed by the blissful cat, the effects of this herb on the feline must be similar to some kind of "high," without the typical accompanying damage. If your cat seems to enjoy it, you can safely give the cat a little bit of loose catnip each day. But not all cats have a passion for the stuff. So don't be disappointed if your pet gives a sniff and walks away.

8. A collar for your cat is not necessary unless it spends a great deal of time outdoors. For hints on choosing the right collar, see pages 148–49, "Strangulation." Flea collars are covered on pages 209–10.

A Word on Discipline

Some of the following pages deal with the various kinds of mischief—sometimes dangerous mischief—your cat can get into. In general, the best way to handle a misbehaving cat is by emitting a firm "NO." Your pet will come to associate your tone of voice with the impermissible act and will thus be trained not to do it anymore. Clapping your hands will only distract the cat momentarily from what it is doing; it will not serve to train it. For more information on training and behavior, see Part III, beginning on page 81.

Try to keep in mind that the new cat might, at first, be overwhelmed by the foreignness of your environment. Give it time. Don't worry or fret if it seems a little shy for a few days. Unlike dogs, who seem to thrive on an abundance of attention, cats sometimes do better when left a bit alone. Apparently, they like taking the initiative and going to people themselves. Whatever you do when you bring your new cat into your home, be patient, gentle and kind as well as firm. I promise you that you and your cat will be fine.

SELECTING A VETERINARIAN

*I*n the entire life of your cat, not many things will be as important as proper veterinary care. So, if it's your "first time out" and you're a novice cat owner who has never needed a veterinarian, I advise you to take some time in making your selection. Don't take *too* much time, however, especially if you've adopted a kitten, you should take the animal for a checkup and immunization immediately.

In choosing a veterinarian, there's nothing quite as important to rely on as a good reputation. Therefore, you might first ask neighbors and friends whom they would recommend. Do stick either to your neighborhood or to an area that is reasonably accessible—you'll find that important on all occasions, and critical in an emergency. Should it be impossible to get a recommendation on the basis of personal experience, give your local chapter of the veterinary medical association a call. The Yellow Pages are another source. Then start asking questions. Most veterinarians will appreciate your concern.

While I'm a big believer in paying attention to what people say in regard to their animal's medical care, you should be skeptical of the lone dissenter. One individual might warn you to steer clear of a particular veterinarian, somberly intoning, "Aunt Jane's cat died in that very office." Don't automatically rule out that practitioner. Aunt Jane's cat could have been 18 years old, with a terminal disease. In a case like that, when most of the people you speak to relate good experiences in dealing with the same veterinarian, give him or her the benefit of the doubt. Go see the veterinarian, view the facilities and draw your own conclusions.

Call in advance and ask the receptionist if you could stop by at a convenient time, briefly meet the veterinarian and take a look at the premises. Almost all veterinarians are extremely interested in expanding their practices. The request to pay a visit is reasonable; any animal doctor should be glad to oblige. If not, erase that name from your list.

Your veterinarian is going to be as important to the health and well-being of your pet as your personal physician is to you. Accordingly, put rapport with the veterinarian very near the top of the points you ought to consider in making your choice. Your cat cannot talk; it's *you* who must be able to communicate clearly with the veterinarian in order to ensure that your pet gets maximum care. At your very first meeting, you should feel confident that:

1. the veterinarian is willing and able to explain medical matters to you in a clear, concise and sympathetic manner
2. he or she conveys a genuine love of animals
3. the veterinarian seems sincerely concerned with *your* pet's health and welfare

During the visit, pay close attention to the facilities. The clinic should be clean and well equipped. Inquire as to what diagnostic services are available. Is there an X-ray machine? Apparatus for gas anesthesia in the event of surgery? An EKG machine—or certainly access to one—is another important diagnostic tool that most veterinarians regularly use. Also, ask about laboratory facilities: find out about the arrangements for analyzing blood and tissue samples should diagnostic investigation be required. Be sure that your questions about these subjects are answered politely, thoroughly and with complete respect for your interest. If the facility or clinic has received certification from AAHA (American Animal Hospital Association) stating that it meets their standards for approval, you can be assured that the facility is well equipped.

One other crucial matter you must explore is what medical facilities exist in the event of a nighttime, weekend or holiday emergency. In some practices a veterinarian is on call twenty-four hours a day, every day of the week, with a nurse on the premises round-the-clock. This sort of situation, of course, is ideal from the client's point of view. Unfortunately, most small practices, especially in suburban settings, cannot offer as complete a service. Just be sure that your veterinarian has specific provisions for emergency coverage during the hours he or she is unavailable. And don't wait until the emergency occurs to discover what those arrangements are. Have the information regarding those provisions ready at all times.

Almost all private practitioners treat either large animals

(horses and other domestic farm animals) or small ones (cats and dogs). Some concentrate on one species—felines, for example. There are many excellent veterinarians who give excellent care to cats and love them too but do not stick solely to treating felines. But some cat breeders and cat aficionados prefer veterinarians who specialize in the treatment of cats. Of course, what really matters most of all is the excellence of the veterinarian and his or her concern for your pet.

VACCINATIONS

*V*accinations are going to be the first order of veterinary business for your kitten and perhaps, depending upon the circumstances, for your older cat as well. A mother cat dutifully nursing her offspring provides her kittens with milk. The first milk to appear and be ingested is known as *colostrum*, which contains maternal antibodies that the kittens must absorb in the first hours of life. Along with being nutritious, colostrum gives early protection against some of the infectious diseases that cats are prone to. Yet, it doesn't give the kittens long-lasting immunity. For this, the kittens must receive a series of vaccinations that begin at 6 to 8 weeks of age.

There are three particular viruses that the vaccinations are intended to prevent: *feline distemper* and two upper-respiratory viruses, *rhinotracheitis* and *calici*. See Part VII (pages 232–35) for essential information about these serious diseases. The immunizations against these illnesses are given in one vaccine, and therefore that vaccine is often referred to as the "three-in-one." The injection will bother you a lot more than it will bother the cat. It takes but a second and your pet will hardly feel a twinge of discomfort.

Most veterinarians will recommend that, after the initial inoculation, there be follow-up shots at 12 weeks and at 16 weeks of age. Possibly, your vet will suggest a different schedule. You have a right to ask why, but he or she undoubtedly has a good reason. Still, no matter what the schedule of the initial shots, the cat should receive a yearly booster vaccination to sustain an adequate level of immunity. As you'll see in Part VII of this book, the three disease entities that this immunization is meant to prevent can be killers. Under no circumstances, however, should a pregnant cat be given a vaccination.

Many owners ask about a vaccination for rabies. As deadly as this disease is, and as serious a threat to public health, in many states cats are not required by law to have this vaccination. The problem of rabies is serious; it doesn't happen to be widespread. However, rabies is something you *must* be concerned about, especially if you live in an area of the country in which cases of rabies have been reported and certainly if you allow your cat freedom to roam outdoors. In the last few years, there has been an increase in the incidence of rabies in several regions of the United States. Raccoons, foxes and skunks are the animals most often afflicted, and bats are also carriers of this dreaded disease. Consult your veterinarian about a yearly rabies vaccination if you live in a rural area, where the risk of contracting the disease is greater than in urban and suburban locales. (Also see pages 253–255 for more information.)

Last year, a new vaccine became available to protect cats against the feline leukemia virus (discussed on pages 246–49). Discuss this vaccine with your veterinarian when your cat receives its "three-in-one."

Occasionally pet owners are concerned that the immunizations themselves are going to make their animals ill. I assure you that's not likely. At the most, your cat may show a decrease in appetite and activity for 24 hours.

By the way, when you take your cat in for its annual booster, expect that the veterinarian will also give the animal a complete physical exam, which takes only a few minutes. If this is not done automatically, I would suggest seeking out other veterinary care in the future.

VETERINARY EXAMINATIONS

*N*o matter how alert and bright-eyed your cat seems to be, you shouldn't take its health for granted. And one of the very best ways to ensure good health for your animal is to be certain that it gets its yearly booster vaccination and, at the same time, its annual physical exam. These visits are never wasted; they provide a chance to catch any possible problem before it gets going full swing. Remember that your cat's comfort is at stake and that its life can be extended. Seeing to it that your cat stays well is surely part of being a responsible owner.

I'm one veterinarian who never minds answering the client who wants to know exactly what I'm looking for when I perform a physical examination; the questions usually point to an owner's interest.

The examination I perform is basically the same as the one a thorough physician would perform on any of his or her human patients; it just takes less time because of the cat's smaller size. Observe the drawings on the next page which illustrate the anatomy of the cat. You might want to refer to this as I discuss the examination procedure.

Most veterinarians begin an examination with the head and work back toward the tail. To help the cat relax, I give it some calm, reassuring strokes. I then study the cat's eyes with a penlight flashlight and/or an ophthalmoscope, which is a special instrument that will help show up any eye problems. Next, I look in the mouth. The tongue and gums should be pink. Gums that are pale or white may indicate anemia, whereas a yellow/orange color is an indication of jaundice. I observe the teeth for tartar and for signs of gingivitis, an inflammation of the gums that accompanies dental disease. The ears must be looked at and the outer canal observed for ear mites or infections.

The following step is to palpate or feel the regional lymph nodes to see if any seem enlarged. The palpable nodes (those that can be felt) are located on each side under the neck, in front of the shoulders, the axillas (the equivalent of the armpit), in the groin and also at the back of each hind leg.

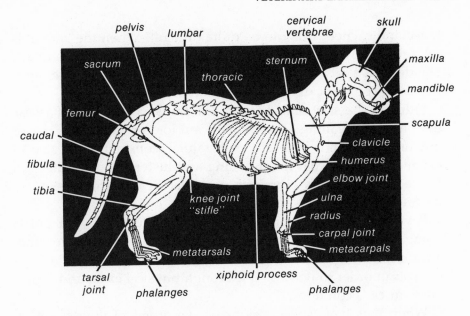

Skeletal anatomy of the cat

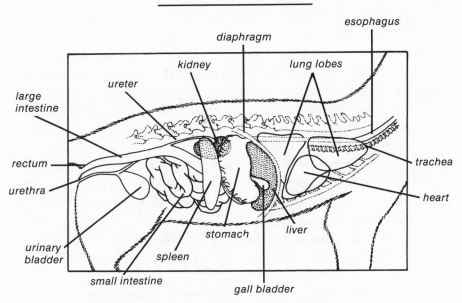

Internal anatomy (organs) of the cat

While taking a rectal temperature, I listen carefully to the pet's heart and lungs with a stethoscope, that familiar doctorly instrument that is so important in detecting abnormalities of the heart and respiratory system.

Finally, the abdomen is palpated. If the cat is obese or very tense and excited, this can be quite difficult. When the animal is relaxed, the liver, the kidneys, the spleen, intestines and urinary bladder can easily be felt for any irregularities; abnormal changes in size or contour can be an indication of a problem.

Either at the start or as I finish, the cat is weighed and I assess the possible meaning of any significant loss or gain. (The loss of one or two pounds in a cat is substantial, considering its size.) I examine the hair coat for shedding and luster; I look at the skin to see if there are any eruptions, scaly patches or disorders of any nature.

If you're a novice owner, you may wonder how your pet is going to react to such an examination. On the rare occasion that a cat does get upset, the veterinarian may have to give it a tranquilizer in order to perform a thorough physical exam and evaluate your cat's condition.

When pets have specific signs or symptoms of illness, veterinarians are obviously going to pay close attention to the part or parts of the body involved. For example, if a cat has difficulty breathing, the chest might have to be radiographed (X-rayed) and an electrocardiogram (EKG) might have to be taken. Any lameness in a limb could call for an X-ray to dismiss or confirm the presence of a fracture or dislocation. At other times, your veterinarian may advise some laboratory tests; the most common are as follows:

1. CBC = Complete Blood Count: This gives the veterinarian information about the red and white blood cells; it reveals the structure and appearance of the cells microscopically, and measures the hematocrit (a measure of red blood cells). All this information is helpful in determining whether an animal has such conditions as an infection, leukemia, anemia or dehydration.

2. Blood Chemistry: A variety of blood measurements taken from one sample of blood and then compared to normal values to help diagnose the overall condition of a pet. The blood chemistry results indicate kidney and liver function test levels, the level of glucose (blood sugar), electrolyte levels as well as other measurements used to evaluate body functions.

3. Urinalysis: As in human beings, a urinalysis can reveal signs

of infection or diabetes and gives information in regard to kidney function.

4. Fecal Examination: This is a means of determining the presence of intestinal parasites.

Follow-up tests are often required during the course of treatment in order to monitor progress.

Keeping a Medical Record

Keeping a record of your cat's medical history may seem a simple, obvious step. But I have had new clients come to me with no recollection of the vaccinations their cat has received, and very little memory of illnesses, treatment, etc. Depending upon the circumstances, this can create dilemmas and complicate procedures. To play it safe, keep track of the medical events in your animal's life.

When you first visit your veterinarian's office, ask him or her to provide you with a medical record book. Most practices have such books to give to their clients. In the event that the practice you choose does not, a request from you might be taken as a good suggestion. In such a little booklet, all pertinent information can be listed in an orderly fashion. Far better to have a detailed, organized account of vaccinations and treatment your pet has received than to have to rack your brains for when and what has medically transpired. Though a number of offices send out reminder cards to inform a client when a pet is in need of routine care or examinations, others do not. You'd be wise to keep track of "due dates" yourself to ensure that your cat is attended to when necessary. Besides, a complete medical record can be immensely useful in case of serious illness; an emergency situation might arise when your own veterinarian and his or her "in-house" records are not available.

Should you move to another city or state, a medical record can be indispensable to the new veterinarian you choose. In addition, a cat that has an extensive medical history because of surgery or serious illness will have an equally extensive medical file in the previous veterinarian's office. Obtain a copy of that file before you move and give it to the new veterinarian to attach to the new medical records.

Health Insurance for Pets

For most people, being sick today is just about impossible without the benefits of a good solid health insurance policy. Along with the advances in medical technology, surgical procedures, modernized equipment and the refining of "wonder" drugs has also come the skyrocketing of hospital expenses and overall medical costs. Veterinary medicine has become equally sophisticated and can, if an animal is seriously ill, become extremely expensive. Certainly, the costs of veterinary care are much lower than the costs for similar procedures in human medicine. Nonetheless, a pet owner is sometimes forced to put a price on his or her animal's life.

For the most part, health insurance programs for pets have been unsuccessful in the past. But to judge by the increasing existence of such plans, the tide seems to be turning. Be aware that coverage is limited. Many plans have exclusions; they do not cover all pets. Nor are these programs available in every state as yet. But if these programs start to become successful, a greater number of animals may benefit and an owner with limited financial resources might still be able to give a pet the best possible veterinary care. The emotionally painful pressure on the pet owner to choose between expensive veterinary care and euthanasia could be eliminated.

You have nothing to lose by inquiring about these plans. Your veterinarian or local veterinary medical association can provide you with details concerning currently available programs.

FEEDING AND NUTRITION

*N*o doubt you've heard the news that cats are finicky eaters. This is not an unfounded rumor started by Morris the cat. Nonetheless, the tendency of the feline to be choosy about its diet can usually be kept within reasonable boundaries, provided that an owner has some knowledge and perseverance.

To an extraordinary degree, the cat is a creature of habit. When consistently fed any one given type or flavor of food—even for a very short time—the cat will quickly get hooked. Try giving it something else after that and you're liable to witness a display of stubbornness such as you've never seen. Admittedly, that stub-

---

CAT FACTS

Water is essential for all of us, so make sure that the cat has clean water to drink. Some cats like to drink from a leaky faucet; others go for the toilet bowl and skip what's in the kitchen. Before assuming that it's sick, check to see if your cat is getting its water on the sly. If you use a deodorizing toilet bowl cleaner, make sure you keep the bowl *covered* when not in use. (The chemicals in that water could harm your pet.) And if there are young kittens in the house make sure they're not in the bathroom when the toilet is flushed. Believe it or not, toilet bowl drownings have been known to occur!

---

bornness makes a good joke. But amusing though it might seem to be, comes the showdown and it really isn't funny: the cat will almost die before it will eat what it doesn't want. I've found that the way to avoid this frustrating behavior is to offer the cat variety from the beginning.

Variety can be quite compatible with nutritional requirements, which are thoroughly met in the major national brands of commercially prepared pet foods. Beware of lower-priced and generic cat foods—many are made with poor ingredients that cats have trouble digesting. Feeding trials, performed by all national brands, are essential to ensure that diets are digestible and nutritious, and in many cases are not performed by the manufacturers of lower-priced foods. If you use a generic or private label product, be sure to write to the company and ask if a feeding trial has been utilized in the formulation of that particular diet. And before you feed your cat "health" food, consult with your veterinarian.

Because the cat is a carnivorous animal, it needs a diet high in protein. Still, its nutritional needs are not fulfilled by meat alone. The commercially prepared foods contain the appropriate additions of cereals, fats, vegetables and fiber as well as minerals and vitamins that enhance the value of the protein they contain. Given a balanced commercial diet, most cats *do not* require supplemental vitamins or minerals. In fact, giving them your idea of extra minerals such as calcium and phosphorus can produce an imbalance. On the other hand, a daily multiple pet vitamin, available from your veterinarian, is not going to harm your cat (it's not very likely to help it either).

Remember, different species of animals have different nutritional requirements. For example, cats require much more protein in their diet than do dogs. Felines also need certain nutrients, such as the amino acid *taurine* (essential for good vision), that is not added to dog foods. Therefore, *never* feed your cat dog food. *Cats should be fed only food prepared for cats.*

I also ask you to beware of table scraps—both for yourself and for the cat. Under no circumstances should scraps constitute more than 10 to 15 percent of the cat's total diet, or the cat's good health will suffer. Let me remind you that the cat knows every trick in the book, from casting starved, beseeching looks to letting forth pitiful wails. One taste of filet of sole and it may refuse its own food, then, with unrelenting determination, pester you until, collapsing from battle fatigue, you give up and hand it more. You're better off not to get started with food from the table at all.

There are three types of commercial cat food: dry, semi-moist and canned, all of which have their merits. Dry food can be advantageous when you take trips and is excellent for snacks; moreover, it helps keep the teeth clean of tartar. As an added benefit, it's inexpensive. Unfortunately, it lacks the moisture of canned food, moisture that is necessary for the cat's body—70 percent of which is water—to be nutritionally stabilized.* People who feed their cats only dry food must be sure that their pets get lots of water.

Semi-moist products vary in nutritive value; some may not be sufficiently complete as a steady diet, especially for growing kittens. Again, for the most adequate diet, count on a well-known brand of canned food. Unfortunately, canned food is also the most expensive and, once opened, it spoils more quickly than the other types. Everything considered, your best bet is to alternate the food supply. Not only will the cat be properly fed, it will be more cooperative and eat what you present it with should your local store run out of your favorite brand or flavor or, even worse, should a special diet be recommended by your veterinarian for medical reasons.

Until it is two months old, a kitten should be fed three to four times a day; this will prevent the onset of hypoglycemia, a potentially life-threatening condition, discussed on pages 213–14. With an older cat, twice a day—beginning when the cat is 6 months old—is sufficient. A normal-sized cat (7 to 9 pounds) will do quite

---

* Dry food should not be given to cats with urinary problems. See pages 223–26.

OLD WIVES' TALES

All cats like fish. There is *no* food that *all* cats can be said to like. This applies to liver, milk and any other food one can mention. The taste buds of the cat seem to be as idiosyncratic as cats themselves. It's rare, though, that a cat will care for sweets.

---

well on a can of food or about 3 to 4 ounces of dry or semi-moist food each day. A kitten, growing by leaps and bounds, will need more, as will an active cat. In cold weather, an outdoor cat will also need more food in order to maintain its body heat. However, owing to the individuality of each and every cat—in terms of size, level of energy, breed and overall nature—strict, inflexible feeding rules are impossible. Giving the cat enough food to maintain its body weight, however, will serve as a general guideline. In other words, if your cat is looking thin, give it more food, and if it seems heavier, give it less. Whether your cat is full-grown or young, don't worry about overfeeding it; most felines have a good sense of how to regulate their intake and will stop ingesting when they've had their proper fill.

As for the eating habits of the cat, one can only assume that they have some instinctual basis. Owners are often annoyed, for instance, to find that the cat likes to dawdle over its food (another reason not to give it its whole day's ration at one time; the food, if canned, will not stay fresh). Some people are dismayed by another habit, the fondness of the cat for scooping its food out of the dish and eating it from the floor. Furthermore, many a cat has a penchant for wanting new food in its dish even though there's plenty there. Taking all this in stride is probably the wisest policy. Of course, if you want your cat to eat promptly and get it over with, you can try removing the food after a while. Maybe the cat will do it *your* way. Then again, maybe it won't.

ADDITIONAL TIPS ON FOOD
- Milk may cause diarrhea, though not always. Try diluting it, using one part milk to two parts water as an occasional treat. Don't leave it out for consumption for more than 1–2 hours because of inevitable spoilage, and never use it as a substitute for water.
- Don't give a cat any kind of bones. After you've feasted on

fish or chicken, dispose of the bones properly. If your cat gets into the garbage it could choke on or swallow one of the bones.
- Always provide fresh water—change it daily.
- Raw foods should not be fed to pets; they may carry parasites.
- Cats enjoy food best when it is served at room temperature.
- Feed your cat at the same time and in the same place every day and you'll succeed in maintaining a degree of regulation.
- Some raw fish can cause a deficiency of the vitamin thiamine (which eventually can lead to neurological problems, such as seizures). Cook fish properly and be certain that bones are removed.
- Raw liver, fed daily in large quantities, has an enzyme that could cause a Vitamin A toxicity, especially if it is fed along with a complete and balanced diet and a vitamin supplement. If a small amount of liver is fed two or three times a week, it should not be harmful.
- Raw egg whites have an enzyme that can destroy the vitamin *biotin*, which cats need in order to survive. If eggs are fed on a regular basis, they should be cooked.

Feeding of Orphan Kittens

Under ordinary circumstances, the basics of feeding a cat require, as I've explained, only a little knowledge and a lot of determination—to see that the cat eats what it should, to be sure that it doesn't eat what it shouldn't, and to lay down household law. Exceptions exist when cats are ill and when kittens must be raised as orphans because of the death of the mother, because of illness in the mother cat or because of inadequate milk production. Sometimes too, though it doesn't happen often, a mother cat will neglect her kittens. A first-time mother can become extremely nervous and leave her babies unattended while she goes off to hide, and you might find yourself with an abandoned litter that you cannot resist. No matter how you've acquired them, you've got a bunch of orphans on your hands. To define the term more accurately, "orphaned kittens" specifically refers to animals under the age of 3–4 weeks (prior to weaning) who have been and are deprived of natural maternal care.

As discussed on page 46, kittens are born without immunity to

---

CAT FACTS

Try not to let your cat get overly accustomed to milk. A little milk given occasionally is all right; too much can cause diarrhea.

The cat's tongue is important for the consumption of liquids. He uses it to lap up or, to be correct, to lap *under* liquids. The tongue curls under into the mouth in much the same manner as an elephant uses its trunk.

---

infectious diseases; if they don't receive colostrum soon after birth they will have no way of fighting off infections and must be kept in a particularly clean environment. While there is no substitute for colostrum, the ingredients of the mother's milk can be nutritionally approximated by a correctly formulated substance. Should you be caring for orphans, you will have to feed them with such a commercial milk replacer (for example, KMR) and nurse them with a bottle. This is a time-consuming proposition, since young animals require a feeding every 3 to 4 hours.

Also, during the first 7 to 10 days after birth, you must rub an orphaned kitten's lower abdomen with a soft cloth moistened with warm water after it is fed. This will stimulate urination and defecation, such as the mother cat would be doing with her tongue were she there to assume maternal responsibility.

As far as the milk replacer and special pet-nursing bottles go, you can get them from most veterinarians and from pet supply stores as well. On the container of the milk replacer, you'll see directions concerning frequency and amounts to be fed. Obviously, there's no sense in looking on the dark side. But whenever a litter is expected, you'd be wise to keep a supply of milk replacer and bottles on hand because, no matter how nice the mother, there's no guarantee that all will go well between her and her baby offspring. If you are unable to obtain a commercial milk replacer, here is a formula you can whip up at home until you can get a commercially prepared product:

    1 cup whole milk
    2 egg yolks
    2 teaspoonfuls of Karo syrup

Feeding the kitten every 3–4 hours, give a total of one teaspoon per ounce of body weight every day.

Although special pet-nursing bottles are available, you can use a small-sized baby bottle if necessary. With a hot sterilized needle or pin, burn several holes in the tip of the nipple. It's best to use a bottle to nurse a young animal. If you use a spoon, an eyedropper or a syringe, use *extreme caution;* give only a little bit at a time, or else the kitten can aspirate (inhale) the liquid and die.

As I've already noted, an orphaned kitten—any kitten, for that matter—*should be fed every 3 to 4* hours. I cannot stress enough, in fact, how important frequent feeding is, particularly in order to avoid *hypoglycemia.* This is an imbalanced condition of subnormal glucose (blood sugar) levels in the blood. The brain is dependent on glucose for energy. Thus, low levels of blood sugar will cause dysfunction of the central nervous system. The kitten will appear to be dazed. It will stagger and become severely depressed and possibly comatose; seizures usually occur. *For any kitten under 4 weeks of age, let feeding every 3 to 4 hours be an unbreakable rule.* The kitten is depending on you or its mother for sustenance.

Sometimes, in spite of one's best efforts, a young kitten simply will not eat. One can't always account for such a loss of appetite, but the most common reason is illness. Always keep a bottle of Karo syrup in the house. In the event the symptoms of hypoglycemia occur, give the kitty 3 to 5 cc's (½–1 teaspoon) of the syrup. It will probably be too thick to go through the nipple of the bottle, but you can administer it carefully with a small syringe or eyedropper; these are available from your veterinarian or pharmacist and the number of cc's is clearly marked on the device. Use it carefully, releasing a little of the syrup at a time into the kitten's mouth as shown in the illustration on page 127. If you prefer, you can use your finger and rub the syrup lightly on the kitten's gums and tongue. After you've given it the proper amount, it should respond quite rapidly. If it is unconscious, has a seizure or fails to return to normal after you've given the Karo syrup, it is essential that you get prompt veterinary care.

When the kitten is 3 to 4 weeks old, you can start on semi-solid foods. Begin with baby foods mixed with water to form a soupy, gruel-like consistency. Most young kittens take quickly to pablum and baby foods made up of strained beef or chicken. Don't assume that the kitten will automatically eat from a bowl. Use your fingertip, put a taste of the food in its mouth and direct the creature toward a shallow dish. At around 6 weeks, and once the kittens are accustomed to semi-solid foods, they can be switched to more substantially textured foods (such as canned cat food). Continue to feed every 6 to 8 hours.

Raising orphan kittens is an extremely difficult task. No matter how attentive you are as a foster parent, you cannot perform miracles and many orphaned kittens do not survive. So if you decide to take on this responsibility, you must be prepared for the sadness of loss as well as the joy of seeing the kittens through.

HOUSEHOLD SAFETY

*T*he parents of any normal toddler take special precautions to protect their child from household hazards. In my judgment, it's not pushing the comparison between young children and pets to say that similar steps have to be taken to prevent injury to animals. This is especially so with cats. In the matter of poking about, cats will stop at nothing, and the younger the feline, the more apt it is to stick its nose into every nook and cranny of the house to see what it can find. Woe to the perky cat if what it discovers—to play with, to chew on, to drink, to swallow—turns out to be lethal.

My warning is simple enough: beware the everyday household product. Many an ordinary disinfectant is plain poison to the cat. Don't leave perfume bottles open. Be careful about discarded bones, the string from Sunday's roast beef, tinsel from the Christmas tree, rubber bands and paper clips. And for heaven's sake, don't let your cat start playing with a needle and thread. One thing you can be sure of too: cats never learn from experience. I remember one cat that had an apparently insatiable taste for needles. That's not unusual; many cats are attracted to shiny objects. Anyway, within 18 months, that cat had downed three needles and, as a result, had undergone three avoidable surgeries. Dumb cat, you say? I would say, "Dumb owner." After sewing, put needles and threads safely away.

Here is a list of items that can be dangerous to your cat:

- Household cleaners
- Household disinfectants
- Household polishes
- Gasoline, kerosene, oil

- Prescription and over-the-counter medications
- Aspirin and Tylenol
- Personal hygiene products
- Insecticides and pesticides
- Perfumes and bath oils
- Antifreeze
- Photographic developing chemicals
- Many plants (see pp. 268–71)
- Rodent and insect baits
- Discarded fish, chicken and even meat bones
- Children's toys—especially those with removable parts; also toys that can be swallowed: marbles, jacks, small rubber balls
- Fishing tackle, hooks
- Holiday decorations and ornaments, assorted knickknacks
- Paints, glues, paint strippers
- Please see pp. 271–76 for a more complete listing of chemical products hazardous to cats.

Don't try lecturing the cat about these items, or punishing it: the animal won't understand. It's *your* job to make sure that these things are not around in the open to tempt your cat. Also, be wary of plastic bags and be on guard about boxes. Cats adore hiding in boxes. Most of the time, this is perfectly harmless. Once, clients of mine could not locate their cat after they'd moved into a new home. Two days later they found it crying in the basement, struggling to get out of the empty refrigerator box. It's therefore a good idea to check any boxes lying about if your cat has disappeared. The same applies to drawers. It doesn't take long to suffocate. To really play it safe, punch holes in cardboard boxes so if your cat climbs in, it will always have air to breathe.

Check your house carefully for potential sources of eye injury. Exposed nails or wires, dried flower arrangements, accumulated dust or wood shavings within the pet's reach should all be cleaned up or eliminated.

Wobbly furniture can be dangerous, too, so fix that shaky bookcase. You don't want a heavy object toppling over to crush the cat. And be especially on your toes about open windows. Contrary to anything you may have heard, a cat will take one giant step right into the great beyond if you give it the chance, and there's no guarantee that it'll land on its feet. Practice prevention. You are responsible for the life of your pet; if all of this

---

OLD WIVES' TALES

Cats always land on their feet. Falling short distances, cats can often twist around, righting themselves to land on their feet. Falls from heights are another story. *Please leave windows closed,* or opened only when a secure screen is in place.

---

strikes you as potentially cramping your style, you have no business owning a cat.

Poisonous Plants

Of the more common household hazards, plants that are poisonous to animals are, in a way, especially dangerous because we tend to take them for granted as an innocuous part of the overall domestic scenery. Poisonous plants are there aplenty in gardens too, and are almost always part of outdoor landscapes. The following ordinary houseplants and flowers are particularly dangerous: *dieffenbachia* or *dumbcane, oleander, philodendron, morning glory, lily of the valley, mistletoe* and *poinsettia.* Rhubarb, tomato vines and mushrooms have also been observed to cause toxicity in pets. Refer to the chart of poisonous plants on pages 268–71 for additional information.

Actually, cats are not interested in greenery as such. Being carnivorous, they have no nutritional need for vegetation. But ruled by curiosity as they are, they will frequently nibble at greenery to see what it's all about. The effects can be disastrous.

Most poisonous plants cause gastrointestinal reactions such as vomiting, diarrhea, nausea and abdominal pain. Some cats may salivate or drool excessively. They may become weak or exhibit labored, slowed-down breathing. Other plants, dieffenbachia among them, bring on neurological reactions such as convulsions, uncoordination and stupor. Poinsettias cause a contact irritation since they contain a sap that inflames the mucous membranes of the mouth, esophagus and stomach. The needles of cacti pierce the lining of the mouth and throat. As for poison ivy and poison oak, pets do seem less susceptible than people, but animals too can suffer severe skin reactions to these plants.

Should you notice that your cat is attracted to houseplants or outdoor flowers and shrubs, try to break the habit immediately by squirting water (use a water pistol) on the cat when it gets

```
┌─────────────────────────────────────────────────────────┐
│                      CAT FACTS                           │
│                      ────────                            │
│                                                           │
│  Cats certainly do not have nine lives, but they can live up to age 25 or 30. │
│  The average life span ranges between 10 and 20 years.    │
│                                                           │
│  Don't be surprised if your cat looks to you for comfort or exhibits some │
│  sort of behavior change as a result of hearing a loud noise; a feline's │
│  hearing is much more sensitive than a human's.           │
└─────────────────────────────────────────────────────────┘
```

near the plant. Better still, raise the plants out of the animal's reach. If the plants are outdoors, try fencing them off. Incidentally, outdoor cats do not seem as intrigued by plants as their indoor counterparts. Possibly the cat outdoors is up to more serious business than the indoor cat, who is more likely to be bored.

Say, however, that your efforts to remove any plants from the animal's reach are unsuccessful and you notice the animal nibbling away at a plant that you're not sure is harmful. Stop it from chewing one leaf more and watch for signs of illness. Refer to page 186 for specific information about what to do if it looks as though the animal is ill, and take it to your veterinarian as soon as possible. In addition, take along a sample of the plant involved. The veterinarian will want to be certain of the plant's identity. Knowing the parts of the plant the cat consumed and how much will also help determine the course of treatment.

There may be some truth in the tale that cats nibble at greenery in order to make themselves vomit because they're actually suffering from some sort of digestive upset. Frankly, we do not know. But if your cat keeps going at your plants and it's driving you to distraction, you can purchase a product such as Kitty Grass, available in pet stores. It is safe for your cat to eat.

A Warning About Electrical Cords

You can hoist the plants up near the ceiling; you can cap the bottle of disinfectant, hide the paint in the basement and keep medicine bottles behind the closed doors of cabinets. But you're not a normal inhabitant of the twentieth century if you can do without electric current, and that means wires and cords. Unfortunately, a tangle of electrical cords can be the playful cat's delight. This is particularly so with many an upstart kitten who loves to fiddle with jumbled wires and, even worse, loves to chew them, especially when teething—which starts at about three

---

CAT FACTS

When a cat swishes its tail from side to side, it's usually an indication of anger, but it's sometimes a sign of physical discomfort. A cat that holds its tail high in the air while standing up straight is saying that it is content and happy. If its tail is curled around its body when standing, this most often indicates a feeling of insecurity and, occasionally, fear.

---

weeks and continues to the age of five or six months, when permanent teeth come in. If your tiny feline is up to kitty mischief, an electric shock can knock it out. At the very least, the kitten might get a mild jolt. But severe burns to the mouth and tongue are possible, as is respiratory distress (which may not develop for several hours following the incident). Immediate death by electrocution can also occur.

An individual who has a great number of household appliances and lighting fixtures has to take special steps to ensure as safe an environment as possible within the circumstances. Wires should be well insulated. Affixing wires to baseboards, making it hard for the cat to get at them, can help. It also makes sense to accustom a cat to playing with toys that are safe; and, by all means, let your cat know that playing with wires is a no-no. Making a loud sound when the cat starts toying with a cord can get results. Of course, you can't always be around to see what the cat is up to. I have a client who disconnects everything in sight when she leaves the house. Her friends think she's obsessive. She figures she's saving herself and her cat from a potential horrendous trauma.

A cat that is chewing on an electric cord can, at that very moment, be dangerous to you as well as to itself. Yell at the cat; or throw a soft object in its direction to distract it from what it's doing rather than putting your hands on the cat. And what if you're too late? The cat's been shocked and is unconscious. If the animal is touching the cord in any way, turn off the current supplying the outlet before you attempt to aid the pet. When this is impossible, move the cat away from the cord with a *dry* stick or a piece of rope. *Do not touch the pet directly!*

You'll find more details about such situations on pages 161–62 in a discussion of electric shock and on page 191 dealing with first aid for shock. For now, let me just emphasize that when burns are evident on the tongue and in the corners of the cat's mouth, shock, respiratory distress and sometimes death can follow. Get the cat to your veterinarian immediately.

On a happier note, it's true that a cat can outgrow the tendency to play with wires and, once it's through teething, it will be much easier to entice it with various safe paraphernalia. Try not to let the fancy for wires become a habit, which, as I've already said, you can do by having the cat associate a loud noise with the prohibited activity. Then too, some cats never show an interest in wires at all. Generally speaking, be as careful as you can and, after that, cross your fingers.

GROOMING: BRUSHING AND BATHING

*C*ats are constantly grooming themselves, licking away at their hair with rough little tongues. A reflection of the feline's fastidious nature, such grooming is done for reasons of hygiene but, to judge by the times at which it occurs, it apparently serves some psychological purpose too. (Notice, for instance, that a cat who is scolded starts a frenzied bout of licking its hair.) So persistent is this grooming that failure to do it can be taken as an indication that something is wrong. In any case, in spite of the cat's own grooming endeavors, it is wise to brush and comb it on a daily basis. This removes loose dead hairs that the cat otherwise ingests as it licks itself, leading to the formation of hairballs (see pages 217–18). Groom your cat and you will also have a lot less hair flying around your home.

Obviously, long-haired cats require more grooming than short-hairs. A coarse metal comb and hard bristle brush are best for working with long-haired breeds; a fine metal comb and soft bristle brush are preferred for short-haired breeds. You can purchase these at a local pet supply store and, while you are at it, get a good shampoo made strictly for use on cats. Like most felines, your pet will probably never need a bath. Uncertainty, however, is part and parcel of living with the feline and you might as well have the proper product on hand.

To remove the loose dead hairs from the deepest layers of the animal's hair coat, brush or comb against the natural direction of

---

CAT FACTS

Cats display an almost obsessive concern with their appearance. (Actually, what looks like concern is just instinctual grooming.) Should all the licking and preening come to a halt, you should definitely be on the alert. It could be a symptom that the cat is ill.

---

growth. After that, you can brush the hair back its natural way. First, use the comb; follow up with brushing. Finally, take a soft towel or cloth and gently rub the hair coat. This will pick up dander and help restore luster to the coat. As for how the cat takes to this, get it accustomed to being groomed when it's young and it will luxuriate in the process. Cats shed the most in warm weather, during which season it's best to increase the number of times you groom your pet.

When might a cat need a bath? Not long ago, I visited some friends who were in the process of moving. I had also come to vaccinate their cats, one of whom seemed to take great offense at being examined and given a shot. After the injection, the animal —a skittish creature always—began running around the room in search of a place to hide. He wound up with a dive right into the fireplace and a leap upward into the chimney. When he fell back down, he was covered with soot—and wouldn't you know, the cat was white! Now, that was a feline in need of a bath.

Any person who says that his cat looks forward to being bathed should be suspected of dreaming. Every once in a while I'll have a client who will tell me that his cat joyfully jumps into the shower or a tub of water and I'm forced to accept the story. Believe me, this is an exception. *Most cats hate baths.* And giving one to the cat can be traumatic—both for the animal and for the person who has to do the job. If a bath is truly necessary, begin with exceptional gentleness and reassurance in your voice and, if at all possible, avoid getting the cat's head wet, or you're likely to emerge with scratched hands and a still-dirty cat.

Place a little cotton in the animal's ears and to protect the eyes use a little plain base ophthalmic ointment or an ointment of 5 percent boric acid. (Both are available from a pharmacy without a prescription.) When wetting down the cat, do not use a spray hose attachment; the noise of the spray will terrify it. Instead, place a shallow wash basin in the tub and fill it with warm water.

CAT FACTS

Purring is one of the cat's unique characteristics. At one time it was believed to have come from the throat, though now some specialists think that it comes from a vibrating motion that arises in the wall of one of the major blood vessels in the chest area. These vibrations are transmitted to the cat's upper air passages, which results in the purring sound. Kittens start purring soon after birth and most cats purr frequently when content; some even purr while sleeping. But cats have also been heard to purr when in pain or nervous or anxious.

It's best to have someone else hold the cat, but if you are alone, use one hand to restrain the pet firmly by grasping the back of the neck. Put the cat gently into the water and, with your free hand, scoop handfuls of water onto the animal until it's thoroughly wet. Then, using a small amount of shampoo, work up a lather and proceed to wash down the legs, the back, the chest and abdomen. After the shampoo, refill the basin with clean warm water and rinse the soap off the cat. With several towels, dry the cat as completely as possible. Any hair dryer you decide to try should be used for several minutes at the most on the lowest setting; keep the nozzle several inches from the cat, or a thermal burn can result. Do not allow the pet to get near a drafty window or an air conditioner or to go out into cold weather until thoroughly dry.

When bathing with water proves impossible, you can use a dry shampoo. Follow the directions on the product.

Here are some other grooming tips:

- Gum, tar, candy or other sticky substances can be removed by rubbing a little mineral oil into the affected area. If doing this doesn't work, carefully cut it out.
  NOTE: I have seen people use kerosene to try to wash tar or grease out of their pet's hair coat. Kerosene causes severe irritation of the skin and may also lead to internal toxicity.
- A greasy haircoat, especially noticeable in some cats down the midline of the back, can be remedied by placing a little cornstarch in the hair. Rub this in and let it remain for several minutes to absorb the excess oil. Then groom the cat in the usual fashion.
- During times of heavy shedding, some owners are tempted to use the hose attachment of a vacuum cleaner to remove

CAT FACTS

A cat's whiskers are extremely sensitive and fall out periodically to be replaced by new ones. Acting as the feline's radar, they let the animal know of any impending collision or, less drastically, of anything it might be about to brush against. Never touch those whiskers with scissors!

Because of genetics, many blue-eyed white cats are deaf.

the loose hair from their cats. *Never do this.* The suction will not only frighten the cat, it could hurt it as well.

- Your veterinarian can recommend a food supplement if your cat has excessively dry hair or skin. The problem is not always diet; environmental temperature and humidity can play a role.
- Any cat that shows areas of hair loss or baldness should be seen by a veterinarian. Such hair loss may be a medical matter, which won't be solved by grooming.

TENDING THE EYES AND EARS

*T*he ears and eyes of the cat are difficult for the animal to clean by itself. Actually, the eyes—unless something untoward should occur that affects them—need less attention than the ears, which are magnets for dirt, wax and mites.

Just as we may accumulate a little dry "sleep" in the corners of our eyes each night, so do some of our pets; Persians, Himalayans, and other short-nose breeds are prone to "tearing," which should be cleaned away before the discharge has a chance to build up. To prevent the stain of "tearing," gently wipe the inner corner of each eye in the morning, using a *moistened* cotton ball or facial tissue. You can moisten the cotton with warm water or with a sterile eye wash (such as Dacriose) available at your pharmacy. Watch out for any change in the amount, color or consistency of any ocular discharge. A greenish-brown discharge that reappears within 1 or 2 hours could be a sign of conjunctivitis (see page 241). A cat with such symptoms should be examined by a veterinarian and treated, if necessary, with a prescribed medication.

OLD WIVES' TALES

Cats can see in the dark. A cat cannot see in total darkness any more than a person can. On the other hand, because of the anatomy of their eyes, cats see better than other animals in semi-darkness; in dim light their vision is keen.

Some cats make a great fuss over having their ears cleaned; others remain quite placid. In either case, cleaning the ears is an important part of grooming. Clean the ears when they appear soiled (about once a month) and the cat won't get an accumulation of wax. Moisten a cotton ball with a little mineral oil (baby oil works fine) and gently wipe the inside of the ear. Do not use cotton swabs: should the cat shake its head—as well it might—the tip of the swab could jam right into the ear canal, injuring the inner ear.

A noticeable odor coming from the ear or repeated scratching or shaking of the head could be signs of infection or the presence of ear mites. Consult your veterinarian.

DENTAL CARE

*B*aby teeth, or what we call deciduous or milk teeth, begin to appear in kittens at two to three weeks of age and are accompanied by typical teething behavior. Permanent teeth replace these by the time a kitten is 5 or 6 months old. At the same time that your cat receives its annual booster shot and physical, its teeth should be examined.

Feline teeth are subject to some of the same problems as those of people. Over the years, tartar begins to accumulate on the surface of the teeth. This is especially true when the cat eats only moist, canned foods. The danger lies in the buildup of too much tartar on the cat's teeth: large amounts will cause gingivitis, or inflammation of the gums. The gums may become red and swollen; they may bleed. Or the cat can get a good old-fashioned case of halitosis (bad breath).

If your cat will allow you to do so, you can wipe the outer surface of the teeth with a gauze pad dipped in a paste made of equal parts of 3 percent hydrogen peroxide and baking soda to prevent the buildup of excessive tartar. Be careful! Cats—unlike most people—like to keep their mouths shut. You don't want to get bitten. If your cat resists too much, give up.

In older cats, abscesses of the tooth roots can occur. This often causes extreme pain as well as fever, a decrease in appetite and depression. As cats age, they might require tooth extractions. Don't worry about the cat's subsequent ability to eat. It will still be able to do so, though, for obvious reasons, it's going to find softer foods easier to consume.

As for professional cleaning, it is usually done by the veterinarian with an ultrasonic machine. A high-frequency sound wave chips tartar off of the teeth; a thin stream of water rinses it away. This procedure, which should be done from time to time as your veterinarian sees fit, does require a short-acting anesthetic. Why should your cat take going to the "dentist" any better than you do?

TRIMMING NAILS

*F*eline nails and the tendency of the cat to scratch with them can become the source of serious difficulty—*if* you allow it to happen. As persistent as feline scratching is, it *needn't* be unduly troublesome. Nor, in my opinion, except under the most unusual of circumstances, does an owner have to take the extreme measure of declawing (pages 71–72) in order to prevent potential destructiveness.

The cat's claws are an important part of its natural defenses. In the wild they are a means for the cat to catch its food. Moreover, the feline uses its claws to climb and, without them, the cat would be at a great disadvantage in fending off the attack of other animals. When the cat scratches, it sheds the sheath of the nail. For all these reasons, the cat has an instinctive drive to sharpen its claws. Many animal behaviorists believe that cats scratch to express their claim to territory, too. If your cat is one that roams out of doors, don't trim its nails. This will happen naturally as it stretches and scratches on tree trunks.

As for the indoor cat, you can save yourself considerable anguish by giving the cat a scratching post. Some cats will rarely scratch at all. The more typical cat *is* a scratcher. In fact, unless you don't mind shredded upholstery, ripped-up carpets and marks in your furniture, a scratching post is imperative (see page

---

CAT FACTS

A cat, even a young kitten, should never be picked up by the scruff of the neck, at any rate not by *you*. So don't copy the mother cat; she's holding her kitten close to the ground, which makes a tremendous difference. Always use two hands to pick up your cat and hold it close to your body so that it feels secure.

---

84). The indoor cat should also have its nails trimmed once or twice a month starting as early as six weeks of age. Then the cat won't snag its nails on the carpet, and if it happens to scratch the furniture, it won't be able to do as much damage as it would with unclipped nails. As it plays with you, it won't be able to scratch you severely either, as sometimes happens when cats get carried away.

The illustration on page 71 shows you how to clip a feline's nails with a pair of cat nail trimmers, which you can get at a pet supply store. I don't recommend an ordinary nail clipper and I am against using manicure scissors. You'll hurt the cat and will do an inadequate job besides. The proper way is to use the cat nail trimmers and trim the sharp points off.

First, take your thumb and forefinger as illustrated and with a very light squeeze, put gentle pressure on the pad of the toe and the top of the claw. In a state of relaxation, the cat's nails are retracted. The slight pressure you're going to apply will cause the nail—which is now between your thumb and forefinger—to extend. Then, with the other hand, use the instrument. Avoid trimming up high where the white hard nail begins to turn into an area of pink. That is the "quick" of the nail, which you surely don't want to cut. Should this happen accidentally, though, apply pressure over the end of the bleeding nail for several minutes using either a clean cloth or a sterile piece of gauze. You can also touch the tip of the nail with a styptic pencil.

Don't be surprised if your cat has extra toes ("extra" meaning more than five). While this is not exactly a routine condition, *polydactylism* is not all that uncommon either. But if it does have extra toes, the nails must be trimmed with regularity. This applies even to cats that exercise out of doors, since these extra nails are not worn down by natural means. One of the problems with extra nails is that they can grow in a circle, piercing back up into the

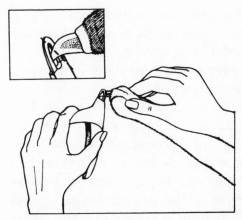

Trimming nails with nail clipper

pad. If this happens, there will be pain and an infection can develop under the skin. Therefore, you must be especially conscientious about trimming these nails.

Most cats resign themselves to having their nails clipped without a lot of commotion. I've even known cats who like it! Should your cat be one that puts up a fierce struggle, you'll have to have the nail trimming done by the veterinarian, but first try this: wrap the cat in a towel, leaving its head and one paw free for clipping. You can also try having someone else help you restrain the cat while you trim.

By the way, cats with trimmed nails should never be allowed out of doors without supervision, because their ability to defend themselves has been impaired.

The Declawing Operation

Every once in a while, a cat will come along that simply cannot be trained to a scratching post. Consequently, the owner may decide to dispose of the animal. Only under such circumstances would I sanction the declawing procedure. Here is what the operation entails:

The animal is anesthetized and a tourniquet is applied on the upper portion of the leg. (In most cases, only the front claws are removed.) Using sterile nail trimmers, the veterinarian must remove the entire last joint of each toe. After all claws have been amputated on the foot, an antiseptic powder is usually applied. Before the tourniquet is released, a tight pressure bandage is placed on the whole leg. Then the procedure is repeated on the other limb. While some veterinarians place sutures into the skin after each toe is removed, many choose not to do so. The bandage is removed one to two days later. Properly, the cat should be hospitalized for at least two days to be sure there is no post-operative bleeding. Even when the cat goes home, it may suffer some degree of pain for several days. It will take five days to a week for the skin to heal over, during which time the pet should be confined to a clean, dry area and discouraged from jumping or being too active. Kitty litter should be removed from its box and replaced with torn-up newspaper or paper toweling for at least five days after surgery. Should the surgery be performed incorrectly, regrowth of nails or painful post-operative infections can result.

Following the operation, some cats will exhibit behavior changes: deprived of their major natural defense, many felines will turn to biting. Others will recover without any noticeable changes.

In my opinion, *a declawed cat must never be allowed outdoors.*

Please do not automatically decide to declaw your cat. First, let the kitten mature and try regular nail trimming and a good scratching post.

ABOUT SPAYING AND NEUTERING

*W*hile detailed information on spaying and neutering can be found in Part IV, on *Reproduction* (see pp. 97–100), they deserve a special mention here. I recommend that the appropriate procedure be performed on your cat as soon as possible; in fact, I consider it a part of basic care, necessary in order to ensure the health of your pet.

In addition, if you neuter your pet, you'll help to curb feline overpopulation. As mentioned earlier, millions of unwanted and homeless cats are born in our country each year. Many are left to wander—easy prey for larger animals, easy targets for automobiles and easy marks for cruel pranksters. If they do survive these

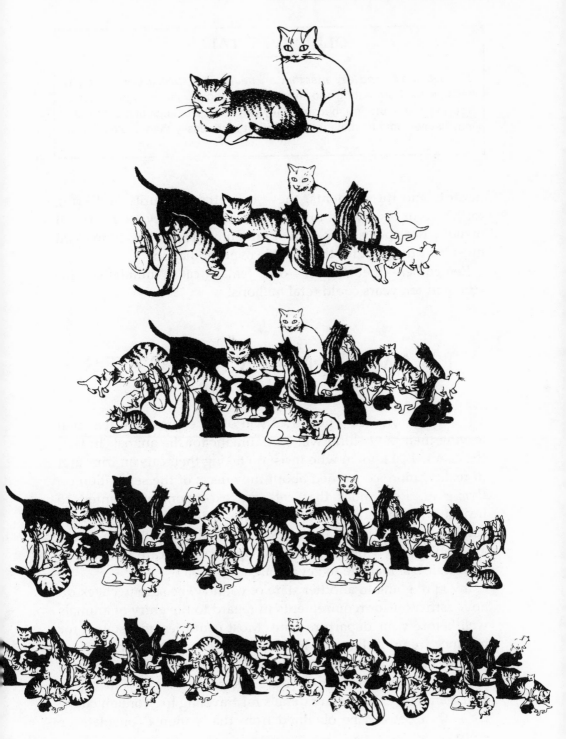

Cat population

OLD WIVES' TALES

Cats become fat and lazy after they are neutered or spayed. Cats generally become fat from eating too much and failing to get enough exercise. Spaying and neutering, because they can effect a change in metabolism, may cause some animals to gain weight more easily than unaltered animals.

hazards and the elements, they soon attain maturity and bring forth five or six kittens to continue this vicious cycle. Every cat owner whose pet is unspayed or unneutered and allowed to roam must bear the guilt for this terrible overpopulation.

Remember—theoretically—one female cat's cumulative offspring in ten years could total millions!

TRAVELING WITH CATS

*C*at owners who travel will often express the fear that leaving their pet behind will be traumatic for the animal. In fact, the clients I've known who insist on taking their cats on trips are, in reality, more concerned about the effects of the separation on *themselves*. Remember that cats are exceptionally oriented to hearth and home and that they have a decided preference for staying put. But there are times when taking a cat along is unavoidable, and while the cat won't particularly care for the upheaval, it will manage to get through.

If you're going to another state or country, be sure to check on any restrictions or requirements in regard to the entry of animals well before your departure date. Most countries and states, for instance, require that cats have had a rabies vaccination within the preceding year. A written health certificate from a veterinarian dated no earlier than ten days before you begin your trip is also mandatory. Necessary details for traveling to a foreign country with a pet can be obtained from that nation's consulate or embassy.

Whether traveling by car, bus, train or plane, cats fare best (as do dogs, for that matter) when safely inside a carrier. Don't be lax about this when traveling by car. A free-roaming pet in an automobile may jump out an open window or be badly hurt even in a minor accident. Furthermore, it can present a serious danger. One playful leap up onto the lap or shoulder (or accelerator) at the wrong moment could cause an accident. So keep your cat in a carrier and concentrate on the road.

Should you be traveling by plane, check with the airline as far in advance as possible about arrangements for your cat. Restrictions vary. Some airlines will allow a small pet to accompany you in the cabin of the plane provided that the carrier will fit beneath the seat. Other airlines insist that pets be placed in a special section of the aircraft, in a special type of carrier. That section is part of the baggage compartment and you can be assured that, at least on the major commercial airlines, the area for animals is temperature-controlled and pressurized too. If you're in doubt, by all means ask.

NOTE: Some modes of public transportation, specifically some trains and buses, will not allow pets on board no matter how small, how cute, how well behaved. In such a case, you obviously have to make other plans.

In addition to providing your pet with any needed vaccinations and giving you a health certificate, your veterinarian just might advise a tranquilizer. I'd say that most cats—even though they'd rather stay home—travel rather well without being medicated. But should your veterinarian prescribe a tranquilizer for your cat, you should try it out ahead of time to check out its possible effects. Sometimes a tranquilizer has an unexpected effect, actually causing the animal to become excited rather than tranquil. It is also imperative that you follow your veterinarian's prescription to the letter. Remember, the purpose of a tranquilizer is to calm the animal down, not knock it out. Be sure, when the time comes, to give the tranquilizer an hour before leaving home and beginning your travels: this will give the medication time to take effect.

Some cats even travel happily—and often. Not too long ago, one of my clients told me that her pet had gone to Paris on the Concorde fifty-five times—which is more than I've done, even once!

For additional information, you can purchase a copy of "Traveling with Your Pet," a comprehensive booklet published by the ASPCA (their address is: ASPCA, Education Department, 441 East 92nd Street, New York, New York 10128).

Whether or Not to Board Your Cat

There's no doubt that your cat will be happiest sitting out your holiday weekend on its own familiar turf. Nor do you have to worry because the cat will be alone—as long as it's healthy and your trip is no longer than three days. Naturally, it is better for the animal to have company. Just take care of the necessities— plenty of water, food (dry), a clean litter box—and the cat will be content holding down the fort. How well it will do depends on the nature of the individual cat. But whether you will be away a long or a short time, it's always best to have a neighbor or friend look in on the animal—to be sure that it's eating, to check on its water supply and to spend some time playing with the pet. And a cat with a history of such disorders as urinary obstruction, diabetes or feline asthma must *never* be left alone unless someone is stopping in daily to make sure it's all right. In the event no friend or neighbor is available, you can hire a professional cat sitter. In many cities, there are people who will either stay with your cat or board it in their home. Speak to your vet or check the Yellow Pages for listings. The service is worth the expense. Your pet need not be made distraught by new surroundings, nor exposed to possible virus infections from close contact with many other animals.

However, should you be going on an extended trip or vacation and you are unable to get someone to stay at your home, a good boarding facility is certainly an option. Visit several to get a feeling for the type of care you can expect your cat to receive. Does the facility look and smell clean? What are the cages like? Are they big enough to allow freedom of movement? Do the animal caretakers convey a real love for cats? If your cat requires a special diet or particular medications, will these be given as directed? Is there sufficient room for exercise? These are the things with which you should be concerned. Don't be deluded either by a place that calls itself an "animal hotel." It may turn out to be very nice—or not. Just remember you're shopping for a suitable boarding facility for a cat you care a lot about, and do your judging accordingly.

CAT FACTS

Any cat that has a history of illness, such as diabetes, urinary obstruction or feline asthma should *never* be left entirely alone. If you've got to leave that cat for a weekend, say, be sure someone comes in to check on it every day.

Before boarding your cat, have it examined by your veterinarian. You want to be sure it receives a clean bill of health and is given any necessary vaccinations. While you are at it, you should obtain a written health certificate. This will protect both you and your cat. Most good kennels will request this certificate anyway and will inquire about the cat's vaccinations and its medical history. Whether a cat sitter or the head of a boarding facility, the party responsible for your cat should always be given the name, address and telephone number of your veterinarian's office.

In the case of a sick or very old cat, you should make every effort to find an alternative to boarding in your absence. The average cat may not like the experience; the stress, however, will affect it less than it will a more delicate creature. Once you've got your pet home again, give it a lot of attention and love. A healthy cat is resilient and will recover; unfortunately, a sick or elderly cat may not.

Cat Travel Tips

Here are eight important suggestions for traveling with your cat in an automobile. I've already made a few of these points, but I want to repeat them for emphasis. By heeding these suggestions, you will increase the chances of a safe and enjoyable trip for both you and your cat.

1. Always take along your cat's own food and water bowls. No matter how short the trip, bring a jug of fresh cool water and offer your pet a drink at regular intervals (every couple of hours).
2. Never give your pet a tranquilizer without your veterinarian's approval. To begin with, it usually isn't necessary, and a tranquilizer can, on occasion, cause a pet to become hyperactive. Therefore, it is wise to try the medication out on your pet a few days before your trip. If you and the veteri-

narian feel the pill is necessary, give the animal the tranquilizer an hour before leaving home so it will have time to take effect.

3. Allow your cat access to its litter box—which you should also take along—at regular intervals along the course of the trip. Take time out to stop where feasible and let the cat get out and walk. CAUTION: Restrain the pet with a collar or harness and leash so you don't get separated.

4. It is best to feed the cat 6 or more hours before you take off. This is especially wise in the case of pets not accustomed to car trips or those that are prone to motion sickness.

5. If it is a long trip and you have to feed the cat in the car, use semi-moist packaged or dry foods rather than meals from a can. You won't have to bother with a can opener, and packaged foods are less messy.

6. Always keep your pet restrained safely inside a secure carrier, especially when car windows are open. Whether the car windows are open or not, the cat could cause an accident.

7. Always keep your cat in the car *with you*. Don't, even if it is confined to a carrier, put it inside a camper or trailer or in the back of a pickup truck.

8. *Never leave your cat unattended in a parked car*. In hot weather the interior of the car heats up like an oven within minutes.

CAT SHOWS: PROS AND CONS

*T*hroughout the country, there are numerous cat shows every year, ranging from minor contests that are mostly for fun to major competitions involving prestige and considerable amounts of money. In major competitions the prize is won by the cat that is anointed "best of breed" or "best of show." The owner of the winner walks away with recognition as a prominent breeder and, consequently, with prospects of what can be sizable breeding fees. Not all cats are allowed in all shows; many are open only to registered purebreds. But the smaller, less serious contests can be a child's delight.

Admittedly, some of these shows are fun; others serve a valuable purpose to the dedicated breeder. At the same time, cat shows can be dangerous to the pet. While precautions are taken to verify the good health of cats to be presented, there is a reasonable chance of a mistaken assessment. This is especially so in the case of upper respiratory viruses, wherein symptoms may not be evident at the time an animal is entered. Following a show, many vaccinated cats come down with a mild URI (upper respiratory infection). In some instances the infection is not so mild. Rather, it is life-threatening and can spread to other cats within a given household or cattery. Deaths do occur. Therefore, if you plan to show your cat, be sure that the pet is in excellent health and up to date on its vaccinations. Confine it to a comfortable carrying case until it is displayed. Before it is shown, keep it in a dry, draft-free area and courteously prevent strangers from handling your pet.

Because of the risk involved, I tend to discourage my clients from showing their pets. I ask the serious breeder to take special precautions, and I point out the hazards to those who regard the minor shows as harmless amusement. They are not always so harmless; the fun is not worth the chance of the animal's contracting disease.

PART THREE

TRAINING AND BEHAVIOR

TRAINING THE CAT

*M*ost people take the training of a dog for granted but somehow reject the idea that training a cat is even a possibility. Granted that the feline is a stubborn creature, a quirky sort that has a mind of its own. Still, the housecat can be trained well enough—up to a point.

When it comes to such routine matters as housebreaking, cats are far easier to teach than dogs. The kitten will have using the litter box "down" by 4–6 weeks. You can also teach your feline to fetch and retrieve light objects such as catnip toys. Cats will sit, beg and roll over too. Reward them with praise and a loving scratch of the neck or with a small treat of cat chow.

The young kitten must be trained to respect the boundaries within your home in which you will allow it to roam. Call it training or behavior modification, you must let the kitten know where and when it can climb, jump or meow. My first cat was 2½ years old when I took her in and she had established behavior patterns that I disliked. For the first month I didn't get much sleep, and a few things were knocked off counters in the course of play. I had to retrain her to fit into my life so that we could coexist harmoniously. The old saying "You can't teach an old dog new tricks" doesn't have to apply to cats. However, teaching a kitten what's right and wrong is easier done than with an adult cat. But give the older cat some time and exert a little extra patience and persistence in your training and, in most cases, the cat will learn new habits and forget the old.

Let the animal know when it's in the wrong. A good stern voice command works well and once the cat knows the meaning of "NO," you'll usually succeed in restraining your pet from going too far out of bounds. Training and discipline can go paw in paw.

The fundamentals of training are basically those of conditioning, but you'll find, especially with the cat, that reward works better than punishment. Be sure you respect the animal's anatomy too: it can't get you the morning newspaper or bark when a stranger comes to the door. And it has a right to maintain its independence besides. Thus, its response to your training will always be somewhat subject to feline whim. Most of the time, a feline treated with great affection will be happy to cooperate. But the cat is *not* a dog. While it will abide by your *rules,* you will have to give a little and abide by *its* terms of endearment.

Having said all this, it's worth noting that in all the years I've been treating cats, I've yet to know a client who really cared whether his or her cat could fetch, roll over or perform a bunch of tricks. Most people will be extremely satisfied to have a well-behaved feline. I've therefore devoted the following section to behavior problems that are of far more concern to the typical owner.

NOTE: Training the older cat or previously outdoor cat that is accustomed to scratching on furniture or trees may prove nearly impossible. But as I advise in the section on declawing (pages 71–72), please try a scratching post (page 84) and nail clipping before resorting to having your cat declawed.

COMMON BEHAVIOR PROBLEMS AND WHAT TO DO ABOUT THEM

*H*ave you ever considered taking your cat for a visit to a psychologist? This is not a laughing matter. Even the most law-abiding of feline citizens may start manifesting "behavior problems" you would never have reason to anticipate. But you, the beleaguered cat owner, do not have to assume unwarranted guilt over the errant ways of your feline pet, spending endless and unproductive hours counting the number of things you must have done wrong to provoke the animal. Chances are, you've done nothing wrong at all. Nor do you have to succumb to being stuck with a "crazy cat." For one thing, your cat's not crazy. (Almost all feline misbehaviors are nothing more than "natural" actions of your pet that, for one reason or another, are being expressed in a manner unsuitable to *you*.) For another, most of these problems are treatable.

In earlier parts of this book, I've discussed two of the most frequent problems that present themselves to cat owners. But the eating of plants (pages 61–62) is easily handled and the scratching of furniture (page 85) need not be the bane of a cat owner's existence if steps are taken to direct the cat's instincts to an appropriate place: i.e., the sturdy, scratchable scratching post your cat will learn to love.

The Scratching Post

The cat is an unredeemable scratcher, and you can't negotiate with instincts. Having a scratching post in your household from the day you get your pet will lessen the chances of ruined carpets and shredded furniture. It is even possible to eliminate destruction entirely.

The majority of commercially available scratching posts are upright stands with carpeted coverings. Unfortunately, the carpet used is all too often overly dense, with a texture of softness that is not too likely to give the cat a surface it will really take to. Being attractive to look at, they seem to have been made to appeal to owners rather than to their cats. Moreover, some of these carpeting materials may confuse the animal too, making it difficult for the pet to distinguish between what's "on-limits" on the post and what's taboo on the floor. However, there is one particular scratching post that I heartily recommend. You can get it from the following manufacturer:

The Felix Company
416 Smith Street
Seattle, Washington 98109

The Felix posts are covered with a sisal hemp material that is suitably rough and also long-lasting. These posts have catnip in them too, with its mysterious allure.

You can also quite successfully make your own. Here are two alternative types:

1. Cut a piece of heavy plywood into a 2-foot square and use this as a base. Attach to this base an upright section of a log with its natural bark intact. This section should be taller than the outstretched length of the cat, which will allow the pet to stretch out its body and obtain the exercise it needs and loves.
2. Make a post similar to those available commercially. Use a strong base like the one I've just described. Attach an up-

right piece cut from a 4" by 4", then cover it with carpeting
—*turned inside out.* With the rough underside exposed, your
cat will find the material more like the bark on a tree than
your living room rug.

Since cats like to stretch and scratch the minute they awake,
you'd be doing yourself and the animal a favor if you keep the
post near the creature's sleeping place. To train the animal, take
it while still a kitten to the scratching post numerous times
throughout the day. Stand the kitten up against it and run its
paws down along the post, letting it know by the way you speak
that you thoroughly approve. The cat ought to get the idea. You
can also sprinkle catnip on and around the post. With some sensible training (and a bit of luck), you can have a feline to whom
the post is as holy as a totem pole. Some behaviorists recommend
that the scratching post be tall enough that the cat can reach up
to it while standing on its hind legs.

NOTE: If you happen to be redecorating your home, consider
covering your couches and chairs in smooth material. Rough material on your furniture doesn't have to mean doom, but there's
simply no doubt that you'll have the edge with less enticing upholstery.

There are two other problems that are considerably more formidable than scratching or plant eating and may, indeed, require
professional attention. The most serious of the common behavioral problems associated with cats are inappropriate eliminations
(urinating and defecating) outside the litter box, and aggression
toward other cats and people.

In Appendix 3 of this book (page 276) you will find a list of cat
behaviorists who could be contacted by your veterinarian for consultation purposes. Before taking such a step, your veterinarian
will want to rule out a physical problem as the underlying cause
of any unusual behavior. *This procedure is a must.* Then, should it
be deemed necessary, the services of an animal behaviorist might
well prove immensely useful in finding a remedy for the "problem," so that you and your cat do not remain at odds. Please
keep in mind that an extra dose of patience and a little time may
be necessary to "cure" the cat. Furthermore, you could very well
run into different opinions on the cause of a problem and its

solution, all depending on which behaviorist you talk to (or whose writings you happen to read). In such a case, you should, of course, follow the advice that works.

Inappropriate Elimination

For the sake of convenience, I've used the term "inappropriate elimination" to cover all the ways a cat "does its business" someplace other than in the litter box. Yet, to be exact, there are two kinds of decidedly different behavior under discussion here. One is simple elimination (urination and defecation) as all of us understand it, i.e., when you've got to go, you've got to go. The other is referred to as *urine marking* or *spraying*. Behaviors of these kinds have different causes and, correspondingly, different treatments. Normal urination and spraying are visibly different activities as well, not to mention powerfully different to the smell. Neither is particularly appealing to human senses, but it is hard to rival the odor of feline urine (especially that of a tomcat) for its overwhelming reek.

SPRAYING

When a cat "sprays" or "urine marks," it is expressing some territorial, competitive or sexually related drive. This is utterly distinct from the typical compulsion to void. When doing the latter, the cat squats with its tail held out parallel with the floor and curving up a bit. The urine is deposited on a horizontal surface—the bottom of the litterbox, you hope. When "spraying," however, the cat does not squat. It holds its tail straight up in the air, and wiggles it. Simultaneously, the animal may do a little two-step with its back legs. Most significantly, the urine is sprayed onto a vertical surface, be it a wall, speaker, piece of furniture—or even a mortified person. Whatever the surface, it is vertical and several inches or more off the floor.

Male animals "mark" much more frequently than females; moreover, they do so at times of the year when hormone levels are highest. Given the hormonal output of the "intact" male cat, it is much more likely to spray than a neutered animal. Nonetheless, neutered males and even females will sometimes spray as well, an occurrence that is almost always restricted to aggressive or competitive behavior between two or more cats. A new cat in the house, for example, may stimulate an aggressive reaction in the resident animal. One or both of the cats could then start a bout of spraying. Also, an indoor cat may react to an outdoor animal by starting a responsive spraying. It is not unheard of, either, for an indoor cat to spray in response to a person toward whom it is aggressive. One thing ought to be clear: *the more cats in the household, the higher the probability of spraying.* Also, cats that have access to the sights and sounds of outdoor animals are more likely to spray than animals who are kept away from outdoor creatures.

While neutering the male cat reduces spraying and usually stops it altogether, castration is not always a complete solution. Be aware that there are also medical means that can be helpful. The administration of the female hormone *progestin* has been found to aid in suppressing urine marking. The catch is that only small doses should be used and this drug therapy cannot be sustained for more than a short time. Therefore, in conjunction with this, other steps should be taken to discourage spraying.

When a cat restricts its spraying to one place in the home, it sometimes works to place its food, water and/or toys right on the spot where it tends to mark. Cats don't like to eliminate where they eat or play, so forcing them to feed, drink or play directly in the usual "line of fire" could help inhibit this unpleasant behavior. An alternative is to place some aversive material (aluminum foil, plastic, newspaper) over the target area, or to blanket the area with some sort of substance which has a repelling effect on the cat. Commercial repellents are available in pet stores, but success with the use of these has not been frequently reported by many of my clients. My sister and brother-in-law discovered that their cat was completely turned off by pieces of grapefruit rind. But such a technique is going to fail if the cat's motivation to spray is strong; all it will do is spray in a new location. Punishing the cat (yelling, hitting or squirting the cat with water) will usually assure only that the cat won't spray while the owner is around. The spraying may continue in the owner's absence and the punishment may merely serve to create fear of the owner.

When the sights and scents of outdoor cats (a female in heat or a tom on the prowl) are the stimulus for the spraying of the indoor animal, obviously, any and all steps that can be taken to get rid of the outdoor animals will help. Sometimes, this is impossible, but efforts can be made to prevent the inside cat from seeing, hearing or smelling the outdoor felines. One could restrict the pet to a part of the house where it won't respond to whatever is going on outdoors. Without doors and windows to the outside, an indoor cat won't be able to see neighboring cats or, more importantly, smell their scents.

In a rare case, a cat will spray in connection with aggressive or fearful feelings toward a person. Then, not only does the cat spray, but it also exhibits other unusual behavior (aggression, for example, or hiding in fear). When something like this occurs, the person who is the focus of the animal's aggression or fear would do well to avoid close contact with the cat for a minimum of 1–2 weeks and then slowly try to make friends. That accomplished, the spraying may cease.

Discuss spraying problems with your veterinarian. Once again, the best results might be obtained by the administration of small doses of progestin in combination with other attempts to change behavior. And always remember, the fewer cats that are around, the less likely you are to encounter this most unpleasant problem.

ELIMINATION PROBLEMS

Owing to pressure on the bladder or bowel, when a cat has the urge to go, it follows that urge, but it does what comes naturally in a location that, at least to you, may be a most unnatural place.

This has nothing to do with the mother cat's failing to teach its kitten where to do its business. A kitten does not have to be taught to use the box, and all your efforts to scratch its paws in the litter will not help if the cat has started to eliminate outside the box. It may also surprise you to hear that, according to some very experienced animal behaviorists, emotional causes—usually lumped together as "stress"—are rarely behind this sort of behavior.

On the simplest level—that which is easiest to understand and to cope with, too—cats have preferences for the feel of material they like to dig into to cover their urine or feces. Sometimes these preferences do not coincide with what we humans provide for the pet. Commercial cat litters are manufactured and bought by people, not felines, and while the manufacturers do their best to please the cat population, they don't always succeed. Fortunately, most cats will use commercial cat litter, but some are less than fond of it; the cat may even be uncertain as to what it wants to do. Thus, a cat could dig and cover in the litter for urinating, avoid it for defecating, or steer clear of it for both. Should something like this occur, the cat is telling you something. It just doesn't like that litter! You, in response, might have to adjust the environment to suit the cat, which is simply to say: try another type of litter.

Today, some pet owners resort to devices to train their cats to use the toilet. Beware! Some of my friends were ecstatic at their own success in training their cat to eliminate in the toilet. The litter box was packed away, until at about 6 months of age, their cat began defecating on the bathroom rug (and elsewhere in the apartment). I suggested they forget the toilet training and put the litter box back out before a bad habit was established. Sure enough, "Garfield" jumped into the litter box and began to scratch away. To this day he hasn't had any more inappropriate eliminations.

Incidentally, one clue that the cat doesn't like the litter is the way it acts toward the litter material. It may fail to scratch in the litter box; it may shake its paws after leaving the box or stand on the edge to eliminate without touching the litter. You may not notice that your cat is showing clear disdain. Dutifully continuing to use the box for a while, it will then discover some other material (your carpet, your bed) that gives it more tactile satisfaction. If clay-based litters don't work, try something different: clay and topsoil mixed, topsoil alone, wooden chips or shredded newspaper.

One of the more interesting causes of elimination problems is an association of scratching on non-litter surfaces. It goes like this: many cats quite happily scratch to cover up the feces or urine in the litter. All would be well if that's where the scratching stopped. But watch a cat and you'll often find that it doesn't. Finished scratching in the litter itself, it will continue to scratch at the smooth sides of the litter box or to use its claws on the walls or floors around the box. All of a sudden, what develops is an association—between the act of eliminating and scratching on smooth surfaces. The next thing you've got is a cat that's doing it on the bathroom floor or in the tub, possibly the sink, what have you. A bathmat or carpet could be in close proximity to the litter box, too, and a similar association could arise, leading a cat to use the carpet. Treatment in a case like this requires "reassociating" the cat to the feel of litter. Place the bath mat (or something similar) near the litterbox—or even *in* it—and gradually change the relative amounts of carpet and litter (bit by bit decreasing the carpet and adding more litter) until the cat is once again acclimated to the litter alone. This process can take considerable forbearance on an owner's part, but in time, the technique should work.

Another thing to consider: surely, if you own a cat, you've noticed that it will decide to sleep on a dining room chair after years of slumber at the foot of the couch. The same sort of location preference can happen with elimination. These preferences can be treated by placing food, water, toys or aversive material in the now coveted spot. Sometimes it's necessary to place a litter box on top of the area involved. The cat begins to use the litter box again. Next, the box can be gradually moved back to the location the owner prefers.

And what of emotional problems? Sometimes, an elimination problem is induced by an environmental change: new furniture in the home, a new baby, another pet. Moving to a new house or changing the location of the litter box are other possibilities, as well as the absence of an owner to whom a cat is profoundly attached. In the past, most elimination problems were blamed on an emotional response that seemed to be correlated to environmental change. However, behaviorists Borchelt and Voith (see list of behaviorists beginning on page 276) have concluded that this is not usually the case. They do not deny that an emotional reaction to environmental change can cause an elimination problem; it is simply their observation that this is not the most common cause. Even when an emotional response initiates the elimination problem, it isn't observed to be the reason it's maintained. They point out that were this so, the cat could be expected to display other behavioral symptoms as well (aggression or hiding), and this is rarely the case. The one emotion that these highly respected authorities have found to be involved in elimination problems is *anxiety due to the prolonged absence of an owner*.

That reminds me of a particular incident involving a client of mine. The client's cat was less active than usual and had taken to hiding under the furniture. Also, it was "making mistakes" outside the litter box now and then. The cat passed his physical exam with flying colors and I was stuck for an explanation of the re-

---

TIPS TO COMBAT
INAPPROPRIATE ELIMINATION

1. Always check with a vet to rule out cystitis.
2. Place a few drops of ammonia in the cat's litter box (it smells like urine).
3. Move the litter box(es) to another location.
4. If you catch the cat in the act, spray it with water.
5. Remove urine from carpet to neutralize the odor (use seltzer).
6. Try different types of litter.
7. Confine the cat and litter box to the bathroom.
8. Take the cat to the litter box after it eats.
9. If the cat urinates in the bathtub or basin, cover the bottom of the fixture with water.

---

ported symptoms. However, after questioning, I found out that the owner's wife had returned to work not long before and that the cat had begun to exhibit the changed behavior around the same time. Call it a "separation-anxiety" response. For the first ten years of his life, the animal always had plenty of company; suddenly he was deprived. But this sort of pattern is an exception; in most cases, you'll be wasting your time trying to blame the cat's failure to use the litter box on some complex emotional response to normal human behavior or to changes in a household environment. As Borchelt and Voith have concluded, these cases are rare.

Needless to say, keeping the litter box clean is essential; a dirty box could certainly cause a cat to eliminate elsewhere. But if you're keeping the box scrupulously clean, and none of the above suggestions works for you, depending upon the severity of the problem, you might benefit greatly by consulting any of the animal behaviorists listed in the Appendix.

Aggression

Hissing, spitting, growling, biting, scratching . . . Aggressive behavior can range from that which is part of an offense to aggression that is strictly defensive. When aggression transpires between cats, it usually involves a bit of both, but aggression against people is less common. Most of these cases occur when the cat (usually young) stalks a person, often biting legs and hands in what the cat understands as *play*.

The play of the cat is closely connected with its predatory instincts. Thus, in stalking, pouncing and biting, it is going after something (or somebody) that moves. Sometimes this behavior can be amusing, but it can also result in injury and, therefore, has to be curbed. Most often, an aggression problem related to play develops when a cat is left alone a lot or isn't played with very much by the owner. The relationship between predatory instincts and play in the feline is crucial. Without the stimulus of playful activity, the cat will resort to releasing its predatory energies in an aggressive or destructive fashion. Not that most owners aren't generous in giving their cats toys to play with. But, unfortunately, most cat toys are "dead," which is to say, they do not move; the cat gets bored and suddenly, you've got an attacking cat.

A play-deprived feline will be very mindful of the movements of an owner or other person, an unnerving matter if ever there was one; that cat will not only watch for movement itself but will be quite alert as to when and where it occurs. That's why many owners report that the cat will attack them only at certain times or in certain places. Remember, cats have location preferences; such preferences can also take the form of lurking in certain rooms of the house in hidden places until—whammo!—the owner walks by. The solution to this sort of play-related aggression is usually fairly simple. Another cat is a possible answer. Of course, some people don't want another cat. In the face of this, an owner can solve the problem most of the time by providing lots of active, interesting *moving* toys for the frustrated feline. Since most toys don't move very easily by themselves (those battery-driven jobs are fairly plunky and don't really grab the cat's attention), the owner who cares will have to devote some time and energy to rerouting the animal's instincts. Thus, a smart owner who knows the cat is probably lurking under the bedspread waiting to spring at his or her ankles, will carry a string that he can wriggle to provide the cat a more appropriate "chase stimulus" than feet or legs. In addition to reducing wear and tear on human limbs, it will also teach the cat to go after inanimate but moving toys even in the context of the owner's own moving presence.

One cat is different from another, of course, and a feline with an exceptionally high level of play behavior will require that the owner be singularly dedicated to solving the problem. Nonetheless, the success rate of treating play aggression problems is extremely high.

CAT VS. CAT AGGRESSION
Fights between cats are typically ferocious and can involve an array of physical movements and manifestations: ears flattened back against the head; pilo erection (when a cat arches its back, and the hairs on the tail and along the back stand up); and sideways motions on approach. The most common type of aggressive behavior between cats involves *fear*. Paradoxically, fear-related aggression often springs up between two or more cats that previously had been living together as best of friends. The cycle is typical: something frightens one of the cats; it then jumps, shrieks, howls, whatever; the other cat mistakes that response as aggression. A fight is on in a second and the previous bond of friendship, believe it or not, is not always easy to reestablish.

The first thing to do is to separate the cats, removing them from each other's sight entirely. Forget all thoughts of letting them fight it out. Often, visual separation for a few days will spur the curiosity of each of the cats as to what has happened to the other. Then, they can be gradually reintroduced by a meal together, a little play, all helped along by a little verbal coaxing by the owner. Done slowly, this will work most of the time. The same procedure is useful in introducing a new cat to the home. Here, the initial hissing and spitting and pilo erection are a result of fear—which will usually dissipate if the cats are gradually reexposed to each other.

Territorial aggression is another matter entirely. This does not usually involve pilo erection and vocalization (hissing, growling). What typically takes place is a prompt and determined chase, with one cat pursuing the other and keeping it out of specific areas of the home. This kind of territorial aggression can be an extremely difficult problem to solve; sometimes, the best solution is to find another home for one of the cats.

Among outdoor cats, fighting is a natural response to territorial or sexual encroachment. If the animal is neutered, it is less likely to stray from home and thus get into fights.

PART FOUR

REPRODUCTION

*I*n this section of the book the feline's reproductive system will be discussed, including the female's estrus (or "heat") cycles, mating and the methods and ramifications of spaying and neutering. The fundamentals of pregnancy and birth will also be covered.

THE FEMALE IN HEAT

*W*hile reproductive behavior in cats is fundamentally the same as in other animal species, one of the more interesting and significant differences between the cat and most other mammals has to do with the nature of the female's ovulation mechanism. We call the female cat (or queen) an "induced ovulator" rather than a "spontaneous" one. What this means is that the release of eggs in the feline is directly brought on by copulation. As a consequence, pregnancy is never a matter of chance. Instead, when copulation occurs between a sexually mature, healthy and fertile male and female cat at just the right stage of the latter's estrus cycle or "heat," the results are inevitable. Sperm and egg unite; the "induced" ovulation is a fact that biologically guarantees impregnation. It may take more than one mating to induce ovulation and in fact the cat will usually mate several times within a few hours. Impregnation does not stop with one act of copulation. Sexually joined with one or more males the female will continue to release a number of eggs as subsequent acts of mating occur. Thus, the female may have some eggs fertilized by the sperm of one male cat and other eggs fertilized by the sperm of a different tom.

The female cat reaches sexual maturity between 6 and 10 months of age, during which time her first "heats" become noticeable, sometimes to the mortification of a startled and naïve owner, who can't comprehend what has possessed the animal. A female in heat is a sight to behold, and often a horror to hear as well, emitting all sorts of vocal "calls" indicating that she's ready to breed. In addition to crying a lot, the queen may roll madly around on the floor, urinate more frequently, engage in persistent rubbing against the owner's feet, or assume peculiar postures (e.g., lifting the tail and raising the hindquarters up in the air. At the sight of that position, many an owner—hitherto petrified that something is wrong with the cat—finally catches on).

Unlike dogs, which "go into heat" semiannually, cats are not as predictable and may experience several heat cycles over the course of the year. Factors influencing the onset of "heat" include nutrition, environmental temperature and, more importantly, length of the day (the period of daylight), which has a significant effect upon hormone levels. That long periods of daylight, such as occur in the spring, stimulate hormonal activity makes enormous sense; this is nature's way of ensuring the birth of kittens in the spring, when they have the best chances of survival. It's very likely, as well, that heat cycles are related to the presence of male cats.

As for the length of heats, they can last for two to seven days. The behavioral changes accompanying heat are a normal manifestation of the female's readiness to be mated. If the queen, in such a state, is out of doors, a whole troup of potential suitors is likely to arrive in an owner's backyard. The queen will not start mating without an interval of "courtship" first; this pre-copulatory behavior can last literally for hours. When she's ready, the chosen tom will clench the back of her neck with his mouth and mount her from behind. After several rapid thrusts in which penetration is accomplished, the tom ejaculates in a matter of seconds. The penis of the tom is barbed and his abrupt withdrawal causes the queen to shriek. After separation the cats will groom themselves (especially the paws and genitals). In just a few minutes mating can occur again and the queen might allow another tom to mount. Hence, in keeping with what I've explained about fertilization, the resultant kittens could have different fathers.

No generalizations can be made about the number of estrus cycles a queen may have each year. Two is normal; so is four; five or six is not unheard of. Nonetheless, even the most understanding owners can be quite upset by a cat that repeatedly goes in and out of heat. Such cats may have what we term "cystic ovaries," which may cause the heat cycle to continue for weeks on end. In this instance, the best remedy is to have the cat spayed.

SPAYING—ALTERING THE FEMALE CAT

*A*s mentioned earlier, it is my opinion that *all* female cats (but a breeding queen) should be neutered. The spaying operation should take place when the animal is 6 to 8 months of age. In medical terms, the procedure is called an "ovariohysterectomy," or an OHE, which refers to the complete removal of both the ovaries and the uterus. The operation is performed while the animal is under a general anesthesia (see pages 119–20), and it feels no pain. In most cases, with post-operative tender loving care (see pages 120–22), your pet will recover rapidly.

The myths about felines are almost as legion as the cat population itself. Let me dismiss one of the weirdest and most prevalent of those myths: *it is not true that a cat will be a better pet if allowed to have a litter before it is spayed.* Spaying, in fact, almost always results in a cat with a more even-tempered disposition. As an added benefit, it certainly prevents outdoor cats from contributing to the problem of overpopulation. Performed at the prescribed age, the operation is fairly routine. In older cats complications can indeed occur, which is another reason why it's important to have the feline spayed when young. The unspayed feline, more often than not, will need female-related surgery eventually. It may develop a uterine infection or breast, ovarian or uterine cancer. The frequency of occurence of breast cancer in older female cats is significant, and approximately 80 percent of these mammary tumors are malignant. If the cat is spayed under a year of age, the incidence is substantially reduced.

Don't worry that your spayed feline will become lazy, fat and inactive. There's no truth to *that* myth either. Naturally, pets—just like people—get a little slower as they age and tend to put on weight. But the cause is the ticking clock; it's got nothing to do with spaying. So encourage your cat to play with toys and thereby get regular exercise; monitor its intake of food and even cut down on the amount it gets if you think it's looking plump. Spayed and content, your cat should remain sleek, active and healthy as it ages.

THE TOM
ON THE PROWL

*T*he male cat reaches sexual maturity between 6 and 10 months. Unlike the female, he is not given to periods of "heat" and is therefore more constantly "on the prowl." Constant prowling, like the stimulation of hormone activity in the female, could be an effect of increased daylight; or it could have more to do with the number of female cats who, for the same reason, are in heat during the months of spring.

Unless you've had no exposure to cats at all, you have probably heard, at one time or another, the horrendous sound of yowling toms interrupting the peace of a quiet spring night. A male cat in pursuit of a female will almost invariably intrude upon the territory of another male who is after the same cat, and the confrontation can wake up the block. Like boxers in a ring, rival cats will circle each other, then start to slug it out. The fights they have are truly terrible, characterized by spitting, hissing, shrieking, ferocious scratching and biting, and what surely look like attempts at the kill. In the middle of all this commotion is the seductive female who—when she's good and ready—will allow one of the males to mount her; succeeding males will follow.

CASTRATION— ALTERING THE MALE CAT

*M*ost veterinarians are all too familiar with owners who get upset about the prospect of allowing the castration of their cats. The nervousness one sees strikes me as somewhat telling, but mine is not the psychoanalyst's mantle. My business is overseeing the health and welfare of animals and, along with that welfare, the contentment of their owners. Because so many clients freeze at the use of the term "castration," the procedure is often referred to as the "altering," "fixing" or "neutering" of a male cat. Regardless of what you want to call it, the operation should be performed when the male cat is between 7 and 9 months of age. As with spaying, the cat is placed under general anesthesia (see pages 119–20). Both testicles are removed and, in most cases, sutures are not necessary to close the wound. What little pain the cat feels will soon subside, and with loving postoperative care (see pages 120–21), your pet will recover rapidly.

Unless you live in the country or suburbs where your cat is able to roam, there is only one valid reason not to neuter a male: that's if you are a breeder and use the cat for stud.

Tomcats are usually very affectionate with people as long as they're not caged. Nonetheless, the problem of "spraying" cannot be stressed too much: the Tom releases a strong-smelling urine that most people cannot stand.

In part, spraying is a territorial act; it is also meant to attract the female. Once a habit of spraying develops, it may continue even after the pet is neutered. To spare yourself the loss of friends, *do not* wait for signs that your cat is spraying before scheduling surgery. Generally speaking, male cats won't begin to spray until they are 10 to 12 months of age. Get it done before that and take my word for it, the "altered" male has no ego problems.

In addition to spraying, intact male cats not used for stud and kept indoors in close quarters often become nervous and aggressive. The neutered male is a wonderfully gentle, even-tempered animal. Also, the altered cat allowed out of doors will tend to stay closer to home and get into fewer of those notorious catfights in which tomcats commonly engage. An abscess that frequently forms following a catfight requires a visit to your veterinarian and that expense will usually exceed the cost of castration. Neuter your cat and you'll also help to curb feline overpopulation. Be sensible and abandon "castration anxiety" if you happen to have it. Your life and the life of the cat will be considerably eased.

BREEDING

*M*any owners who've purchased purebred cats get it into their heads that they will "breed" their animals and make a "return on their investment." I ask you to reconsider any such thoughts and leave breeding to the professionals.

Cats are mated to bring out the best characteristics in a breed (e.g., size, color, length of tail) and the resulting offspring should "improve" the breed. The time and energy involved is much more than most pet owners would be ready for by a mile. Breeders will be the first to tell you that they aren't really in it for the money, *per se*. The popularity of a breed depends on the particular country or area; the price will reflect that too. A breeder must have a reputation to attract customers to the "product"; such a reputation is hardly acquired overnight. Any owner who fancies that the Persian kitten resulting from the mating of his cat with the Persian who lives next door will be a prize is in for a big disappointment. That kitten may be adorable and its cuteness worth the price of gold—but only in the metaphorical sense. In real dollars, its value is a far cry from the worth of a Persian kitten descended from a carefully selected pair of champions.

Expenses, too, take a big chunk out of any profits for the serious breeder. Just to give an example, if a pregnant pet doesn't have a routine delivery, then a cesarean section (see pages 105–106) must be performed and, depending on where you live, may cost more than double the expense of a routine ovariohysterectomy. Aside from the expense, the general maintenance for cats that are meant to be bred is costly. So forget the return on your investment. If you want a purebred cat, you're best off if you want it for other reasons.

Sometimes, pet owners will foster a pregnancy because they want their children to experience the "miracle of birth." A miracle it definitely is. But the majority of cats have their kittens when no one is around to disturb them. Most public schools and many libraries have excellent films available for educational purposes; let your children learn the miracle of birth from sources like these.

Should you really want to become a professional breeder, that is another matter, and a fine endeavor—as long as you know what you're getting into. Otherwise, as discussed on pages 97–98 and 99–100, I urge you to neuter or spay your animal. Thousands of cats are euthanized—*every day*—because of overpopulation.

On the following pages I discuss the birth process at some length—because I know it happens, *not* because I want to encourage the event. If you are unable to find homes for the kittens produced by your pet and if you have to give them up to a local pound, you may find that your children's experience with the "miracle of birth" has turned into a real nightmare.

NOTE: If there is an accidental pregnancy, the cat can be spayed (within the first few weeks following mating). But why put your animal through this? Get it spayed *now!*

PREGNANCY AND
GIVING BIRTH

*Y*ou may suspect that your cat is pregnant because of an increase in the size of her abdomen. Most likely, your pregnant pet will also show a marked increase in appetite, to which you should of course respond by giving her extra food.

Yet, other than providing her with a comfortable home and your continued love and attention, you don't have to give the cat any special care during the bulk of her pregnancy. Not even nutritional supplements are necessary as long as you feed her a balanced diet. Under normal circumstances, an office visit is unnecessary; generally, a healthy, vaccinated cat will have an uneventful pregnancy. (It's preferable not to vaccinate or give booster shots to a pregnant cat.) The gestation period, i.e., the length of time from conception until birth, lasts approximately 63 days. This may vary one or two days either way, but usually not more unless there are complications.

Keep the cat safely inside your home during the 2 months she is expecting; avoid her having contact with ill animals. Do not give her any medications unless instructed to by your veterinarian. Mind you, there's no need to be overprotective. These precautions are mentioned merely to better ensure that the fetuses develop fully and that the pregnancy ends with the birth of a healthy litter.

During the last weeks of the pregnancy, you may notice a change in the cat's behavior and she may, at that time, need pampering. After all, she's entitled. Because of her increasing size, for example, it may be difficult for her to groom herself adequately. With a cat that has long hair, I would advise cutting some of the fur around the anus, the vulva and the nipples; this will help her keep those areas clean, and you might assist her by using a little mild soap and water in these areas. In the last few days of the pregnancy, the mammary glands fill up with milk; many cats have seepage which hardens around the nipples, causing some irritation if left alone. Take a moist cloth and soak the area for a few minutes before wiping it off. Meanwhile, routine combing and brushing ought to be continued throughout the pregnancy and after "queening," a commonly used term for the delivery of kittens.

It is during the approach to delivery time that the fascinating part of pregnancy begins. That's when your cat will begin the search for what is to *her* (though not always to you) the perfect spot for bringing her babies into the world. As her search becomes obvious, don't get nervous. I say this because some owners work themselves up into a state of anxiety and are much more concerned than the pet. Try to stay relaxed. Set up a special box for delivery if you wish, possibly near your pet's sleeping place. Always remember that peace and quiet are critical for the "queening" cat. Line the box with newspaper, paper toweling or some other absorbent material and place it in a dry, warm, draft-free and dimly lit area.

The best idea is to set the box up several weeks early so the cat will have plenty of time to get used to it. But be aware that the cat could pull a fast one, choosing another spot at the very last minute. It could be a closet with laundry piled on the floor; it could be a freshly made bed—*yours.* If your cat starts to queen in one of these places, *do not* pick her up in the middle of the process and move her to the box. Let her deliver and start to nurse the kittens. Once she has settled down, bring the box close to her and gently put her in it. Very tenderly, place the kittens beside her.

In any case, be sure to provide a box that is of good size, ample enough to allow the cat and her kittens plenty of room. Every once in a while, a kitten will be killed during the first few days of life because the mother has accidentally rolled over on top of it and squashed it.

As for delivery, allow some leeway in your mind regarding the normal length of gestation. While it is usually 63 days, as I have said, it can occur anywhere between the 61st and 70th day. Start to observe the cat more carefully after the 61st day. Here is a way to know when labor might begin: Take a rectal temperature (see pages 116–17), because the day preceding the onset of labor, the body temperature usually falls below 100 degrees F. With the onset of labor itself, the cat becomes somewhat restless and begins to breathe more rapidly, often with an open mouth. Frequently, this is followed by a vaginal discharge that is clear at first and then gradually tinged with blood. *If the discharge has a bad odor, is discolored or seems inordinately bloody, you must get prompt veterinary care; this can be a sign of complications,* such as fetal death.

Next come the abdominal contractions—starting within the hour or hours—signaling the active stages of labor. These straining motions will occur at shorter and shorter intervals and finally in quick succession as the animal gets close to delivering the first of her kittens. While this is going on, keep the delivery area quiet and dimly lit; this is serious business. If a kitten has not come forth within six hours after contractions begin, you must notify your veterinarian. Such a delay often indicates a "breech birth" (hind end first, rather than head first) or a kitten that is too large to pass through the cervical canal. The cat might need a cesarean section, although this is rarely the case: the majority of feline births occur without complications.

The first thing you will notice passing through the genital opening is the amniotic sac, one of the fluid-filled pouches within which each kitten develops inside the uterus. Providing a protective barrier around the kitten as it goes through the birth canal, the amniotic sac also supplies some natural lubrication that smooths the passage of the kitten into the world. If that amniotic sac happens to break before the kitten is fully delivered, the passage of the kitten can be slowed down; the kitten can be "stuck," half-in, half-out. In such an instance, after 10 to 15 minutes, you can aid the situation by applying a small amount of lubricating jelly (K-Y jelly will do) around the vaginal opening. Grasp the exposed portion of the kitten with your fingertips and don't be scared. Pull gently, with steady pressure, away from the mother. The tension of your pull along with the mother's contractions should bring the kitten out quite easily.

As soon as the kitten is born, the mother will begin to vigorously lick the amniotic sac from around its mouth and nose, thus stimulating the animal to breathe. Normally, she'll bite the umbilical cord and eat the placenta (afterbirth), which is passed after each kitten. You ought to pick this up before she consumes it, for it can give her an upset stomach. Also, watch to be sure that after each kitten's delivery an afterbirth is passed. Retained afterbirths can trigger a uterine infection. If they are not passed, relay this fact to the veterinarian, who may want to give the cat an injection to dispel the retained placenta.

It *can* happen that a cat will fail to act in the proper motherly fashion of licking away the amniotic sac. If, in a minute or two, the mother does not start to clean the kitten and to stimulate it to breathe, you must gently rupture the sac yourself (assuming the sac is intact). Then cut the umbilical cord approximately 1 inch from the belly of the kitten. *Do not* pull on that cord. You can sever it gently with your fingertips or cut it with a sterilized scissors. In the event there is bleeding, tie the cord with some thread, making the knot between the kitten and the severed end of the cord. Then rub the kitten gently but vigorously in a dry clean towel to stimulate breathing.

The mother cat is a real trouper. She can have one kitten, six, or more. After she's passed the first, she may take a longer time expelling the following kittens, although usually the time between kittens is relatively short once the process has begun. Think of it this way: if she can take it, so can you. In most cases, the entire birthing process occurs within a period of 30 minutes to several hours; if there are more than 6 hours between delivery of each kitten you *must* call your veterinarian.

Dystocia and C-Section

When a queen goes into labor and is unable to deliver because of her own physical inabilities (e.g., inadequate dilation of cervix or weak contractions), or the size or position (e.g., breech presentation) of the kittens, we say she is experiencing *dystocia*. (This problem occurs much more often in dogs than in cats.) In examining the cat, your veterinarian will determine the cause of the dystocia. Occasionally, medication can be administered to strengthen contractions, allowing for normal delivery. When such treatment is not successful, surgical intervention (a C-section, or cesarean section) is necessary. This is accomplished most often by a mid-abdominal incision which enables the litter to be rescued. Because future dystocias are likely after the first one, your veterinarian will probably recommend that the cat be spayed.

Having delivered her litter, the mother will begin to nurse her babies. If she ignores them, place them up close to a nipple so the suckling can begin. In a rare instance a queen will refuse to nurse her kittens or she may not have sufficient milk. See pages 56–58 for instructions on the feeding of orphan kittens.

Occasionally, when a queen neglects to bite the umbilical cords as her offspring are born, the kittens get all twisted up in those cords, and in the mother's tail. Watch carefully and assist in cutting the cords as I've instructed.

Once again, in most cases, delivery is uneventful. It is best to keep your distance—don't distract, handle, or annoy the cat—and do not interfere unless a real problem develops. Should that happen, remember to be very gentle as you assist. Any difficulty that you can't handle calls for help from your veterinarian as quickly as possible.

KITTENING

*O*nce the litter of kittens is born, there is surprisingly little that anyone has to do—other than adjust to one's own obsession with watching the little creatures grow. Just be sure that the mother is given plenty to eat. After all, she's eating for herself and her family; naturally, her appetite will be hearty. This is an occasion when I depart from my usual stand on vitamins, which I normally do not recommend, as long as the pet receives a balanced diet. During the time when the mother is nursing and for several weeks afterward, she should be given a vitamin supplement such as feline Pet-Tabs or Felovite, even when she's fed a balanced diet.

Be on the alert for any change in the mother's health. Look out for decreased appetite, diarrhea, vomiting, sneezing or listlessness. Also, you must see that each of those tiny kittens is getting equal attention. You've heard of the runt of the litter? Well, that runt—while cute—may not be strong or pushy enough to look out for its own interests; the stronger kittens may push it away from a nipple and you must help it out. Be sure, moreover, to keep the housing box clean and change the lining daily. A towel will afford extra warmth and comfort. Just be careful that the bedding is fitted tight up against every side of the box so that one of the kittens doesn't bury himself underneath and suffocate.

The mother might continue to have minimal amounts of a

slightly bloody vaginal discharge for 7 to 10 days after queening. Again, a foul odor or a discharge that seems excessive or that turns into heavy bleeding are reasons to notify your veterinarian.

As for the way in which the mother cat deals with the kittens' waste, don't be squeamish and do accept the wonders of nature with grace. What she does is to lick the kittens' anal regions, thus stimulating evacuation. The fecal material and urine is cleaned up and ingested by the mother until such time as the kittens are ready to defecate on their own (something that starts to happen when they are 2 to 3 weeks of age).

At birth, the eyes are closed, but between the first and second week, they will start to open. Initially, those eyes are always blue; adult color begins to be evident at approximately 3 months of age. Once the eyes are open, clean them with Dacriose or warm water, using a cotton ball soaked with the liquid. Some discharge from the eyes of young kittens is common. If not cleaned away, it may harden and seal up the eye. In some cases the kitten can contract an infection and a puslike material accumulates beneath the lids; left untreated, this may result in blindness. So watch the eyes carefully during the second week. Any sign that they are not opening, or of swelling beneath the lid, and you should consult your veterinarian immediately.

If you can resist watching the kittens develop, you're a tougher person than I am, because the sight of it could truly melt the hardest heart. By about three weeks of age, the kitten's ears start to stand upright and the animal starts to walk about. Of course, it looks a wee bit drunk, but within a few days, its wobbly steps will get stronger. At around 3 to 4 weeks of age, the mother begins to train the kittens to use the litter box.

A friend of mine watched the following occur when the kittens her cat had borne were approximately three weeks old. In its very first act of elimination, one of the kittens did its business on the kitchen floor, letting out an astonished squeak in the process. Along came the observing mother cat. Expressing her disapproval, she took her front paw and lightly socked the tiny creature—zap!—right in the face. Then taking the kitten by the nape of the neck with her mouth, she dumped it into the litter box. How's that for training and discipline!

When the kittens are between 6 and 8 weeks of age, they should have a medical examination and their first vaccinations.

Submit to the doctor a stool specimen to be examined for parasites (see pages 219–22).

Sometimes the presence of a new kitten will provoke an older resident cat, who will resent the invasion of its domain. Giving the kitten a swat, the older cat can scratch the little one's eyes. Watch the animals carefully for this, especially during the first few weeks of life.

Weaning Kittens

Weaning ought to begin when the kittens are between 3 and 4 weeks of age, a time that coincides with the development of baby teeth. Kittens not weaned when those teeth come in can cause enormous irritation to the mother's mammary tissue. Also, be mindful that problems can ensue when weaning is done too abruptly. So make it a gradual process by alternating at first, giving the kittens food and allowing them to nurse.

On occasion, the milk production of a mother cat slows down or ceases altogether after only a week or two of nursing. In such cases the offspring must be bottle-fed with a commercial milk replacer (see pages 57–58). Any time a litter is expected, milk replacer should be kept on hand.

Do not take it for granted that a baby animal will eat from a bowl just because it's placed before it. Maybe the kitten is merely used to having it easy, but it won't know what to do and will need guidance. Using your fingertip, place a little taste of food in its mouth and then direct it toward a *shallow* dish or plate. Try to appreciate the obstacle that a deep bowl presents to a little creature who's very hungry yet can't get to its food without climbing right in on top of it. Start out with baby foods mixed with water to form a soupy, gruel-like consistency. Pablum and a mixture of strained meat and vegetable baby foods are accepted well by most young animals. Once the kittens get used to semi-solids, they can be switched to gruels made from commercial canned cat food.

During the first week of weaning, as I've said, alternate several times a day between feeding and allowing the kittens to nurse. Bit by bit, lessen the amount of nursing time and the frequency with which it takes place. Kittens should be completely weaned by the time they are 5 to 6 weeks of age. Be certain that the weaning is completed before finding new homes for the little kittens. A young, helpless pet, separated too quickly from its mother and not thoroughly weaned, may refuse to eat to the point of starvation.

Mastitis

In connection with nursing, there's a particular condition called "mastitis," of which you'd best be aware. This is an inflammation and infection of the breast tissue that sometimes occurs while a female is nursing a litter. In most cases, only one or two glands are involved. But those glands get swollen and inflamed, causing pain to the cat when touched. The cat may have a fever and exhibit a decrease in appetite. In addition, the gland or glands may abscess, although this happens only in the most extreme cases. Whenever mastitis arises, the lives of the kittens are threatened. For one thing, the queen is too sore to allow them to nurse. For another, owing to infection, the milk (which will probably look discolored) contains bacteria and toxins which are dangerous to the little ones. The kittens, in fact, may shun the milk or, if they take it, may start to look poorly. The mother cat herself should be treated by your veterinarian as soon as possible since systemic antibiotics must be administered. Meanwhile, you'll have a problem with the kittens, who have no natural source of milk. In the event that you are unable to receive prompt care for the mother cat, don't allow the kittens to nurse. Separate them from the queen and feed them with a commercial milk replacer. As for the mother, until you can get veterinary attention, apply warm compresses to the affected mammary gland or glands for 10-minute intervals, 3 to 4 times a day. When a mammary abscess has developed, your veterinarian might have to perform surgical drainage.

Among other things, mastitis can occur as the result of sudden weaning. Sometimes, owing to a sudden withdrawal of the kittens, the mammary glands become "engorged," especially when the queen is a heavy milk producer. Gradual weaning allows the queen's body to reduce milk production in steps; engorgement of the mammary glands and the resultant inflammation is less likely. Once again, however, if mastitis does occur, warm compresses will give the queen some physical relief.

KITTEN MORTALITY COMPLEX

*T*he first veterinary researcher who is able to discover the cause of what is known as kitten mortality complex (KMC) will have achieved an important breakthrough in the field of animal medicine. Like crib death in human beings, kitten mortality complex currently defies satisfactory explanation. Unlike crib death, however, which affects only infants, kitten mortality complex can affect mother cats as well, and its effects can spread to other grown cats.

Kitten mortality complex is a relatively new and mysterious disease entity. Its manifestations, in a general sense, are death in young kittens, and an increased failure to reproduce successfully in breeding female cats. There may be some sort of correlation with feline infectious peritonitis (see page 250), but the specific cause is not known. In fact, we don't actually know what it is; we only know what it does. KMC probably is a result of a combination of conditions. Feline leukemia virus (FeLV) contributes to this syndrome by causing atrophy of the thymus gland and suppression of the kitten's immune system. If a kitten dies, and if KMC is suspected, its mother should be checked for FeLV.

As a disease entity, the syndrome we call *kitten mortality complex* includes such reproductive failures as spontaneous abortions, stillbirths and congenital birth defects, including malformations of newborn kittens. However it starts and progresses, it may be related to the development of congestive cardiomyopathy (heart disease) in young kittens, feline infectious peritonitis and, more commonly, "fading kitten syndrome." In this last case, kittens may be born emaciated and weak and die in the first days of life or, starting out healthy, may gradually stop eating, appear depressed, lose weight and die. Adult female cats exposed to KMC may also suffer uterine infections, respiratory illnesses, fever and cardiovascular diseases.

According to the Cornell Feline Research Laboratory, *kitten mortality complex* has been reported primarily in catteries and breeding colonies. It is believed to be carried by some sort of infectious agent, probably a virus passed on to the developing fetuses "in utero." Once a breeding cat has had reproductive problems connected with KMC, the animal will usually be affected in subsequent breedings too. (Apparently, the animal carries the causative agent for months or even years.)

A number of breeds have been known to be affected, including Himalayans, Siamese, Burmese, Abyssinians and Persians, as well as domestic shorthairs. It can surface in a young cat having her very first pregnancy, but also in older cats that have been successful breeders. No correlation with diet or routine vaccinations has been established. Kitten mortality complex is of greater concern to breeders than it is to individuals with a single cat in residence, but it is important for any cat owner to know of this sad disease.

PART FIVE

WHEN YOUR CAT IS SICK

I've already stressed the importance of keeping an accurate record of your cat's medical history. Also it's essential to be aware of your pet's regular habits. You needn't become obsessed with its every move: just know your cat well enough to observe changes in food or water consumption, or amounts urinated or defecated. Weigh your cat periodically to monitor any loss of weight.

This information will help the veterinarian, if called upon, to diagnose your cat. After all, if *you* don't know how much your cat is inclined to eat when it's well, how is the vet supposed to know? Without this basic information, how can you yourself be sure of any deviation from the norm? The same applies to the pet's typical behavior patterns. Know what they are and you'll be able to spot a change that could very well indicate the beginnings of a medical problem. And, as with people, the earlier a problem is spotted, the better.

I hope you'll be seeing a veterinarian only for your cat's annual checkup. There may, however, be times when you think your cat is acting "funny." Cats are hearty creatures, but they, too, suffer their share of illness. After reading this part of the book you'll be better equipped to deal with any illness that your cat may encounter. You'll learn how to spot the most common symptoms of illness, how to check your cat's vital signs, how to administer medication and how to comfort a convalescing cat.

GENERAL SIGNS
OF ILLNESS

*W*ould you sit down and tackle a big steak dinner if you were feeling sick? It's not very likely that you would. Similarly, among the symptoms of illness in the cat, loss of appetite ranks at the top as probably the single best indication that something is really wrong. This can be tricky, however, with a very finicky feline who—for reasons known to the cat alone—may suddenly refuse to eat. And since *all* cats are probably finicky to one degree or another, it is advisable to watch for other symptoms as well.

Any animal that isn't eating, or seems to be eating without its usual gusto, should be observed for signs of depression reflected in a lowered level of activity. Leave a new toy on the floor and see if the cat is interested, or throw a wadded-up paper bag across the room and watch for a reaction. An unresponsive pet that lies around and cannot be aroused to engage in its usual play may well be trying to tell you that it isn't feeling up to par. Also, be very concerned about a cat that starts to hide, perhaps in a closet. That may be a very sick cat indeed. As for vomiting, this is not necessarily a cause for alarm (see pages 169–70); but if it is persistent it is another matter, and a valid reason to be anxious, as is diarrhea (see pages 171–72) that continues for more than 24 hours.

In addition to the above symptoms, animals can run a fever just like people; a high temperature is a sure sign of some kind of malady. Instructions for taking the temperature of a cat are to be found on pages 116–17.

Another symptom of illness, which can be an extremely serious matter in and of itself, is *dehydration*, a condition referring to a deficit of water in the body. Without consuming sufficient water, the animal's body will dry up like a lake in a drought.

Even under normal circumstances, the cat does not consume the amount of water that a dog is prone to drink. But water is important to the cat, too. When a feline fails to drink for a prolonged period—something it may do when ill—it will start to suffer dehydration. A cat can also lose water and become dehydrated because of a fever, heat, stress, vomiting, or diarrhea. Dehydration commonly accompanies kidney disease (see pages 226–28).

One of the symptoms of dehydration is a marked decrease in saliva and urine production. You can perform a specific test to see if dehydration is occurring: lift up the skin over the upper portion of the animal's back and then let go. Normally, the skin is very elastic and will snap right back; skin that falls back slowly or simply "stands up" is a sign of clinical dehydration. This condition is accompanied by imbalance of the electrolytes (sodium, chloride and potassium) in the body and can cause death if the balance is not restored.

Water can be given to the cat by mouth with a syringe if the pet will accept it and is not vomiting. However, in most cases, prompt veterinary care is imperative in order to determine the cause of the illness and to administer subcutaneous or intravenous fluids (depending on the degree of dehydration). These will rehydrate and maintain the cat until it is eating and drinking on its own.

The appearance of a raised "third eyelid," or nictitating membrane (see illustration on page 242), can simply be a sign of something wrong with the eye(s). For reasons not fully understood, however, it is—at times—indicative of a systemic illness (such as FIP or feline leukemia virus).

TAKING YOUR CAT'S TEMPERATURE/PULSE/ RESPIRATION

*I*n the event that you suspect that your cat is sick, you should be prepared to measure its temperature, pulse and respiration. Although I can explain to you how to take these readings, I believe you'll benefit from a demonstration in the veterinarian's office. Make it a point, then, to request a lesson when you take your kitten in for one of its early checkups. Actually, it's as simple to take the temperature of your cat as it is to take the temperature of a young child, except for the obvious—that the child is bound to be more cooperative.

The normal body temperature of the cat ranges between 101

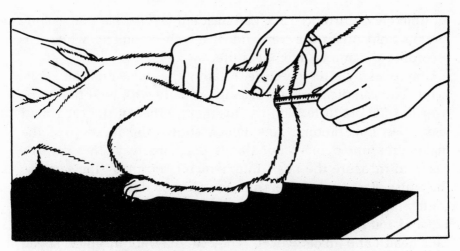

Rectal thermometer—taking the cat's temperature

and 102.5 degrees F. If your pet's temperature is above 103 degrees (which is considered to be a fever) or below 100 degrees F., your veterinarian should be informed.

Use the standard human rectal thermometer you'll have on hand in your first-aid kit (see page 134). Before you start to insert it, speak reassuringly to the pet and restrain the animal, preferably with someone else's help. Shake the thermometer down and apply a small amount of lubricating jelly or Vaseline to the tip and gently insert the thermometer into the rectum about one-third its length. (The opening *directly* below the base of the tail is the anal opening. See illustration above.) The cat will undoubtedly tighten its anal sphincter, making it difficult to push the thermometer inward. You can manage to do it, however, by applying gentle, steady pressure until the cat relaxes, which it ought to do within 10 to 30 seconds. Leave the thermometer in place for approximately two minutes and *hold on to the exposed end*. Otherwise, it could fall out and break. In a rare instance, it could also be pushed up entirely into the rectum. Should this happen, don't panic! Such a situation is not as bad as you might think. Rather than getting hysterical, place the cat in the litter box as quickly as possible. Usually, the animal will defecate in short order and pass the thermometer. Sometimes, though, an enema is required. DO NOT GIVE AN ENEMA WITHOUT DIRECTIONS FROM YOUR VETERINARIAN. If the thermometer is not passed naturally within an hour, get the animal to the veterinarian's office, where the procedure can be safely performed. Understand that this is an unlikely occurrence. Such an incident *will not* happen as long as you hold on to the free end of the thermometer while it is recording the animal's temperature.

Unlike taking a temperature, locating the pulse on a cat is difficult. You can pick it up by placing pressure with your fingertips over the femoral artery on the inside of either of the cat's hind legs. (See illustration below which shows the location of the major pressure points.) But this is the hard way. In a cat, it's easier to measure the heart rate, which is normally the same as the pulse. Put your fingers on one side of the chest and your thumb on the opposite side (see illustration, page 149). Between 120 and 160 beats per minute is normal. This may vary with the cat's health and anxiety level. (The beat may, for instance, speed up during an examination in the veterinarian's office.) Should you find the heart rate to be outside the given parameters, you ought to notify your veterinarian.

As far as the feline's breathing is concerned, under normal circumstances it is almost undetectable. But counting the respirations per minute is not necessary. Instead, pay close attention to the way your cat breathes when it is healthy. Should the animal's breathing pattern vary, becoming erratic or labored, you will quickly notice. If you hear any coughing, you should observe the animal's respirations and act accordingly, getting medical advice if the breathing seems abnormal.

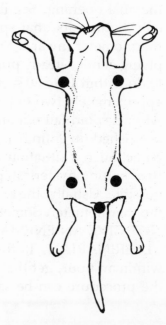

Arterial pressure points of the cat

A WORD ABOUT SURGERY AND ANESTHESIA

*F*acing an operation, a cat will usually have to be fasted the night before, with all food and water withheld from the animal for 12 to 18 hours before it enters the hospital. Although this is generally standard procedure, medical problems may exist that would make fasting inadvisable. So follow the instructions given by your veterinarian.

When a pet has to undergo surgery, it is placed under anesthesia in much the same way that a person is. Approximately one hour prior to surgery, the animal is given an injection of a pre-anesthetic. For very short procedures, many veterinarians will opt for heavy tranquilization rather than a complete anesthetic. In the case of longer procedures, however, the cat will receive an intravenous injection of sodium pentothal or a similar drug, after the pre-anesthetic. Once the cat is "asleep," it is "intubated" with one end of a breathing tube inserted into the windpipe while the other end is connected to an anesthetic machine; thus a means is provided for administering a mixture of oxygen and anesthetic gas.

Following surgery, the veterinarian and/or veterinary assistant will keep a careful watch on the animal until it has fully recovered from the anesthetic. The period of rallying to consciousness after surgery is critical. Owing to the instability of the animal's condition during this time, your veterinarian will usually want the cat to stay overnight in veterinary quarters following an operation. In addition to permitting the cat to regain full consciousness in protected surroundings, the overnight stay will enable the veterinarian to observe the animal's overall state for signs of any post-operative complications, and to be sure that the pet is kept extremely quiet for at least 24 hours after the operation. Recovery from anesthesia for castration, dentistry or the treatment of an abscess is usually rapid and in these cases the cat is often sent home the same day.

NOTE: Most veterinarians will want to keep a pet in the hospital only long enough to be certain that the animal has safely recovered from the anesthesia. This is especially true with cats, since it is generally recognized that they are profoundly sensitive to separation from their home environment. Abide by your veterinarian's advice; the animal must have professional supervision in the immediate aftermath of surgery, but you can be sure that a competent veterinarian will want you to have your cat back home as quickly as possible.

When dealing with middle-aged and older cats (six years or more) requiring surgery, your veterinarian might ask permission to perform some routine tests prior to the operation. He or she is not just trying to take your money. The tests are necessary to assess the pet's liver and kidney functions. Since anesthetics are metabolized by these organs, it is essential to know whether the aging kidneys and liver can adequately do the job.

To be sure, there are risks for animals undergoing anesthesia. But just as with people, the risks involved are minimal and far less in most cases than those of withholding necessary surgery.

POST-OPERATIVE CARE AND THE CONVALESCING CAT

*Y*our cat has returned from a visit to the veterinarian's office. However busy you may be, don't ignore the needs of your pet. Put first things first: it's time for a dose of TLC, every ounce you can give. Any trip to the veterinarian—even a routine one—will probably be unsettling to the cat; take this into account. If the visit has involved an operation, it's also time for an exceptional degree of peace and quiet. Following surgery, the cat will be weaker than usual and should be kept from getting into its usual mischief. Probably, the cat will appear somewhat dazed as a result of anesthesia, which may not have completely worn off by its first day home. But occasionally the cat will try to be active even though it's "hungover." *The pet is not up to it and could get hurt.* Encourage the animal to lie down on a soft blanket in a peaceful place it's fond of. Following some surgeries (e.g., castration, declawing), your veterinarian should recommend replacing kitty litter with torn-up paper towels or newspaper for about 5 days.

On the first day following an operation, the cat might have to be restrained from overeating. Take your veterinarian's advice in this regard. Any special directions for feeding should be observed; make sure they are explained before you take the cat home. You don't want to end up calling the office and finding it closed for the night. Also, be scrupulous in following directions for the administration of medications. All prescriptions should be used for the length of time specified on the label. Just because symptoms have disappeared is no reason to withdraw medication; unless the full course is given, the symptoms might return.

As far as follow-up visits are concerned, in most cases where surgery has been involved, a veterinarian will want you to make an appointment for a checkup and/or suture removal within 7 to 10 days of the animal's discharge. Whenever you are directed to return for follow-up care, be sure to do so or your pet may suffer needlessly.

NOTE: Clients are often concerned because a cat licks or scratches at its sutures, but in most cases this will not occur. Rely on the judgment of your veterinarian. He or she may recommend covering the wound only in an extreme case; it's important that the wound be exposed to air, so that it will heal more quickly. Try to keep the cat inside so that the affected area will remain dry and clean. If you notice a discoloration or swelling of the incision, or if the pet is persistently licking it, your cat should be reexamined by your veterinarian.

ADMINISTERING MEDICATION

Topical Medications

*I*f a topical medication has been prescribed for your cat, you have to be sure you're applying it properly. Otherwise, the medication will not only fail to have effect; you could inadvertently harm the cat. For example, get a product for skin irritation into the eye of the animal and the creature may really suffer. So watch what you're up to and, in addition to listening to the veterinarian, follow the instructions of the printed label (unless they are contradicted by your veterinarian). Topical medications come in three basic forms: liquid drops, ointments and creams. Following instructions pertains not only to the method of application but to frequency and duration of use.

It's common for a client to report that a cat has licked a medication off its skin the minute after application. To prevent that from happening—at least as best you can—rub the cream or ointment into the skin and allow the medication to be absorbed for several minutes while keeping your eye (and your hands, if necessary) on the cat. Very few medications will harm the animal when licked. Some are so bitter, in fact, that the cat will quickly be discouraged from further licking. But the problem is not harm to the cat from the ointment or cream; rather, it's that the animal may bring about a worsening of the skin irritation for which the medication is being used in the first place. In a rare case where excessive licking persists, an Elizabethan collar (see illustration below) might have to be used, which makes it impossible for the cat to reach the area with its tongue. These collars fit quite comfortably around the neck; the cat can sleep and eat with one on. Just be sure there is a space of two fingers' width between the cat's neck and the collar.

When placing medication in the eyes, tilt the head of the animal upward, then spread the upper and lower eyelid margins apart as shown in the illustration (page 123). *Do not* touch the applicator tip with your finger, or allow it to touch the eye directly. After you've placed the medication into the eye, close the margins of the lids together; this will spread the medication over the entire surface of the eye.

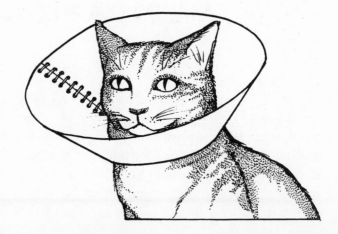

Elizabethan collar

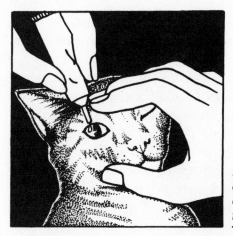

Placing ointment or drops in the eye: Tilt head upward, spread eyelids apart with your thumb and fingertips.

Putting topical medications into the ear should always be done when the ear is clean. Remove waxy debris and excess medication from the ear on a daily basis and you will facilitate better treatment. Tilt the head slightly up, take a cotton ball and wipe out the inside of the ear. Remember, don't use cotton-tip applicators to clean an animal's ears. If the cat shakes its head, the applicator could be jammed deep down into the ear canal, thereby causing serious injury. Little risk is involved in using a fingertip with a cotton ball.

Pills

Most cat owners complain that giving a pill to the family cat is a real pain. I don't want to put up a vigorous argument, but I really believe it's fairly simple once one gets the knack. Observe the illustrations on page 124, which should help you become more proficient at the task. My first piece of advice is that you learn to be quick and a little forceful, enough to let the cat know you mean business. Otherwise, "pill-popping" becomes a game and your cat is going to win it; repeatedly, the animal will spit the pill right out. Some people find it easier to cover the tablet or capsule with a bit of butter or margarine. This will help the pill slide down the feline's throat. But initial mastery of getting the pill into the back of the mouth is the first and most important trick.

Place your cat up on an elevated slippery surface; a tabletop will do just fine. In treating animals, we veterinarians find that the scents of other creatures and that slippery stainless steel tabletop serve to distract the animal in question. Similarly, you ought to find that putting the cat on a tabletop confuses it a bit or "disarms" it to some degree, making it easier for you to do the job.

Take one hand and put it over the top of the animal's head. (Use your left hand if you are right-handed and vice versa if you are left-handed.) Get a firm hold on either side of the upper jaw. With the tablet in your *other* hand (your right hand if you are right-handed), open the lower jaw with that hand and quickly place the pill in the center of the mouth, as far back on the tongue as possible. Close the mouth, hold it closed, tilt the head upward and gently massage the cat's throat. This will stimulate the pet to swallow. When you let go, if the animal licks its nose, you can be pretty sure that the pill is on its way down. Some cats, however, will be stubborn beyond belief, simply refusing to swallow.

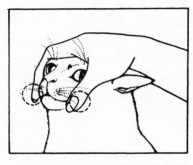

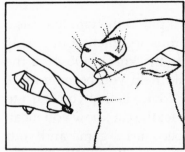

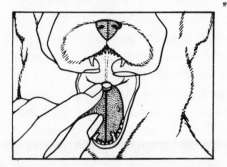

Giving the cat a pill:
a. Tilt head backward with thumb
   and fingertips on either
   side of jaw.
b. Open mouth using fingertip of
   free hand (with pill).
c. Place pill as far back on the
   tongue as possible. Close
   the mouth, holding it tilted
   upward, massaging the throat to
   stimulate a swallowing reflex.

Should this be the case with your cat, you can place a couple of drops of water on the tip of its nose. In licking the water away, it will wind up swallowing the pill. You can also blow gently on the animal's nose. The main thing is to act without delay, never giving the cat a chance to get suspicious and prepare for a one-upmanship at which it can excel.

If all this trickery doesn't work, you can try hiding the medicine in something your cat is crazy about, maybe a piece of cheese. In this way, you might be able to trick the pet into taking the pill, while the animals *thinks* it's getting a treat. This works better with dogs, though. The cat is not so easily fooled.

Liquid Medications

Giving liquid medication to a cat is harder than giving a pill. So if your veterinarian prescribes a liquid medication, ask for a syringe to make the administration easier. Using a teaspoon is almost impossible. Even if you don't spill half the liquid on the way to the animal's mouth, you're probably going to loose a good deal of it while attempting to place the spoon inside the animal's mouth. Stick with a syringe and you'll do much better.

As with giving a pill, it's best to place the cat on a tabletop. The animal won't feel as secure up there as it would on the floor and you'll have the advantage. A second pair of hands to restrain the pet will be of enormous help. Without such assistance, you'll have to do the best you can.

Whenever administering a liquid, give a small amount at a time and allow the pet to swallow the medicine before you give it more. *Do not fight with an animal that puts up a serious struggle.* The cat could take a breath as you give the medication and inhale (aspirate) the liquid into the lungs. The results could be life-threatening. I don't mean to alarm you; be gentle and patient and this is most unlikely to occur. But should the animal resist too much, give up for a while and try again when the cat is more receptive.

NOTE: Many pet owners are inclined to give their cats periodic doses of mineral oil. I advise against this and recommend cat laxative preparations or Vaseline (see page 218), as aspiration of the oil could occur and be life-threatening.

Incline the cat's head slightly upward and place the end of the

WHAT *NOT* TO GIVE YOUR CAT

Aspirin
It is generally recommended not to give aspirin to cats. Although veterinarians may occasionally use aspirin cautiously and at low doses, cats cannot tolerate high doses. A single aspirin tablet (usually 5 grains or 325 mg) constitutes a high dose for a cat. The poisoning from aspirin will affect the nervous system and damage the liver.

Acetaminophen
Acetaminophen is the generic name of the painkiller best known by the brand name *Tylenol*. The drug acetaminophen is now found in literally hundreds of brands of pain remedies and combination medications sold over the counter (without a prescription). A single dose of acetaminophen is deadly for cats. It impairs the ability of the hemoglobin molecule in blood cells to carry oxygen and destroys red blood cells. It causes severe breathing difficulty, a bluish color of the gums (cyanosis) and swelling around the head and neck, and can lead to death.

Fleet Enemas
Since constipation occurs in cats, they are sometimes given enemas. Soap and water enemas or enemas containing stool softeners such as dioctyl sodium sulfosuccinate are fine. Fleet enemas and some other brands of pre-packaged enemas are called "phosphate enemas." These can cause problems in cats because they induce an imbalance of the calcium levels in the blood. Normal calcium levels are essential for normal muscle and heart function. The result of this imbalance is muscle tremors and convulsions, and it has resulted in fatalities.

Urinary Acidifiers
Cats are often given drugs to make the urine more acidic. This is helpful in treating several urinary tract disorders. One of the drugs used for this purpose is ammonium chloride. This drug is safe and effective in adult cats but not kittens. Kittens do not possess adequate liver function to handle this drug, and they exhibit signs of ammonia poisoning which include stupor, incoordination and seizures. Be particularly cautious of urinary acidifiers prescribed to be used as food additives. These can be used appropriately for adult cats, but if kittens have access to the medicated food, poisoning can result.

Administering liquids by mouth: Tilt the head slightly up with the tip of syringe or eyedropper on either side of mouth. Massage the throat to stimulate swallowing.

syringe in the side of the animal's mouth as illustrated above. Once again, allow the cat time to swallow as you depress the syringe. The cat may hate the taste of some medications. You may find that the animal will shake its head quite violently to get rid of the stuff, some of which will land on your floor and walls. Accept the situation and clean the liquid up. The veterinarian would not prescribe the medication unless it was needed.

Be scrupulous in following the prescribed dosage and administering it for the length of time advised. (If an animal spits out most of the dose, then it's usually safe to administer another one.)

PART SIX

FIRST AID

*C*uriosity may not always kill the cat, but it surely can cause some very close calls. You do not have to be a worrisome fool or an overanxious owner to concern yourself with the possible results of all that feline poking around. Just be sure that this ever-so-fascinating trait of the cat keeps you sensibly on your toes. First, one admonition. I wish I didn't have to issue it so sternly, but in the years of my experience, I've seen uncountable injuries and deaths that could have been totally avoided. What I mean is this: common sense ought to tell you to remove from sight objects and temptations that might doom your nosy cat to pain, irreparable damage or terminal complications. An open can of paint, for instance, is plainly an enticement as far as the cat is concerned, a delicious invitation to be lapped right up. Nor are many felines going to resist chewing on the chewable leaves of a poisonous philodendron that sits in a tub on the floor. Leave a needle and thread around for your baby kitten to get ahold of and you may live to regret it—though your kitten might not have the same luck. Obviously, outside hazards are harder to control, but do you have to let the nestful of hornets in the garden go on thriving?

Cats get broken bones, and may be poisoned, cut, burned, bitten, bruised, stung, drowned, electrocuted and smothered. They choke on bones, get hit by cars and attacked by dogs and yes, by other cats. They fall off roofs and terraces while pussy-footing it on the edge and any old cat, no matter how smart, will make a headlong plunge from any height if intrigued enough by a bird, a plane or a leaf floating by on the breeze.

A scary list? There's no more reason to panic about these things than about the far more frightening travails that accompany childhood. Yet accidents happen in a flash. I'm not suggesting that what you can do for your cat will supplant the experienced care administered by your veterinarian, to whom—if it is in any way possible—you must rush your cat as immediately after an accident as you can. What I am about to discuss are traditional and basic first-aid techniques that may make all the difference in the world between the continuance of life and the demise of a cat. My hope, in other words, is to familiarize you with what you can do to help save your injured cat when time, calm and instant action are everything. So if and when emergencies do occur, you will be better able to cope.

USING THE FIRST-AID SECTION OF THIS BOOK

*W*ere a child of yours involved, I doubt I'd have to advise you to read up on and learn ahead of time those first-aid measures you can take to deal with typical emergencies. No matter how farfetched the eventuality of any given accident, you'd make it your business to know what you are supposed to do should the unexpected occur. Avoiding panic is not easy, but surely it can only help you stay calm and cool if you have some idea of the steps you must take in life and death situations. Therefore, my first piece of advice is to read through this first-aid section *now*. For your sake and the sake of your pet, I hope you never have to use this part of the book, but you can only benefit by being prepared.

The various emergency situations your cat could encounter are listed in the table of contents and in the index. For your further convenience, they are presented in the text in alphabetical order. In each instance of possible emergency, the causes, symptoms and necessary care are discussed. But before we move on to the specifics below, here are six important general steps you should always keep in mind. They are especially critical when you are unsure of the cause of a given condition or if you might become too panicked to find immediately the page dealing with a particular problem.

1. If you can identify the cause of the animal's illness or injury, take steps to eliminate it. (The animal has a bone in its mouth? Get it out. The animal's been hit by a car? Take it out of the street so it won't be in further danger.)
2. Most housecats don't wear collars. You probably have (you certainly *should* have) one for your outdoor cat. In the event that the cat collapses, loses unconsciousness and has difficulty breathing, check to see that it isn't being choked by that collar. Should you find that the collar is not the problem, carefully look to see that the mouth is clear of any foreign material that could be obstructing the passage of air into the lungs.

3. When the animal isn't breathing or if its heart has stopped, use CPR—cardiopulmonary resuscitation. This is clearly described beginning on page 144.
4. Take appropriate steps to control any visible external bleeding by applying direct pressure, pressure bandages or a tourniquet—depending upon the place and type of bleeding. (Described on pages 196–99.)
5. An unconscious animal or one that has collapsed should always be inclined slightly so that its head is a little lower than its body. This prevents aspiration (inhalation) into the lungs—of blood, saliva or vomitus that often accumulates in the mouth when an animal is severely injured or very sick.
6. Cover the cat with an old jacket, shirt or blanket to try and conserve its body heat. When an animal is severely hurt or ill and especially if it goes into shock or drifts into an unconscious state, the body mechanisms that maintain and conserve body temperature fail to function properly. You want to keep the animal warm.

Your next concern is to get to the *veterinarian*. Let me stress the importance of keeping close at hand the phone number of your veterinarian and any telephone numbers for emergency coverage after office hours. These numbers and any instructions should always be written down and kept in one location. That location should furthermore be known by all members of the household. The time you waste frantically looking for a telephone number could mean the difference between life and death. When possible, leave for the vet's immediately. Have someone else call the veterinary facility you're headed for to tell them you are on your way and to describe the cat's condition, to better ensure quick, appropriate treatment when you and your pet arrive. *Drive carefully.*

There are two important points I want to repeat.

1. As you read the first-aid sections of this book, note the causes I have listed for the different types of emergencies. Once again, I'm getting back to the matter of prevention. Insofar as it's possible, I would ask you to so arrange the life of your cat that you will never have to use any of these first-aid procedures.

2. Practice some of the restraint methods and first-aid techniques. Explain these techniques to the younger members of the family and let them try to practice them too. Your cat will get used to the extra attention and handling; everyone will be prepared for the proper steps to take. Keep in mind, however, that when I recommend practice, I am referring mostly to techniques that will help you become familiar with the materials you should use and the ways in which you would restrain the cat in any given emergency. You might, for instance, practice applying a bandage or giving a medication. If you were to attempt to induce vomiting or to practice CPR, you would not only frighten the animal, you might unintentionally cause it serious harm. Just use your common sense.

In any emergency, try to think clearly and calmly. Believe me, in a stress situation, everyone has to stop, take a deep breath or two and try to relax—even veterinarians.

FIRST-AID KIT

*C*ertainly nothing can stimulate panic in a medical emergency quite as much as not being able to find a necessary item— a bandage, a bottle of antiseptic, a roll of cotton, what have you. Instead of keeping such products around in a haphazard fashion, as do many people, do yourself and your cat a service by collecting every item that might be needed in case of an emergency in one neat, accessible kit. You can purchase a commercially marketed first-aid kit in your local pet store or pharmacy. Most of these, however, are small and compact; the contents and the quantities of material contained may not be sufficient for every eventuality. I recommend that you compile your own kit. Choose a good-sized, clean container, preferably one that is waterproof and also has a lid. You can get such a container at your hardware store. An empty toolbox or tackle box will work just fine.

Here is a list of the most important contents of a good first-aid kit:

- 1 standard rectal thermometer (in a case)
- 1 pair tweezers
- 1 pair scissors
- 1 pair needle-nosed pliers
- 1 penlight flashlight
- 6 tongue depressors
- 1 dozen Q-tips
- 1 small package cotton balls
- 1 small jar Vaseline
- 1 roll cotton batting
- 2 1-inch rolls of adhesive tape
- 1 2-inch roll of adhesive tape
- 1 ½-inch roll of adhesive tape
- 1 2-inch roll of gauze wrap
- 1 3-inch roll of gauze wrap
- 1 dozen sterile gauze pads (large)
- 1 dozen sterile gauze pads (small)
- 1 Ace bandage
- 1 clean cloth or handkerchief (to use as a pressure bandage)
- 1 bottle 3 percent hydrogen peroxide
- 1 bottle rubbing alcohol
- 1 bottle Kaopectate
- 1 bottle Milk of Magnesia
- 1 tube sterile 5 percent boric acid or plain-base ophthalmic (eye) ointment (hereafter referred to as ophthalmic ointment)
- 1 small bottle of antiseptic powder or spray
- 1 small bottle of mineral oil
- 1 styptic pencil (or powder)
- 1 bar of soap or bottle of pHisoDerm/Betadyne Scrub
- 1 container of activated charcoal

Some of these items will rarely be used; others you'll need more often. As your supply becomes diminished over time, remember to restock those items you have used, so that you won't be caught short.

If you have a family, especially one with youngsters who share in caring for the cat, I recommend that each and every member know what is in your kit. Be sure it is kept consistently in one place, within reach. (I except the reach of very young children, who could misuse or abuse the listed items.)

In addition to having the first-aid kit, you would be wise to have on hand a blanket, a piece of rope (or an old necktie) and a flat board on which to transport an injured pet. These should obviously be in a convenient location. The ways in which all these materials, including those in the first-aid kit, are utilized, will be clearly explained in upcoming sections.

Hydrogen Peroxide: Special Information

One of the most important and useful medicinal products that you should keep in your animal's first-aid kit is hydrogen peroxide solution. The standard strength available is 3 percent, meaning that the solution is 3 percent hydrogen peroxide and 97 percent water. Here are some of its uses:

AS A DISINFECTANT
The 3 percent solution can be used full strength as a cleansing wash for abrasions and minor cuts of the skin. If your cat steps on glass or wire or receives a puncture wound, perhaps in a fight with another animal, wash the wounded area with mild soap and water and then rinse it off with a liberal amount of peroxide. Its antiseptic, anti-infective action can prevent serious bacterial infections from developing. (In the case of a deep puncture wound, a severe burn or when redness, swelling and pain persist, don't count on the peroxide but get to your veterinarian. Often topical cleansing is not sufficient to prevent infection, and antibiotics are necessary).

FOR CLEANING SUBSTANCES FROM HAIR
Hydrogen peroxide can be used to get rid of stains in a cat's hair coat caused by blood, food or saliva. Mix 3 parts water to 1 part peroxide and be careful not to get any in the animal's eyes. Wipe gently over the affected area. Then rinse with clean, warm water.

TO INDUCE VOMITING
In cases in which a pet swallows something toxic and you are directed to induce vomiting, you can accomplish this by giving the cat a teaspoonful of hydrogen peroxide. See page 125 regarding the administration of liquid medications.

FOR CLEANING TEETH

A small amount of baking soda mixed with an equal part of peroxide makes an excellent paste for this purpose. Cleaning your feline's teeth is something you should do from time to time in any case—*assuming you have a cooperative cat.* If the pet has had dental work, the cleaning is all the more important. Unless the animal fights you off, wipe the outer surface of the teeth with a piece of gauze dipped in the baking soda–peroxide preparation. Repeating this procedure every other day will lessen the amount of tartar that accumulates on the pet's teeth and will reduce the need for future dentistry.

Whenever you use peroxide, open the container carefully. You mustn't let the liquid splatter in your face or into the animal's eyes, where it might cause irritation.

Keep the container tightly closed and store in a dark, clean, cool area. Heat, dust and exposure to light can all cause this disinfectant to deteriorate.

APPROACHING THE ANIMAL: PICKING IT UP

*I*n the unfortunate event that your cat becomes suddenly sick or injured, everything you can do to assess its situation will help you to maintain your calm and to go into action. You will want to prevent further injury if the cat has had an accident and you will certainly want to alleviate any pain (for example, by removing the cat's paw from an object in which it is entrapped). Possibly, you'll have to perform first aid; should the cat be injured, you'll undoubtedly have to rush it to the veterinarian. Whatever the case, you'll have to do *something.* Nothing is possible without touching the animal, an activity that—in such abnormal circumstances—causes many an owner a good deal of anxiety. Fear being what it is, one can hardly tell an individual not to feel it. But provided that you know your cat and that you've accustomed it to being handled, you ought to be able to prevail.

Both for your own personal safety and that of the cat, it is imperative that you approach the cat in a non-threatening manner. No matter how friendly and affectionate your cat is most of the time, it might display an aggressive side when frightened or in pain. You cannot muzzle a cat as you can a dog and in warding off what it perceives as a threat, it may use not only its mouth but all four feet as well in defense. In other words, a frightened cat that struggles as you attempt to come to its aid can—if you approach it ineffectively—give you a nasty bite or scratch. As far as the animal's condition is concerned, it can worsen in a struggle, causing weakening if the cat is ill or bringing about the compounding of any injuries. Your method of nearing and handling the cat is therefore critical.

As you approach the cat, speak to it in a quiet and soothing tone of voice. And no matter how desperate you are to get to the cat, never move toward it in a sudden rush or attempt, in haste, to pick it up. Walk toward it slowly or move in a stooping position (an excellent way of getting near the cat) and be as gentle as possible in whatever you must do. Touch the cat lightly on the back of the head, softly stroke the back of its neck and continue speaking to it in soothing tones.

Before you approach the cat, make some quick observations as to the animal's condition. As you touch it, judge the possiblity of picking it up without special precautionary measures. While it is critical that you be gentle, you must do your best to make the animal feel you are in command of the situation. You will have to employ your instincts as well as your sense of self-defense in order to communicate to the cat that you are in control. A tender but unshaky hand on the back of the head will help, and if you pick the cat up, a firm support hold is mandatory. Very often, it is not only fear or pain on the part of the cat that will cause it to bite or scratch. Being unable to talk, the cat has very few ways of expressing itself in a dramatic fashion; scratching and biting is one of them. The cat may merely be saying, "I hurt." Your response, a soft voice, a firm gentle touch, will tell the cat you understand. But the firmer you are, without being rough, the more the cat will relax.

Holding the animal by the scruff of the neck or by the lower chest and front limbs provides no support for the lower part of the body (see illustrations on page 138). A cat doesn't enjoy being

Incorrect way to hold a cat   *Correct way to hold a cat*

dangled in the air any more than you would. Instead, place one hand in front of or underneath the forelimbs and around the chest; use your other hand to support the hindlimbs. Then draw the pet up into your arms and hold it close to your chest. The cat is now secure. If the cat is unconscious, has been hit by a car or suffered other severe trauma, be careful how you move it. It's best to place it on a flat suface, such as a board. If it's acting wild, is in severe pain and is frightened, try to get it into a box or some other container. Handling a strange cat is another matter, requiring special alertness, caution and, most of all, confidence. Wear gloves if possible, or else use a towel or a blanket as a buffer between the two of you so that you won't get bitten.

Although you will often know what is the matter with the cat, you should keep in mind that your veterinarian is the best person to determine the exact nature of the animal's malady. Occasionally, though, an animal will be impossible to handle and before you can get it to the veterinarian, it will require special restraint. You will have to count on your observations to know this, and then on the techniques I describe in the following section.

RESTRAINT AND TRANSPORT

*P*roper restraint techniques are not harmful to the pet: they are meant to secure the animal in such a way that it can do no further injury to itself or injure you. Unlike a dog, a cat cannot be muzzled; its head is small and its nose too short. A cat can furthermore be difficult to clasp; it has a spectacular ability to wriggle out of a hold. If a cat is hard to deal with, these are the best ways to restrain it:

1. Wrap the cat in an old shirt, jacket or large bath towel. In my experience, the latter works best. Observe the illustration (below) and practice the technique. Obviously, you want to avoid hurting any part of the body that is injured. So if a cat has a wound on one leg, for instance, wrap the other three legs, leaving the affected leg exposed so that you can examine it and apply a pressure bandage over the wound. If you're having trouble restraining the cat, you might want to cover its head. (Completely wrapping its head, however, is not necessary.) Just be sure to leave space for the cat to breathe.

2. Using the 1-inch adhesive tape in your first-aid kit, tear off two strips, each approximately 12 inches in length. Gently place the animal on its side and extend the hind legs. Wrap the tape around the lower portion of the legs and be sure that the legs are held close together or the cat will squirm free. Fold the last inch

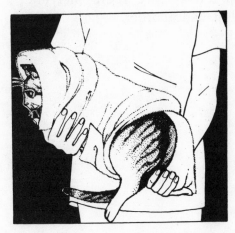

Restraining an injured cat: Wrap in a large towel, leaving the injured leg free but supported from beneath.

of tape back on itself so that it may easily be removed. Then repeat this procedure with the forelegs. Restrained like this, the cat will not be able to scratch you, but you must still watch out for the animal's teeth. Don't use this technique if the cat is suffering from an injured limb.

When a cat is extremely fractious and difficult to handle, the towel works best. I also recommend a towel or jacket should you stumble upon an injured cat that you don't know—certainly unless the animal clearly appears to be docile. Otherwise, with cats that are well behaved and let you touch them, try the tape method. If the cat is docile, these restraints aren't usually necessary. Taping is more traumatic than using a towel, so you would never use this procedure on a docile cat.

If you yourself just plain object to restraint and really expect the cat to be gentle, you can hold it without resorting to towel or tape. But for your own personal safety, you are wisest to use a firm, secure restraint.

When leaving your home with your cat to get to the veterinarian, always be sure to take it inside a good, sturdy carrier. In an emergency situation, however, you can get the cat to the veterinarian in a large towel, blanket, pillow case or canvas bag. My gym bag has worked quite well in a couple of situations where I was on the street with only that bag and came across an injured cat or abandoned kittens.

This section of the book covers specific accidents or mishaps that might require first aid. Again, you should read it through entirely at a time of leisure. For convenience in an emergency, the problems discussed are in alphabetical order.

ACCIDENTS WITH CARS/ COMPARABLE TRAUMAS

*T*he injuries sustained in a traumatic incident, as when a cat is hit by an automobile or falls from a window, range from minor to very serious. Many animals die immediately because of the force of a trauma, whatever its cause. But for the animal that survives, your quick assessment of the injuries and subsequent actions might save its life. Read the section on approaching an injured animal (pages 136–38) so that you will be able to avoid further harm to the cat and also won't place yourself in jeopardy should the animal become defensive out of fright or pain. Observe the cat carefully to try to determine how severely it has been hurt. Then, keep these points in mind and give them the listed priority:

1. If there is any sign of major bleeding, take steps to stop it (pages 196–99) in order to prevent the cat from going into shock as a result of the bleeding.
2. Administer CPR (pages 144–48) to an animal that is experiencing respiratory difficulty.
3. Keep the cat covered with a blanket or shirt in order to maintain its body heat.
4. Apply a splint or similar device (page 167) to severely fractured limbs to prevent a worsening of the injury.
   NOTE: Theoretically this is sound advice; however, it is often too difficult to accomplish since most homemade splints are inadequate and in the process of putting one on the owner may be bitten. Therefore, it might be best to gently place the cat in a cushioned box and bring it to your veterinarian.
5. Transport the animal to a veterinary facility as quickly as possible. Not only should the visible injuries be professionally treated; internal injuries may also have been incurred and the animal may die if not treated with intravenous fluids and other supportive care.

ALLERGIC REACTIONS

*W*hat we call an allergic reaction occurs when the immune system of an animal (or, obviously, of a person) fails to perform normally in response to the invasion of foreign substances or organisms. The substances that cause allergic reactions are known as *allergens* and they can be just about anything. In the case of animals, "anything" can range from flea collars (common) to nylon rugs (rare). As sometimes happens with people, the reaction to the allergen occasionally becomes worse with repeated exposure.

There are two general types of allergic reactions:

1. By far the most common is a delayed, *slow response,* often restricted to one portion of the body, such as the head or neck, where it manifests itself as hives or localized swelling. Hives are raised swellings of the skin which frequently cause intense itching. A cat that begins to paw persistently at its head or neck might well be scratching such hives. This kind of reaction is rarely life-threatening and, most often, the symptoms subside as soon as the offending allergen is removed.

2. A less common but far more threatening reaction is called *anaphylaxis.* This is an acute, hypersensitivity reaction to a given allergen and it occurs immediately after contact. The animal has difficulty breathing; it collapses, goes into shock and without treatment will often die within minutes. An anaphylactic reaction like this would follow "injection" into the body of an offending substance. Insect bites, drugs and sometimes vaccines are the most frequent causes. To a certain extent, however, I am speaking of these in a theoretical context. Though I have dealt with reactions to insect bites (page 180), in all my years of practice, I have not yet encountered such a severe acute reaction to any drug or vaccine although such reactions have occasionally been reported following the administration of the new FeLV vaccine.

Allergic reactions can be produced by substances that are inhaled, injected, ingested or touched. Here is a list of some of the most common causative agents:

Those inhaled:	Pollens from trees, weeds, and grasses
	Dust
	Environmental pollutants
Those injected:	Drugs/medications/vaccines (rare in my own experience)
	Insect bites and stings from bees, wasps, fleas
Those swallowed:	Spoiled foods
	Table foods such as milk, cheese, eggs, cereals, seafood, meats
Those contacted:	Carpeting
	Clothing
	Household items: cleaning materials, polishes
	Collars—especially flea collars
	Plastic food and water dishes

Some pets will never exhibit any sign of an allergic reaction; others will be mildly affected only on occasion; and some are severely affected over and over. Generally speaking, cats are less subject to allergic reactions than dogs. You should, nonetheless, be familiar with the most frequent symptoms:

Usually associated with a delayed reaction:	Hives
	Localized swelling—especially of the face
	Sneezing
	Coughing
	Scratching
	Rubbing of the eyes and face along furniture and on the floor
	Licking and/or biting of the paws
Usually associated with an anaphylactic reaction:	Restlessness
	Panting
	Difficulty breathing—may be asthma-like
	Vomiting
	Diarrhea
	Collapse

First Aid for Allergic Reactions

When an animal suffers an acute, anaphylactic reaction, it must receive adrenaline intravenously to counteract the effects of the allergen. If the cat collapses and has difficulty breathing, keep it warm and be sure that it has an open airway for breathing (see "Choking," pages 156–59). *Get the pet to your veterinarian immediately.*

If you suspect that your cat is suffering a slow, delayed allergic reaction, you should take the following steps.

1. Try to determine what is causing the allergic response and remove it. One of the most common causes of an allergic reaction is the flea collar. So if your cat develops an irritation around its neck and it's wearing a flea collar, simply remove it. Flea bite allergies are also common. Check for fleas, which you'll want to rid the cat of in any case (see pages 208–10).
2. In the case of other contact allergens, you must rinse the substance away. Wash the cat thoroughly with mild soap and water. After that, a cool water bath or soaking in water will give the pet some temporary relief from itching.
3. Observe the animal for any respiratory distress. If this occurs or the animal's condition worsens, consult your veterinarian.
4. In many cases you don't know the cause of an allergic reaction. Fortunately, treatment for allergic reactions is standard and you should be concerned only if reactions occur repeatedly.

ARTIFICIAL RESPIRATION AND CPR

*A*ny number of problems stemming from serious illness or traumatic injury can cause an animal to stop breathing or bring on cardiac arrest. In either case the body—deprived of oxygen and the normal circulation of blood—will rapidly deteriorate; in a matter of minutes, unless something constructive is done, death will ensue. Because the unexpected, no matter how unlikely, can always happen, I advise you to become familiar with the techniques of cardiopulmonary resuscitation, frequently referred to as CPR. Your cat's life could be at stake.

The following symptoms may indicate that respiratory arrest is imminent:

1. Labored or difficult breathing. (This is a very noticeable phenomenon since the normal respirations of the cat are so shallow that they are almost imperceptible.) Gasping and breathing with an open mouth are signs of a respiratory problem.
2. A bluish coloration (cyanosis) of the animal's tongue and gums indicating inadequate oxygen supply.
3. A stretching back of the neck in an obvious and strained attempt to get into a position in which easier breathing is possible.
4. Unconsciousness and respiratory arrest.

In these circumstances, the cat is in immediate need of artificial respiration, the act of forcing air (thus oxygen) into the lungs. Specifically, the techniques involve increasing and decreasing the expansion of the chest in an effort to restore normal breathing. There are two methods. Before proceeding with either, be sure you take these steps:

1. First, check the mouth and nose for any object that may be obstructing the air passage. To do this, carefully open the cat's mouth (you could be bitten if the jaws close automatically) and grab the tongue with a piece of cloth and pull it outward, following the steps for removing foreign objects on page 158. Two people can do this more easily than one: observe the illustration on page 146, which shows how one individual can hold open the animal's mouth with two lengths of gauze while another removes a foreign object. Gauze or cotton swabs can be used to wipe out vomitus, saliva or blood from the back of the oral cavity.
2. If the cat has been submerged in water, or has a lot of saliva or vomitus in the mouth, pick the cat up by its hind legs; then, with its head downward, suspend the cat for 10 to 15 seconds. As you hold the cat downward, shake its body a

couple of times to clean the airway and let the liquid drain from the animal's mouth (see illustration on the next page).

3. Lay the cat on its side with the body elevated slightly higher than the head. Remove any collar or harness.

4. Extend the head and neck outward in a straight line with the animal's back, a position that will help maintain an open airway.

How to administer artificial respiration. Carefully observe the illustrations on pages 148 and 149.

1. *Manual method:* Place your hands on either side of the cat's body at the level of the chest as shown in the illustration. Using a quick, sharp motion, compress the ribs between the palms of your hands. *Do not be too forceful!* Repeat this step 15 times per minute or until the cat begins to breathe on its own.

2. *Mouth-to-nose method:* This technique (the human counterpart is mouth-to-mouth) should be used if the manual method fails; it is preferred if an injury has caused a puncture wound in the animal's chest. Again, the head and neck of the cat should be extended. Place one hand firmly around the cat's muzzle, ensuring that the animal's mouth is closed. Place your mouth over the cat's nose and then blow gently in. Blow air in for 3 seconds; remove your mouth for 2 seconds. Keep repeating the process. Soon you should see the sides of the cat's chest begin to rise and fall, a sign that the animal is starting a return to normal breathing.

Removing a foreign object from the mouth

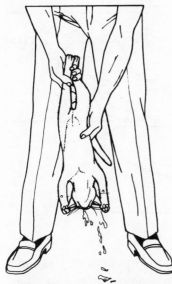

Suspending a cat to drain water or vomitus from mouth when unconscious

Whether performed manually or by the mouth-to-nose method, artificial respiration should be continued until the cat is breathing on its own or, at the very least, until you reach your veterinarian's office. Even though an animal has been resuscitated, it will invariably need further medical care. Whenever respiratory arrest has occurred, first attempt to get the cat breathing again and *then* get it to the veterinarian with all due speed.

Cardiac Arrest and Cardiac Resuscitation

Cardiac arrest occurs when the heart stops pumping blood through the body. *This usually follows respiratory arrest within a short period of time.* If artificial respiration is performed without delay, it will usually keep the heart beating. You'll know that the heart is beating by placing your hand on the lower portion of the cat's chest on the animal's left side as shown on page 149 and gently squeezing the chest between your fingers and thumbs. But if the heart is not beating, do as follows:

1. Put the cat in the same position as you would for artificial respiration (see illustration on page 148).
2. Compress the chest between your hands at the level shown in the illustration on page 149, just behind the elbow.

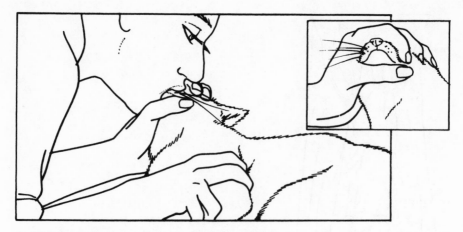

Artificial respiration, mouth-to-nose technique

3. Use a quick, firm compressing motion repeated at 1-second intervals for 30 to 60 seconds. *Do not squeeze your hands completely together.* Assuming that the heartbeat returns, watch to see that the cat is breathing on its own. If there's no heartbeat begin artificial respiration and, once again, get the cat to the veterinarian as fast as you can.

Know the Causes of Respiratory or Cardiac Arrest

1. *Obstruction of the airways to the lungs:* A bone, a piece of food or any other type of foreign material can lodge in the pharynx or opening of the trachea (see "Choking," pages 156–59). Accumulations of vomitus, saliva or blood in these passages—a common danger following an accident or illness accompanied by a state of shock or unconsciousness—can also cause obstruction.

2. *Asphyxiation:* The cutting off of oxygen (suffocation) is a considerable danger with cats because of their fondness for crawling into enclosed spaces such as boxes and drawers. When an animal is deprived of air, its oxygen level will diminish in short order. Asphyxiation can also result from high levels of carbon monoxide and other poisonous gases, and from smoke inhalation.

3. *Strangulation:* This is almost always due to a collar that is too tight. Certainly, an outdoor cat ought to have a collar for identification, but the apparatus should have an elastic portion allowing the collar to stretch in case it gets hooked on a branch or

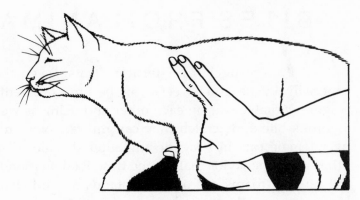

Cardiopulmonary resuscitation, placement of hands

fence. Sometimes, too, owners put collars on kittens and then forget that these must be periodically checked and sized to accommodate the growth of the kitten's neck. A tight collar can cut deep into the growing cat's neck, causing a serious and painful injury.

4. *Drowning:* People with backyard swimming pools should have them well enclosed at the very least, or covered to prevent animals from falling in. Although cats (and other animals) have a natural ability to swim, they can't easily climb out of the ordinary pool. In struggling to get out of the water, even a tough little animal can tire and easily drown.

5. *Chest trauma:* Injuries resulting from falls, animal fights and accidents often include rib fractures, a punctured lung, *pneumothorax* (an accumulation of air within the chest cavity that interferes with breathing) or a *diaphragmatic hernia* (in which the diaphragm is torn and abdominal organs are pushed into the chest cavity). All these conditions limit the animal's breathing capacity.

6. *Fluid in the chest:* As a result of some disease processes—cardiomyopathy (a form of heart disease) being one example (see page 203)—fluid may accumulate within the chest cavity, inhibiting the ability of the lungs to expand and fill with air.

In any of these situations, the cat may expire if not aided within a matter of minutes.

BITES FROM ANIMALS

*I*n a struggle over territory, cats—even those that are especially docile and sweet—can become decidedly ferocious, waging veritable war on each other and using as weapons every vigorous bite and scratch they can muster. Nor, in competition over female cats in heat, do unneutered males display toward other males behavior that can be described as friendly. In short, the cat that roams out of doors stands a good chance of being bitten. Because the wounds are usually tiny punctures, an owner may not notice them right away. The surface of the skin heals rapidly; meanwhile, infections resulting from the bites themselves can build up, unseen, beneath the surface. The usual outcome of an infected bite is an ugly, painful abscess, which is a swollen accumulation of pus. If your outdoor cat suddenly becomes inactive, seems to lose interest in eating and reacts with obvious pain to the touch over any specific portion of its body, assume that it probably got into some sort of scrap and sustained at least one bite—and possibly more.

1. Locate the wound—and be sure not to overlook the possibility of more than one puncture.
2. Clean the punctures with 3 percent hydrogen peroxide or mild soap (or Betadyne or pHisoDerm). Be sure to rinse well with water. Repeat this process 3 to 4 times daily for several days.
3. Carefully clip the hairs around the wound(s). The air that will then be able to reach the wound will help promote healing and will also make it easier for you to keep an eye on any inflammation or swelling.
4. Warm compresses should be applied 3 to 4 times daily for 10 minutes at a time. This will alleviate pain as well as help draw out infection.
5. Watch for an abnormal swelling at the site of the bite. This localized infection, if left untreated, can spread throughout the body, causing fever, a loss of appetite, listlessness and discomfort.
6. The following is a special problem with long-haired cats: An abscess sometimes comes to a head and breaks open before

any symptoms are noticed. Quite simply, both the bite wounds and the abscess are hidden in all that hair. The pressure that results from the unnoticed abscess often causes the death of a large area of skin covering the abscess site. As the skin sloughs off, the abscess breaks apart. A large opening is left, exposing a very messy, infected wound, which should be cleaned as described for bites. But the cat must also be seen promptly by your veterinarian. Surgical removal (debridement) of the dead tissue is often necessary, as is the administration of antibiotics.

7. Abscesses are almost always a predictable result of a real cat fight. Following feline battle, any wounds should be cleaned well and warm compresses applied for 2 or 3 days.

If bites are treated promptly, following these steps, an abscess will not usually develop except in the case of a severe or deep puncture, in which case antibiotic treatment should be administered as close to the time of injury as possible. Since it's impossible for most pet owners to determine whether a wound is superficial or deep, watch the injury for several days and if it looks as if it's healing properly and the animal is acting normally, you needn't see a veterinarian.

In the case of dog bites, you may not even see any puncture wounds on your cat. But the pressure of the canine's jaws can cause serious internal injuries; the cat may also go into shock. See pages 190–91 for instructions on how to treat shock, and then get your cat to the veterinarian *immediately*.

NOTE: As far as rabies and cat fights are concerned (pages 253–255), you have nothing to worry about if your cat has been vaccinated. Moreover, rabies is not widespread in domestic felines. But if you live in the country or don't know what bit your pet, don't rule out the possibility that it may have been a rabid animal (most likely, a skunk, raccoon, fox or bat rather than a dog or cat). In this instance take your pet to the veterinarian with all due speed! *And be sure to report the situation to the city or local health department immediately.*

For information on bleeding, see "Wounds," pages 196–99.

BURNS

*A*nimals suffer burns less frequently than do people. Normally, the hair coat of the cat insulates its body from extremes of heat and cold. (In the case of a fire, however, the cat is in horrendous trouble, because its hair coat will ignite in seconds. Thus a cat trapped in a burning building is usually lost to the fire.)

But most of the burns I've had occasion to treat have resulted from simple human carelessness: a small, unnecessary fire in the house, a dropped pot of scalding water, a flippantly tossed cigarette. The untutored child who wants to set a cat's tail on fire can be a cause as well. An exception to a burn brought about by human carelessness (or the cruelty of an ignorant child) would be one caused by a cat's own uncontrollable urge—say, to check out what's cooking on the stove. Unlike the rest of the feline's body, the pads of the feet are very vulnerable to heat. The stove-top burn is fairly common.

Any burn, be it from fire, steam, scalding water, chemicals, radiation, electricity or some kind of general heat, is an injury to the cells of the skin and possibly the tissues underneath. Depending on both length of exposure and the intensity of the burning agent, the damage is going to vary. You will find a discussion of chemical burns on pages 155–56 and electric burns in the section on electric shock, pages 161–62.

Veterinary care in the case of serious burns is absolutely imperative. And even when a cat sustains superficial burns (first degree) that involve a small portion of its body, it's best to have it medically checked. First aid in burn cases should include steps to relieve the pain, to protect the wound from bacterial contamination, to prevent shock (or to treat for shock should it occur) and to promote the healing of the burned tissues. I have included the appropriate first-aid steps for all degrees of burns. (The degree of injury depends on the length of time the animal is exposed to the source of the burn.) But should your cat be exposed to a raging fire, try to get it to a veterinarian immediately if at all possible. It would hardly make sense to take all the proper first aid steps and thereby consume the time that could have you in your veterinarian's office. Use your head.

Classification of Burns and Corresponding First-Aid Treatment

FIRST DEGREE

These are minor burns wherein superficial skin areas are reddened and hairs are singed. These burns may be painful for 24 to 36 hours. Nonetheless, they usually heal quickly and completely.

First Aid:
1. Either apply a cold compress (a hand towel soaked in cold water will do) directly over the burn or soak the area in a cold water bath. *Never use ice packs or ice water*—they could cause tissue damage.
2. After the initial soaking, keep the area dry and clean. Inspect the area hourly for the next few hours, looking for any signs of blistering or oozing, which would indicate a more serious injury.
3. *Do not apply butter or margarine* (this treatment, used in the past, is now contraindicated). A thin coating of pure aloe vera gel is all right to use, however, to alleviate discomfort.

SECOND DEGREE

These are deeper burns in which the cells that make up the outer layer of the skin are often destroyed. The skin appears sore and red; blisters develop and if the skin surface opens, a clear fluid may seep from the area. Since the skin acts as a protective organ that normally preserves these fluids, significant burns over a large portion of a cat's body are a very serious injury.

First Aid:
1. Cold water soaking by compresses or by immersion. Once again, *do not use ice.*
2. Dry the area gently with a clean cloth and blot the wound; be careful not to rub it.
3. Wrap a clean, dry cloth or sterile gauze over the wound. Never use cotton batting or cotton balls to cover any type of burn since particles of cotton will stick to the damaged skin.
4. Leave blisters and burned skin intact. Never attempt to puncture blisters or peel off skin.

154 · FIRST AID

5. Do not apply butter, margarine, antiseptic ointments, sprays or, for that matter, any other product unless directed to do so by your veterinarian.

THIRD DEGREE

The burned areas appear charred or whitish in coloration and the destruction of tissues is very deep. When large portions of the body suffer second- and third-degree burns, significant fluid losses can lead to shock and subsequent death in a matter of hours, even with prompt medical care.

First Aid:
1. Do not attempt to clean the burn; leave it alone.
2. *Do not immerse the entire animal in water.* (When the animal has suffered extensive burns, it is usually in shock and the body therefore cannot regulate its own temperature. Immersing the animal might actually increase the degree of shock.) Cold compresses might provide some relief, although most nerve endings in the skin will have been destroyed.
3. Do not apply butter, margarine, antiseptic ointment or sprays.
4. Cover with a thick layer of sterile gauze or a clean cloth.
5. Keep the animal quiet and lying down; cover it with a blanket.
6. If respiratory problems develop, maintain an open airway (see "Choking," pages 156–59).
7. In cases in which the delay in reaching a veterinarian is going to be greater than one hour, do as follows if the cat *is conscious and has not vomited:* Mix a solution of 1 level teaspoonful of salt and ½ teaspoonful of baking soda into 1 quart of water (room temperature). Give the cat 4 to 5 teaspoonfuls by mouth.

As with human burn victims, many pets survive the initial complications resulting from extensive burns. Their bodies, however, become more highly susceptible to bacterial infections than under normal circumstances. They can therefore be weakened by infection and die 1 or 2 weeks after the initial injury.

Chemical Burns

Don't underestimate the potential danger to your cat posed by dishwasher and laundry detergents. Along with drain cleaners and other cleaning agents, these everyday products can cause serious injuries if splashed onto an animal's skin or into its eyes. Both the strength of the chemical and the period of time it remains on the animal's body or eyes will determine the extent and nature of the burn. Thus, the most critical first-aid step you can take is to wash the product off.

Use a steady stream of fresh clean water or a sterile eyewash such as Dacriose to rinse away the chemical from the animal's skin or eyes. Be careful that you neither touch the substance yourself nor spread it farther over parts of the animal's body that are not already affected. In order to avoid this, place the cat in a sink or bathtub and, preferably using a hose attachment, direct the water over the region of the body where the chemical has been spilled. As long as you are extremely careful, a pitcher of water, repeatedly refilled, will do. Then, place a clean cloth or sterile gauze bandage over the skin. (Remember, *never use cotton batting or cotton balls to cover any type of burn since particles of cotton will stick to the damaged skin.*) Take the cat to your veterinarian for further medical care.

Chemicals sprayed at or spilled on the animal's face may cause exceptional pain, and also affect vision. Act quickly. Place the pet on its side: hold its eyelids open and pour *water* over the eyes and

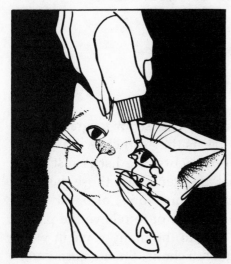

Washing chemicals out of eyes: Tilt head back and rinse away from the other eye.

face as illustrated on page 155. *If only one eye is affected, avoid getting the chemical into the other.* You can accomplish this by being sure that the affected eye is the one closest to the surface on which you have placed the cat. After rinsing away the chemical, cover the eye(s) with a dry, clean cloth or a piece of sterile gauze, using adhesive tape to hold it in place. Try to prevent the cat from scratching at the bandage or rubbing the injury.

Special steps should be taken when an acid (such as Mace or a toilet-bowl cleaner) is splashed on the skin or in the eyes: Prepare a mixture of 1 quart of water and 1 teaspoonful of baking soda to use in rinsing the affected area. *Never try this mixture with an alkali (such as a drain cleaner), however, since more irritation could result.* It is always a good idea to read the label on any product you think has caused an injury. Follow any specific first-aid directions listed there; cats can be treated in the same way that people are. *Regardless of whether an acid or an alkali has been the cause of a chemical burn, the cat should be taken to the veterinarian right after you've rinsed the chemical away.*

Dangerous chemicals should always be stored in areas out of the reach of pets and children. In addition to causing chemical burns, these household products can be very dangerous when inhaled or swallowed. (For first aid, see "Poisoning," pages 183–187). Please take to heart all I've said about household safety (see page 59). Be sensible. When using cleaning products, pesticides, insecticides, hair sprays, spray deodorants and similar chemical agents, keep your cat in another part of your home.

CHOKING

*F*or any number of reasons, cats seem to gravitate toward any foreign material and objects they can chew on. Bones, marbles, jacks, balls, needles, ornaments; the list is just about endless, and the only objects that are exempt are those that can't fit in the mouth. Curiosity is the driving force; also, all young animals will chew on objects in an attempt to relieve the pain of teething. A cat owner must be alert to the many ways in which foreign objects can cause an animal to choke. Such objects can be wedged in the mouth, swallowed or stuck somewhere along the digestive tract—the back of the throat, the esophagus or anywhere else in the gastrointestinal system.

The following objects can be dangerous to your cat:

1. Bones: Fish, chicken and chop bones are the most likely to interest the feline. Once in the stomach, small pieces of chicken bone will usually be broken down by the digestive juices and rendered harmless, but before that happens, they can also become lodged in the mouth or throat. *Never give a bone to any pet no matter what type it is or how big the animal.* Some people may argue with this advice; nonetheless, it is my experience that the dangers far outweigh any benefit. *Get rid of garbage containing bones.*
2. Small stones, marbles, the removable parts of play toys.
3. Pieces of stick, nuts, olive and fruit pits, pieces of plastic wrap or aluminum foil.
4. Needles, pins, fishing hooks and tackle, thread, yarn and string from roasts.

NOTE: If your cat enjoys playing with yarn or string, allow it to do so only when you're present to supervise. Your pet could swallow them.

An object stuck in the roof of the mouth or between the teeth will cause the cat to salivate or drool excessively. The pet may rub its face on the floor or exhibit obvious signs that it is attempting to dislodge something from its mouth. It might smack and lick its lips or have difficulty eating and swallowing food. If it is possible to grasp the object and remove it easily, you should do this with a tweezers or needle-nosed pliers—*unless the object is a needle* (see pages 159–61).

A pet that is *choking* on something will usually try to dislodge the material by a frenzied pawing at its face and mouth. Trapped in the mouth or throat where it can block the airway, the object will make the cat gag, gasp or gulp. Initially, the cat will show signs of anxiety or excitement. Should the supply of oxygen be cut off, the tongue and mucous membranes of the mouth will turn blue and the animal will collapse. Quick first aid is essential.

Don't let the steps I am about to describe alarm you. You are to proceed to remove the object manually in the following fashion *only if it is possible to do so.* Keep in mind, moreover, that a choking animal will be distracted by intense discomfort and may therefore be more cooperative than you might expect. (Also, the cat may be unconscious, in which case cooperation will hardly be your main concern.) Obviously, this procedure will be easier if done by two people.

1. Restrain the cat, if necessary, by wrapping it in a shirt or towel. Leave the head exposed.
2. Open the animal's mouth and with a dry cloth or piece of gauze wrapped around your fingertips, pull its tongue forward. Look for any foreign material. The penlight flashlight in your first-aid kit will help you see down the cat's throat (see illustration on page 146).
3. If you see the object: using your fingertips, a tweezers, a forceps or a needle-nosed pliers, get a grip on the object and remove it with a gentle, steady pulling motion. *Never do this if the object is a string, thread or needle (to which a thread could be attached).* These types of obstructions will not interfere with breathing and should be removed only by your veterinarian as quickly as possible.

If you can't see the object, or if you can see it but are unable to remove it, you can employ a modification of the Heimlich maneuver used to aid choking human beings:

1. Place the animal on its side. With your hands positioned on either side of the cat just behind the last rib, as shown in the illustration on page 159, compress inward and slightly upward. The thrusting motion should be quick and firm.
2. Release, then repeat this step several times in quick succession. This should force the foreign object upward and outward, clearing the airway.
3. Check the mouth for the presence of any foreign material; remove any you find.
4. Assuming that you've been able to remove the object, and in the event that the animal is not breathing, start artificial respiration (see pages 144–48). Continue until the pet begins to breathe on its own or until you reach the veterinarian's office.

Objects that become entrapped in the digestive system and cause obstruction in the gastrointestinal tract must be removed by your veterinarian.

Modified Heimlich maneuver: Place hands below ribcage; gently thrust forward and inward to expel object.

One day when I was working at the ASPCA in New York City, a large cat was presented to me for treatment. He was gagging and having trouble swallowing. It was immediately obvious why: there was a small stick protruding from his mouth. The cat was placed under anesthesia and the stick—all seven inches of it— was gently removed, without surgery. Perhaps that will convince you—as it did me—that an animal will try to swallow almost anything, notwithstanding how impossible it may seem.

Of all the objects that can get into the feline's mouth, there to get stuck or swallowed, none is as common as the needle, whose shininess makes it especially attractive to the cat. No other object in the mouth presents a situation quite as precarious, either. Bad enough that the needle can get stuck or swallowed; all too often, however, attached to that needle is a thread. Only if you catch the cat just as it gets a needle in its mouth, and only if you feel no tension in the thread as you gently test the chances of pulling it out, should you attempt to remove it. Otherwise, leave it alone and promptly get the cat to the veterinarian. The same would apply should a thread be wrapped around the base of the tongue. If you fail to act by getting to the veterinarian, this is what can occur:

When a linear foreign body—whether a string, thread or yarn —is trapped with one end in the mouth and the other end down in the stomach and intestines, a digestive process is set in motion that can threaten the life of the cat. The peristaltic, wave-like motion of the intestines pulls along whatever is being digested down into the intestinal tract. With one end held in the mouth and the other encompassed in the moving gut, the thread is automatically going to get tightened. Now taut as a stretched-out wire, that linear material will, in time, cut through the walls of the intestines—unless it is surgically removed. This gruesome occurrence might take a day to begin. But the more quickly a cat in this situation is rushed to a veterinarian, the better its chances of survival. Needless to say, people who sew should practice special caution. *Never leave needles or threads around your house.*

Obstructions can occur anywhere else in the gastrointestinal tract, including the esophagus. Caught in the esophageal passageway between the mouth and the stomach, an object will cause the animal to salivate excessively and to make repeated attempts to swallow. Any food consumed will be vomited up almost immediately. The symptoms vary when an object is obstructing other parts of the intestinal tract, the indications depending on the size and shape of the foreign body and whether the obstruction is partial or complete. For example, severe abdominal pain and persistent and violent vomiting can be a signal that something is caught in the digestive system, as can lethargy, dehydration and shock, all of which will follow without appropriate treatment. Sometimes, a foreign object may not cause obstruction or discomfort until it gets to the very end of the pet's digestive system. A few years ago, I examined a cat that was straining to defecate. What I found was a staple wedged across the anal orifice (which I was easily able to remove).

If, over the course of 24 hours, an animal shows persistent vomiting, abdominal pain, difficulty swallowing or defecating, you should definitely be suspicious. Withhold all food and water and take the pet for prompt veterinary treatment. Your veterinarian may perform X-rays or a "GI" series to locate a suspected foreign body. Such an object may be removed by surgery, or sometimes by an *endoscopic* instrument. This is special equipment that is passed down through the mouth and the conducting passages into the stomach. Often it makes possible removal of a foreign object without an operation (see pages 218–19).

Certainly, it can also happen that an object swallowed by an animal does not cause a problem. Instead, it can pass harmlessly through the system. If you see your cat swallow a small pin, needle, tack or any sharp object, do not panic. Feed the pet small amounts of a *bulky food.* You want to surround the object with a protective barrier so that whatever has gone into the gut will pass through the digestive tract and not pierce the intestinal walls. Small pieces of dry food or bread soaked in chicken or beef broth or milk will serve the purpose well. Give the animal the food every hour for several hours. Provided that the pet then exhibits no abnormal symptoms and continues to eat and act normally, you can more or less relax and simply watch to see what occurs. By all means, call your veterinarian, but you needn't act with hysteria or haste. For very small objects, such as a staple, the following day will be soon enough to X-ray the cat and to be sure that the object is safely passing along.

One final word regarding a linear foreign body (thread, string or yarn) that has been swallowed and seems to be going through the entire digestive system. You might observe one end of the material passing out of the cat's anal orifice. *Do not pull on this.* Should you notice this, or any intense straining to defecate, get your cat to your veterinarian for immediate medical care.

ELECTRIC SHOCK

*T*he tendency of a cat—particularly when young and teething—to chew on cords and wires makes it extremely susceptible to electric shock. Protecting your cat from this type of injury should be a top priority. Keep all electrical cords out of reach or hidden under protective cover, and if possible steer your cat to other objects (throw one of its toys in another direction to distract it). After a while it may willingly desert chewing on wires and take up safer play.

If you catch the cat in the act of chewing on an electrical cord, you can stop it quickly. A good loud yell will do. Unfortunately, your pet—if determined enough—will get at wires when you don't happen to be around. Often, the only evidence of resulting injury is inflammation of one or both corners of the mouth and possibly the adjacent lip folds. The burns are most commonly first- or second-degree and appear relatively innocuous at first.

(This is not always true; the burns can be severe.) Even minor burns on the mouth must never be ignored, since they may be a sign that the cat has been in contact with an electric current. Whatever the resulting condition of the mouth, respiratory complications (pulmonary edema) can result from contact with the electric current within a matter of minutes and may prove fatal.

Aside from the appearance of burns on either side of the mouth, affected pets frequently salivate profusely owing to soreness of the mouth, and then sometimes develop trouble in breathing. After electric shock, fluid often builds up in the lungs (this is called pulmonary edema; see page 235). The cat needs medical care. Even when there is no problem breathing, a cat with burns on its mouth sustained from electric shock should be taken to the veterinarian's, where it can be observed. Possibly, no respiratory complications will develop; maybe the symptoms will subside. But you cannot take that chance. Frequently, a cat that has received an electric shock will require placement in an oxygen cage and treatment with drugs to reduce fluid accumulation in the lungs.

For your own safety, I want to repeat a warning: *Never touch an animal that is itself touching an exposed electric wire.* Turn off the current. Use a dry stick to get the cat away from the wire. If the cat is unconscious, it may be suffering from shock (see pages 190–91). Keep it warm by covering it with a jacket or towel. Administer CPR or artificial respiration (see the section beginning on page 144) if necessary. But in any event, *get your cat to a veterinarian as soon as possible.*

EYE INJURIES

*E*ye injuries are among the most painful a pet can sustain; they can also lead to some degree of vision loss. Though the indoor cat is not immune to such an injury, the chances are increased for the animal that has unrestricted freedom out of doors. The sources of eye injuries are numerous:

1. Scratches on the outermost surface of the eyeball (the cornea) can be caused by sticks, twigs and branches. Such scratches can also occur during a fight with another animal,

especially with another cat. Not treated promptly and properly, superficial scratches may erode deeper into the cornea and cause the eyeball to rupture.

2. Dust, particles of dirt, thorns and seeds, glass or hair can blow into the eye. Lodged beneath the eyelid, they can irritate the cornea and also inflame the conjunctiva (see illustration, page 240).

3. Damage can be inflicted by chemical irritants sprayed or thrown into the animal's eyes. Before you use any insecticides, repellants or household cleaners, make sure your cat is in another room.

4. Any traumatic incident—an auto accident, a fight—can cause a laceration of the eyelid(s) or eyeball(s). Some of these traumas result in puncture wounds in which a foreign object becomes embedded in the eye.

5. Occasionally, a pet will receive a blow to the head which causes an eye to protrude (prolapse). Breeds of cats like the Persian that have short noses and somewhat bulging eyes are most susceptible to this injury. As a consequence of their anatomy, the eyeball is not well protected and a blow to the head can easily cause protrusion.

Depending on the nature and extent of damage, the following different symptoms can arise:

1. Redness or inflammation
2. Excessive tearing or discharge from the eye(s)
3. Squinting due either to pain or to increased sensitivity to bright light
4. Swelling of the eyelid(s) or surrounding area (sometimes to the extent that the eyelids may be closed)
5. Rubbing of the face along the floor or against furniture or furious pawing at the eye
6. Bleeding from the eye(s) or eyelid(s)
7. Crying or pulling away when the eye is touched
8. Abnormal appearance of the cornea: a bluish-white discoloration; a cloudy or opaque condition
9. The third eyelid (nictitating membrane) may be raised up, partially covering the eye*

---

* What is known as the "third eyelid" emerges in response to trauma to act as a protective membrane against further injury. The illustration on page 242 shows the third eyelid both in its normal position and when prolapsed.

Always wash your hands before trying to look in the animal's eye(s); the cat should also be properly restrained. This will help you assess the injury, facilitate first aid and prevent the cat from further harm as a result of any self-inflicted trauma. Any injury to the eye, even if it appears minor, must be taken seriously. *Be sure the cat is examined as soon as possible after you have administered first aid.*

First-Aid Measures

NOTE: Treating a chemical burn to the eyes is discussed under *Burns,* pages 155–56.

REMOVING A FOREIGN BODY FROM THE EYE
1. Gently pull down the lower eyelid and raise the upper eyelid to examine for foreign material.
2. Having located foreign matter, *wet* the corner of a clean handkerchief, a tissue or cotton ball and touch this lightly to the object in order to remove it. *Never use DRY cotton in cleaning the eye.*
3. As an alternate method when step number 2 doesn't work, take a small bulb syringe and flush the eye with clean, room-temperature water, or an eyewash such as Dacriose. Simply direct a fine stream toward the eyeball and the eyelids. Foreign objects not embedded should easily wash away.
4. Apply a small amount of ophthalmic ointment to the eye.
5. Should your efforts be unsuccessful or should the cat still be uncomfortable, take it to your veterinarian.

DEALING WITH INJURY TO THE EYELID
1. Apply gentle, direct pressure over the wound with a dry, clean cloth to control the bleeding.
2. Flush with a sterile eyewash solution (such as Dacriose).
3. Cover the eye with a dry, clean bandage as shown in the illustration on the next page.
4. Keep the eye covered. Restrain the cat to prevent it from scratching at the eye until you arrive at your veterinarian's office.

Bandaging an eye: Place a large gauze pad or clean handkerchief over the eye(s), wrap around head and ears with roll gauze, then tape end of gauze in place.

TREATING CORNEAL LACERATIONS/ULCERATIONS

These are extremely painful. The cat will usually squint. The third eyelid may also be raised. Another symptom is a whitish discoloration on the corneal surface; there may be bleeding if the conjunctival tissue or the edge of the eyelid is affected.

1. Flush the eye gently with sterile eyewash and apply a liberal amount of ophthalmic ointment.
2. Cover *both* eyes with a clean, dry dressing if possible. See illustration above. Transport the cat to your veterinarian.

PROLAPSED EYEBALL/PENETRATING EYE INJURY

Both a *prolapsed eyeball* and a *penetrating eye injury* present extreme emergencies:

1. *The prolapsed eyeball:* Apply a liberal amount of the ophthalmic ointment to the eye every 10 to 15 minutes until you reach the veterinarian's office. (You may also use a contact lens solution.) This is to help prevent the surface of the eyeball from drying out. If there is to be any chance of saving the eye, only your veterinarian can do it; the cat must get *immediate* veterinary care.
2. *Penetrating eye injuries:* When sharp objects have penetrated or become embedded in the eyeball, or in the event the eyeball has been ruptured, prompt veterinary care is essential. *Do not try to remove the foreign object and do not flush out the eye.* Apply a loose, clean, dry bandage over *both* eyes. Keep the cat as quiet as possible while you transport it to the veterinarian.

In regard to all eye injuries, be conscientious in following the steps prescribed by your veterinarian. Adhere strictly to the time schedule given for application of medicines and be sure to make follow-up visits when they have been recommended.

FRACTURES, DISLOCATIONS, SPRAINS AND STRAINS

*I*t usually takes quite a forceful trauma to produce an actual fracture of the bone. Some of these traumas, however—being hit by a car, pinned under a piece of furniture, or falling from a height onto a hard surface—are often sufficiently severe to cause bleeding, shock and internal injuries. These conditions must *always* take top priority (see pages 131–33) and only when such life-threatening conditions are ruled out or eliminated should you tend to a fracture. Dislocations, strains and sprains can occur under less extreme circumstances but can cause the feline a good deal of pain as well.

Fractures

Most of the time, the symptoms of a fracture are obvious. If the cat can walk at all, it will hold its affected leg slightly up in the air to relieve the pain, which can be considerable. *If the animal is limping, it must be examined by your veterinarian as soon as possible. The cat must also be kept very still.* A "greenstick" fracture (wherein the bone is cracked, but not completely broken) or a "simple" fracture (in which the bone is broken, but the skin surface is intact) can easily be worsened if the unrestrained animal falls on the already injured leg.

Be mindful that not all animals will raise a fractured limb in the air. (Your cat may be a stoic!) Following any traumas that logically might have produced a break, make sure your pet is not limping or dragging a limb. Fractures will often produce a great amount of swelling, too.

It is much easier to tell when a cat has suffered a "compound" fracture (when there has been a complete break and the bone has broken through the surface of the skin) or a "comminuted" fracture (when the bone is shattered and pieces have splintered off). In such cases the leg will usually appear deformed. No matter how messy the fracture appears, *do not attempt to clean the area.* Rather, cover it with sterile gauze, applying pressure if you see gushing blood (see page 197). Under no circumstances should you touch any visible fragments of bone. Just restrain the cat and immobilize the limb in order to prevent any worsening of the condition.

This is the procedure to follow in all types of fractures:

A temporary splint can be fashioned from a newspaper or from two narrow pieces of wood (such as tongue depressors). Study the illustrations below. You will see that strips of adhesive tape or cloth can be applied or tied in several places to hold the splint. You must never put these at the point of an obvious fracture. Put a thin padding of cotton or cloth between the splint and the leg, and always be sure the splint extends the length of the leg, so that it is both below and above the break. Gently place the pet with its good side down before applying the splint. *If the animal struggles as you attempt to put on the splint, however, you'd be better off to abandon the effort (since you might worsen the injury in the struggle) and concentrate on keeping the kitty still and quiet until you can get it to the veterinarian.*

Once your veterinarian puts on an appropriate splint or cast, or performs the necessary surgery to stabilize a fracture, it will take 4 to 8 weeks (or more) for a fracture to heal, depending upon

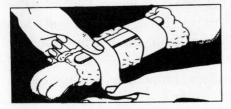

Applying a temporary splint: Wrap cotton padding around injured limb, applying tongue depressors on either side for support. Tape at intervals above and below the point of injury.

the animal's age, its nutritional state and the type and location of the fracture. Splints, slings, casts and bandages should be checked by your veterinarian at least every 7 to 10 days (or according to your veterinarian's directions), as such external devices may cause damage if they are too tight or become wet. If the cat chews and licks at the splint, cast or bandage, or if it becomes wet or gives off an offensive odor, this usually indicates a problem—possibly an infection—calling for prompt veterinary attention.

Fractures are generally the result of traumatic injury. Sometimes, though, they can accompany an unbalanced diet or chronic kidney disease or bone tumors, all of which can produce "demineralization" of the bones, which causes fracture even in the absence of forceful injury.

Dislocations

The hip is a "ball and socket" joint. When the head of the femur (the ball) slips out of the acetabulum (the socket), a dislocation occurs. As with a fracture, the cat will walk on its other three legs. You may also notice a visible swelling over the injured hip. If the hind legs are pulled back together, one will usually appear shorter than the other. (However, you shouldn't attempt to do this.) The cat will experience pain; X-rays must be taken to rule out a fracture. The dislocated joint must be put back in place under general anesthesia and the affected limb placed in a sling. As for first aid, it's best to avoid placing any pressure against the affected leg. Try to keep the cat still and lying on its opposite side until you get to the veterinarian.

Sprains and Strains

These are more common in dogs than in cats. When they occur in felines usually the pet is middle-aged or overweight. Most of the time, these injuries are not serious. Though the cat will often place partial weight on the affected limb, after a few days of supervised rest the cat should show rapid improvement. Very little localized swelling will be evident. Immediately following the injury, you can either apply cold compresses (wrapped around the leg) or soak the limb in cool water. The following day, *warm* compresses or soaks should be applied for 10 to 15 minutes every 4 to 6 hours. Be sure the cat rests until it resumes normal walking. Keep it confined to a large carrier or inside a small room where it is unable to jump or run about (thereby worsening the initial injury and causing prolonged pain). If, after a few days, the cat has shown no improvement, make certain it is seen by your veterinarian.

NOTE: In their roughhousing, kittens can bump or twist a leg, let out a shriek and become acutely lame. Before you assume a serious injury has occurred, observe the kitten and see if there is any obvious sign of fracture or dislocation. If not, keep the little pet quiet for a few hours; see if the lameness persists. I've had many a worried client who came rushing in with a limping kitten that, when placed on the exam table, proceeded to walk comfortably as if nothing had happened at all.

GASTROINTESTINAL DISORDERS

*D*igestive upsets are common in cats. If a cat vomits, has diarrhea or constipation, there is no need to panic. What a cat eats and how it eats will affect its digestive system. In addition, stress and anxiety as well as systemic illnesses can cause digestive upset. Watch the frequency of symptoms and be alert to unusual signs that seem to exceed normal digestive disturbance. Whenever conservative first aid is not effective within a 12-hour period, though, it is time to call your veterinarian.

Vomiting

Many cats vomit occasionally and show no other signs of illness. If this happens and the cat seems otherwise fine, you don't need to seek veterinary care. Vomiting is a natural reaction of the body to rid its digestive system of any offending substance. Cats also vomit to rid themselves of hairballs. This is normal.

Sometimes cats eat grass for other than nutritional reasons. This consumption is a natural attempt to create an irritation in the stomach so that the animal vomits and rids itself of the initial source of a digestive upset. For the cat that has an attraction to grass, there are products such as Kitty Grass. As I've previously mentioned, these products may keep your cat from eating house plants, some of which could be poisonous.

Regardless of the reasons, if your cat is vomiting you should observe the frequency, the appearance of the vomitus (for blood, yellow-green bile or foreign material like hair, glass or string) and the relationship to feeding time (e.g., "the cat always vomits three hours after eating or drinking anything"). This sort of information will help your veterinarian determine the cause of the digestive upset.

FIRST AID FOR VOMITING
1. Keep the cat as quiet as possible.
2. Give it 1 teaspoon Pepto-Bismol or Kaopectate (see pages 125 and 127 for administering liquid medications). Repeat every 8 hours for 24 to 36 hours.
3. Withhold *all* food and most water for 18 to 24 hours; this is a critical step since consumption of food and water will only irritate the system. You may place several ice cubes in the cat's water dish; as these melt the cat can lap up small amounts of water.
4. After 18 to 24 hours—assuming vomiting has ceased— begin to feed the cat small quantities of bland foods such as boiled hamburger or chicken and rice (which you can prepare), or commercial strained-meat baby foods. (I prefer the latter since they are so easily digested.) Continue this form of feeding for two days, offering small amounts every few hours.
5. Provided no further vomiting occurs, the cat may be returned to its normal diet on the third day.

NOTE: *Persistent vomiting indicates a serious problem and can cause rapid dehydration.* Take your cat to the veterinarian if:
    a. it has vomited more than two or three times within a 12-hour period.
    b. there is any blood in the vomitus.
    c. the cat appears weak or otherwise ill.

Diarrhea

Feeding your cat a good, balanced, commercially prepared diet is the best preventive treatment for this all too familiar condition. Rich, starchy, fatty "people food," milk products or spoiled foods are often the cause of both diarrhea and vomiting. Avoid overfeeding.

FIRST AID FOR DIARRHEA
1. Give 1 teaspoon Kaopectate every 8 hours for 48 hours.
2. As with vomiting, feed small quantities of bland food, such as boiled hamburger or chicken and rice, or strained-meat baby foods. Give the cat small amounts throughout the day rather than one large meal. Allow it to drink only small amounts of water.
3. After 2 to 3 days of a bland diet, and provided that the diarrhea has ceased, resume normal feedings.
4. Drop off a sample of the cat's stool (after the diarrhea has been resolved) at your veterinarian's office, to be analyzed for parasites, which can be the cause of diarrhea and vomiting.

NOTE: Your cat ought to respond to home treatment within 24 hours. Should the diarrhea continue or should there be any blood in the stool, take your cat to the veterinarian immediately. Afflicted with persistent and severe diarrhea, an animal may become dehydrated. Moreover, the disturbance could be related to a systemic infection (e.g., a virus), the presence of intestinal parasites, a food allergy or stress. An absorption disorder, in which the normal absorption of food through the intestinal walls fails to occur, could be responsible, as could a more serious disorder such as cancer.

Constipation

Sometimes a cat will skip a day without having a bowel movement, just as people sometimes do. This may be for no other reason than the cat ate less food than normal the day before.

Every once in a while, I'll hear from a client who is in a panic because his or her cat has not had a bowel movement for 24 hours. My first question—especially when the cat is male—is "are you sure the cat is urinating?" When a cat has a urinary obstruction (see pages 223–26), its attempts to pass urine may be confused with straining to defecate.

As long as the cat *is* urinating and is *not* uncomfortable, there is no reason to be concerned unless it goes without a bowel movement for more than 48 to 72 hours. Then you should definitely consult your veterinarian, who may recommend that you give the pet a laxative (see page 218).

Some cats develop trouble with constipation as they age. At times an older cat becomes obstipated, meaning that the stool has accumulated and "backed up" in the intestinal tract. Usually, the animal will stop eating, become inactive and may vomit. Your veterinarian will have to treat the cat with an enema, and often must anesthetize it in order to "clean it out."

NOTE: Do not give your cat enemas, laxatives, stool softeners or mineral oil without specific instructions from a veterinarian.

HEAD AND NECK TRAUMA

*S*evere blows to the head and neck usually occur out of doors and result when an animal falls or is hit by a car. Occasionally, veterinarians see cases of head and neck trauma in cats confined indoors, especially when the animals are young. The little kitten, in pursuit of fun, can easily cause a heavy object to topple onto its head. Any heavy object that has an unstable foundation should therefore be removed. It's important too to watch your step—literally. Consider how easily the young cat could get right under your foot or be in the way just as you slam the door. A little kitten is quite fragile.

Most of the time, you will know when a cat has sustained a serious injury to the head. Often such a trauma is accompanied by profuse bleeding from the nose and by bleeding lacerations, since the head, nose, mouth and ears are well supplied with tiny blood vessels. Bleeding certainly requires attention. But you should also be alert to the possibility of brain or spinal cord in-

jury, and heed the following warnings in administering first aid
for any head wound:

1. *Do not clean wounds of the head.* This could aggravate bleeding. Cleaning could also spread glass, dirt, hair or other
   foreign material into deeper tissues—such as the brain—if
   the skull has been fractured.
2. When applying direct pressure over a bleeding wound (see
   page 196), *do not use great force.* You could compress any
   fractures into the brain or spinal cord.
3. Do not give the cat any food or water.
4. Handle the cat gently and move it as little as possible.

There is very little you yourself can do about injuries to the
brain and spinal cord other than to get the cat immediate veterinary care. Whenever an animal has injured its head or neck, keep
it as quiet as possible and observe the pet for these symptoms:

1. Inability to walk or move; any kind of paralysis, incoordination
2. A clear or blood-tinged fluid, or blood, draining from the
   nose or ears (this may indicate a skull fracture)
3. Seizures or muscle twitching
4. Loss of consciousness (intermittent or total)
5. Loss of control over bladder or bowel functions
6. Signs of shock (e.g., pale gums and/or tongue; see page 190)
7. Vomiting
8. Difference in the pupil size (when both eyes are compared)
9. Exaggerated extension of the neck and stiff jutting out of
   the forelegs. (Should these be evident, a serious spinal cord
   injury is likely to have occurred; *any movement of the animal
   should be minimal.* It should be kept still and held support-
   ively to prevent twisting or turning of the neck. *Rush to your
   veterinarian.*)

FIRST AID
1. Keep the pet lying down quietly on its side and cover it
   with a towel or blanket to keep it warm.
2. Apply a clean, dry dressing over any bleeding wounds.

3. Any nose bleeding can be controlled by applying pressure over the affected nostril, and then a cold compress or ice pack for several minutes.
4. Check the mouth for any accumulation of blood or saliva or vomitus, and clean these out to assure an open airway.
5. Be prepared to administer artificial respiration if necessary (see pages 144–48).
6. Being as gentle as possible and keeping the animal immobile, quickly get the cat to your veterinarian so that the extent of the trauma can be evaluated and treated accordingly.

NOTE: In some cases, a pet that has received a strong blow to the head or neck will not seem to be hurt too badly at first. With the passing of time, however, the animal's condition worsens. *Do not wait for this to happen.* Get to the veterinarian without delay. Time is essential with injuries to the brain or spinal cord. Delay getting treatment, and any fracture could cause compression on either the brain or spinal cord, possibly causing permanent damage or death.

HEATSTROKE/ HYPOTHERMIA/ FROSTBITE/SUNBURN

*D*espite their protective hair coats, animals are not immune to temperature extremes. Your cat looks to you for shelter —from excessive heat in warm weather and, in the winter, from the cold and the whipping force of icy winds.

Heatstroke

Everyone, including animals, has a built-in mechanism that keeps the body temperature constant. The normal body temperature of the cat ranges between 101 and 102.5 degrees F. When heatstroke occurs, the body temperature rises to over 106 degrees.

Heatstroke (hyperthermia) occurs much less often in cats than in dogs. But because of their "pushed-in" faces, breeds such as the Persian are the most susceptible. All cats should have fresh, cool water available to them, especially in warm weather. Outdoor cats should have some sort of shaded shelter, while indoor cats should be kept in a portion of the house with good ventilation.

The greatest number of animal deaths from heatstroke occur in parked cars, the result of an owner's carelessness or callousness. *Never* leave a pet alone inside a parked car while you run even the briefest of errands. No matter that the car is in the shade or that the window is partially open; the air circulation will be inadequate. On a warm day, the temperature in the automobile will rise in a matter of minutes, transforming the interior of the vehicle into a stifling "oven."

Cats, like dogs, do not perspire as we do. Rather, they get rid of excess body heat through opened-mouth breathing and panting as well as through the pads of their feet. Cats that are very young or very old and those that are sick or debilitated are more apt to become victims of heatstroke. Any animal with a history of heatstroke should be carefully watched in warm weather since it is more inclined than other animals to have repeated episodes.

Consider heatstroke if the following symptoms occur during warm weather: open-mouthed breathing and uncontrollable panting; drooling or foaming at the mouth; signs of anxiety and agitation; gums and tongue turning bluish or gray.

Take the cat's rectal temperature as instructed on page 116. In the event of heatstroke, the mercury could rise right off the scale, showing that the animal's temperature is higher than the thermometer can measure. To repeat: in warm weather, a rectal temperature in excess of 105 degrees F. is a probable sign of heatstroke.

FIRST AID
It is critical that the animal's body temperature be reduced as rapidly as possible.

1. If the room or area in which the cat is confined is hot, take the pet to a cooler part of the house.

2. Place the cat in the sink or bathtub and hose it down or immerse its body in cold water. (Be careful not to submerge its head.)
3. When no sink or tub is available, wrap the cat in a cold, water-soaked towel and apply an ice pack to the top of the animal's head. In addition, a fan can be directed toward the pet and some rubbing alcohol poured over the cat's feet and back.
4. Monitor the cat's temperature; discontinue the cooling measures once the temperature has been lowered to 103 degrees F. Otherwise, you could produce hypothermia (low body temperature) which could be equally dangerous.
5. Administer artificial respiration (see pages 144–47) if the cat stops breathing.
6. Allow the pet to drink small quantities of cool, fresh water frequently. *Never force liquids into the mouth of an unconscious cat.*
7. An unconscious cat should be taken immediately to a veterinary facility for care.

NOTE: Following any occurrence of heatstroke, *take the pet to your veterinarian* as soon as you have the pet cooled down. Even though the cat has apparently recovered, life-threatening complications frequently arise after an episode of hyperthermia.

Hypothermia

This condition exists when an animal's body temperature falls way below normal and the mechanisms that conserve body heat are not functioning. Such a state is often precipitated by prolonged exposure to cold but may also be the result of severe illness, or may occur if an animal goes into shock following a traumatic incident.

Symptoms: The pet will be inactive, listless, depressed and feel cold to the touch. A rectal temperature of less than 100 degrees F. would indicate hypothermia. Below 97 degrees F. is considered serious and may be life-threatening.

FIRST AID
Immediate steps must be taken to warm the animal and restore its normal body temperature.

1. Cover the cat with a towel or blanket.
2. If you have a hot water bottle, fill it with *warm* water and place it on the outer side of the towel, so it's not in direct contact with the animal; a plastic milk or juice container is a useful substitute.
3. A heating pad can also be employed, on LOW heat, as long as you put a towel between the pet and the heating pad.
4. When hypothermia results from illness or physical trauma, the body must be kept warm. When an animal has become hypothermic as a result of exposure to environmental cold it should be physically stimulated. *Gently massage* the body and legs; vigorous rubbing can cause further tissue damage. You can encourage the pet to drink small amounts of warm liquids (water, milk or broth).
5. If the animal is in shock (see page 190), or remains listless and depressed, or should the body temperature not be restored to normal in 1 to 2 hours, obtain prompt veterinary care.

NOTE: Never use a heating pad or blow dryer when frostbite is suspected.

Frostbite

Frostbite is the freezing of tissues caused by exposure to very low temperature; small ice crystals form in the fluids and tissues of the skin and underlying layers, causing destruction and impairing the circulation of blood in the area. Hair covering and pigmentation of skin may make it difficult to determine the presence and degree of freezing in some pets. But it is the pads of the feet, the tail and the tips of the ears that are the most susceptible. Very young, debilitated or older animals are the most prone to frostbite.

SYMPTOMS

1. Initially, the skin becomes pale because of diminished blood supplies; soon after, it becomes reddened, hot and painful to the touch; swelling often occurs.
2. The hair may fall out and the superficial layers of the skin may peel.

3. The animal is sensitive to the irritation and scratches at the area.

4. Great pain and swelling would indicate that freezing has affected the deeper, underlying tissues. Necrosis (death) of these tissues can lead to the development of gangrene.

FIRST AID

Be gentle in handling frostbitten areas and do not overheat the animal.

1. Immerse the affected area in lukewarm water, increasing the warmth of the water over the next few minutes. You can place the whole animal's body in the bathtub or sink for 15 to 20 minutes. Just be sure that the water is no warmer than is comfortable for your own hand and do not submerse the head.

2. Afterward, dry the animal *gently* with a towel. *Do not use* a blow dryer when aiding a frostbitten animal.

3. Apply a thin coating of either Vaseline or an antiseptic ointment to the frostbitten areas to protect and soothe the skin. (Don't worry if the cat licks it off unless a large area is involved or the licking is excessive. Then ask your veterinarian for an Elizabethan collar [see page 122]).

4. Wrap the pet in a warm blanket to conserve its body heat.

5. Treat the animal for shock if necessary (see page 190). (Treatment for shock by artificial respiration will be required only in very severe cases of prolonged exposure, i.e., hypothermia.)

6. Have your cat checked by a veterinarian as soon as possible.

7. Following emergency care, gently massage the area on a daily basis. *Do not rub*. This will help restore the circulation of blood to the tissue and will also reduce the pain.

Any animal that has been frostbitten should be protected from further exposure to cold. Frostbitten tissues are more susceptible to repeated freezing.

NOTE: Cats that have had frostbitten ears often have rounded ear tips after the episode owing to the destruction of the outer edge of the ear. Moreover, after healing, regrowth of hair is often sparse. The hair may also grow back white.

Sunburn

The occurrence of "sunburn" in pets is almost nonexistent. However, cats with thin hair coats and those with white or light-colored hair should be kept from excessive exposure to direct sunlight, especially at midday. These animals could be burned and are more subject to certain types of skin cancer than other pets.

Some animals suffer an irritation known as solar dermatitis on their noses and the tips of their ears. The affected areas become crusty, cracked and sore. Pets that suffer from this irritation should also be removed from direct sunlight during the midday. In addition, before these pets are allowed out of doors, topical application of a lotion containing suncreens (use any commercial brand made for people) may be applied to the areas of skin that have no protective hair covering.

INSECT STINGS
AND BITES

Despite its powerful streak of curiosity, the cat exhibits a surprising degree of caution. The cagey feline animal is not, for example, as likely as a dog to blunder right into a hive of buzzing bees. Fortunately, too, first aid for the majority of insect bites and stings is relatively simple; and reaction to all but a few bites and stings is minor.

Insect Stings

Stings from bees, wasps, yellow jackets and hornets usually occur on the head, especially in the area of the mouth and nose. In addition to having to endure an acute burst of extremely nasty pain, the cat will show pronounced localized swelling and will experience observable discomfort.

Ideally, any stinger the insect leaves behind should be removed with a tweezers. Owing to the density of a cat's hair, however, this is actually very difficult, so unless the stinger can easily be found, it is best to proceed with measures to reduce the swelling.

First, clean the area with mild soap and water and then disinfect the site of the sting with hydrogen peroxide or alcohol. Either an ice pack or cold compress should then be applied. You may also apply a *thin* coat of a paste-like mixture of baking soda and water to help relieve itching.

Should a cat be subjected to repeated stings such as those inflicted by a horde of insects, it could definitely have a life-threatening allergic and "anaphylactic" type of reaction (see pages 142–144). Although such dreadful attacks do happen, they are rare. In addition, the very rare cat will have an acute allergic reaction to a single sting. Any signs of abnormal reaction should provoke immediate life-saving steps. If the cat exhibits trouble breathing or collapses, try to keep an open airway for breathing. To keep the animal breathing, give it artificial respiration (see pages 144–147). Then get the cat to your veterinarian as quickly as possible.

Insect Bites

Bites from fleas, mosquitoes, gnats, chiggers, ants and lice are less serious than the stings of flying insects. (NOTE: Mosquitoes do carry heartworms, but the problem is more significant with dogs than it is with cats.) Insect bites cause localized irritation rather than swelling and terrible pain. Sometimes there is heavy infestation, however, which makes the irritation more generalized. The result can be intense, persistent itching which brings on vigorous scratching and licking, all of which cause trauma to the skin. This is especially true when cats have an allergy to flea bites; only one or two flea bites can produce a severe allergic dermatitis.

Do the same as you would with a sting. Clean the area. Apply cold compresses. Put on a thin coat of baking soda paste to reduce the itching. And see pages 208–10 for more general advice about fleas.

For information about *ticks,* see page 211.

Spiders

Most spiders found in the United States are harmless. The two major exceptions are the *black widow* and *brown recluse* spider. The bite of a black widow will produce first a slight local reaction, then intense pain (caused by a nerve toxin), nausea, abdominal pain and labored breathing. You have to treat the cat for the symptoms you see and then get it to the veterinarian.

The venom in the bite of a brown recluse spider initially produces a local reaction followed 10 to 14 days later by the formation of an open sore. Other symptoms often include fever, chills, vomiting and pain. Veterinary care is necessary. In the case of poisonous insect bites the veterinarian's treatment is primarily supportive care until the symptoms subside.

As far as *tarantulas* are concerned, most of us have heard stories that they're real killers. They are not; a tarantula's bite causes only a localized wound which can be treated as you would the swelling from an insect sting.

Scorpions

Scorpions are found primarily in the southwestern United States. They have a stinger located in their tail through which they inject venom into their victims. The toxicity of the venom varies with the species. Symptoms from a sting include severe localized pain, vomiting, shock, convulsions and even death. You can do nothing but get the cat to a veterinarian, who will institute the necessary supportive care (intravenous fluids, oxygen, etc.) to sustain life until the animal's body is rid of the toxin.

INTERNAL INJURIES

*A*t times, injuries to animals caused by severe traumatic incidents—such as automobile accidents or falls—include damage to internal organs and thereby cause internal bleeding. A ruptured spleen or tear in a major blood vessel is accompanied by significant bleeding (hemorrhage) and can put the pet's life in jeopardy. As a result the animal will usually go into shock. (See pages 190–91 for symptoms and recommended first aid.) In the event that your cat receives a severe blow or has fallen, you must always consider the possibility of internal injuries and bleeding.

Emergency first aid (CPR or artificial respiration, treatment for shock; see pages 144–47 and 190–91) should be administered as you transport your cat to the veterinarian. Usually, the veterinarian must perform emergency procedures and also operate because, in the face of internal bleeding, only rapidly performed surgery can circumvent death.

In observing an animal immediately following an accident, you may, at first, find no apparent evidence of injury. But *always* check for the presence of the following symptoms, which could indicate internal bleeding:

1. A cool and clammy feel to the animal's body
2. A pale or white color to the gums and tongue
3. Signs of great pain and tenderness in the abdomen, evident when touched; extreme restlessness
4. Blood coughed up or vomited; the presence of blood in the urine or stool
5. Signs of shock: due to the falling of the animal's blood pressure, a loss of consciousness may occur as a sign of serious hemorrhage

FIRST AID
1. Keep the animal lying quietly on its side, moving it as little as possible. Any bleeding may be worsened by sudden motion or pressure placed on the chest or abdomen.
2. Maintain an open airway for breathing. If the cat stops breathing, administer artificial respiration (see pages 144–147).
3. Take measures to prevent shock if necessary (see pages 190–191).
4. Rush the pet to your veterinarian but do so with exceptional gentleness. It's best to transport the cat on a flat surface or wrapped in a blanket or towel, keeping the head exposed.

NOTE: Withhold all food and water until you are sure there are no internal injuries.

POISONING

It is quite impossible to overemphasize the necessity of protecting the cat from the dangers of its own instincts. This is surely the case when it comes to the hazards of poisons, particularly in light of their presence in the typical home. Many everyday household products and plants (see pages 268–76) are toxic to varying degrees and can sometimes cause fatality. *All medications, pesticides, cleaning agents and chemicals should be tightly sealed and out of the reach of children and pets.* Always remember that your cat, like a young child, is blind to reason and its safety is up to you.

Nonetheless, despite the best of intentions and efforts to prevent them, accidents do happen. Poisoning occurs in four ways: by absorption through the surface of the skin, by injection via a sting or bite, by inhalation through the nose or mouth, and by ingestion.* Of all these avenues, poisoning as the result of ingestion is by far the most common.

Symptoms of Poisoning by Ingestion

- Acute onset of illness which may include pain, nausea, vomiting and/or collapse
- Burns around the mouth, lips and tongue (indicating that an acid or alkali, such as an oven cleaner or floor wax, has been swallowed)
- An abnormal odor to the feline's breath; coughing or bloody vomitus (indicating that a petroleum product such as kerosene or gasoline has been swallowed)
- Hemorrhaging (indicating the ingestion of an anticoagulant, such as warfarin compound, contained in some rat poisons)

When poisoning has occurred, it is always preferable to get veterinary care immediately, as different poisons sometimes re-

---

* For information on how to treat poisons absorbed through the skin, see page 155, "Chemical Burns." Insect bites and stings are covered on pages 179–81 and snakebites on pages 193–95.

quire varied treatments. *Only when getting prompt professional care is impossible should you proceed to take emergency measures of your own.*

Before administering first aid, *read* the label on the product involved to check for prescribed antidotes and directions (which can be applied to both people and pets)—but do not take those directions as the final word. Confirm these directions with a veterinarian or your local Poison Control Center. Keep the telephone number of Poison Control in a place you can easily find. (A good location would be next to the number of your veterinarian.)

Make sure that the pet is breathing properly; if it's not, administer artificial respiration or CPR (see pages 144–47).

NOTE: DO NOT give a pet anything by mouth if it is unconscious, vomiting or having seizures.

FIRST AID
When poisoning has occurred, there are two options for emergency treatment: 1) diluting the poison or 2) inducing vomiting.

1. *Diluting the poison:*
   • Follow this procedure if the cat has swallowed an *acid, alkali* or *petroleum product,* such as battery acid, brush or drain cleaner, floor or furniture polish, gasoline, kerosene, lye, paint thinner, shoe polish, toilet bowl cleaner or wax *and/or*
   • the cat has burns on the mouth, lips and tongue *or* is coughing or has a strong, abnormal breath odor.

   • Restrain the cat by wrapping it in an old shirt, jacket or towel, leaving its head exposed.
   • Give the cat small amounts of milk and water (up to one cup).
   • Check to make sure the cat does not go into shock (see pages 190–91). If the cat loses consciousness, be sure to maintain an open airway. Apply artificial respiration and CPR (cardiopulmonary resuscitation) when necessary (see pages 144–48).
   • See your veterinarian as soon as possible and bring a sample of the product swallowed and the label/bottle.

2. *Inducing the animal to vomit:*
   - Follow this procedure if the cat has swallowed a *noncorrosive substance*, such as after-shave lotion, alcohol, antifreeze, bleach, boric acid, cologne, cosmetics, DDT, detergent, drugs or pills, fabric softener, hair dye, ink, insecticide, lead paint, matches, medication, mothballs, nail polish remover, perfume, pesticides, or roach poison, strychnine, turpentine or weed killer *and/or* the cat is panting, in pain or coma, lacking coordination, vomiting or convulsing.

   - DO NOT induce vomiting if the animal has swallowed a strong acid, alkali or petroleum product such as gasoline or kerosene. Acids and alkalis are caustic and burn the mouth almost immediately. Oral tissues would already be burned from swallowing these products; vomiting them up would only cause more damage to the mouth and throat. In these cases, DILUTION (no. 1, page 184) would be the proper method of dealing with the poison.

   - Restain the cat by wrapping it in an old shirt, jacket or towel, leaving its head exposed.
   - Give the cat (only if conscious) *one-half to one teaspoonful of syrup of Ipecac; or 3 percent hydrogen peroxide* by mouth every five minutes until vomiting occurs (*do not exceed a dosage of 3 teaspoonfuls*).
   - After the cat has finished vomiting, give it the antidote listed on the bottle or label. If the specific antidote is unknown, dilute the poison by giving the pet *water or milk mixed with several teaspoonfuls of activated charcoal* (from your first-aid kit).
   - Check to make sure the cat does not go into shock (see pages 190–91) and if the cat loses consciousness, be sure to maintain an open airway. Apply artificial respiration and CPR (cardiopulmonary resuscitation) when necessary (see pages 144–48).
   - Always save a sample of the vomitus and bring it, along with some of the product swallowed, to the veterinarian when you bring in your pet.

Ingesting Poisonous Plants

Only if you witness your cat eating a poisonous plant (see list on pages 268–71) should you treat it for poisoning.

FIRST AID
Check to make sure the cat does not go into shock (see pages 190–91) and if the cat loses consciousness, be sure to maintain an open airway. Apply artificial respiration and CPR when necessary (see pages 144–48).

Follow steps to induce vomiting (see no. 2, page 185) *but only if the cat is conscious.*

Generally speaking, poisons are almost always ingested by accident, though there are some people around who think it's cute to give their pets drugs. In fact, Valium and marijuana are two of the most common drug toxicities for which pets are taken to veterinarians. Drug overdoses can cause an animal to become severely depressed once these products are absorbed in the system. With a large overdose, prompt veterinary care is often necessary to keep the animal alive until the body metabolizes the drug (breaks it down and rids it from the body via the liver and kidneys). When only small quantities have been consumed and if the animal appears depressed, it can—in the absence of veterinary care—be given a mild stimulant such as a few teaspoonfuls of coffee or tea. In the meantime, keep prescribed medications—and any other drugs such as marijuana—out of the cat's reach.

Mouse and Rat Poison

Many rodent baits can poison our pets. They often contain ingredients such as warfarin compound, that have anticoagulant (blood-thinning) properties. When consumed by a cat, life-threatening hemorrhage can result (e.g., internal bleeding, blood in the urine or stool, bleeding gums, subconjunctival hemorrhage in the eye [see page 241] and nose bleeding). *Please place rodent poisons where pets and children can't get into them.*

FIRST AID
If you catch your cat in the act of swallowing these products, induce vomiting immediately (see no. 2, page 185). Follow this

up with a prompt visit to your veterinarian, who will administer Vitamin K and observe your pet for signs of hemorrhage.

POISONING BY INHALATION

*A*s with people, the following gases can be dangerous to cats if inhaled: ammonia, carbon monoxide, fumes from burning plastics or insulation, heating or cooking gas.

Symptoms of Poisoning by Inhalation

- Animal will appear weak and dizzy.
- There is apparent respiratory difficulty.
- Lips and tongue may be bright red (indicating carbon monoxide poisoning).

FIRST AID
- Remove the pet from the area (do not do this at the expense of your own life!).
- Observe the animal for shock (see pages 190–91) and if the cat loses consciousness make sure it has an open airway for breathing and apply artificial respiration and CPR if necessary (see pages 144–48).
- Your pet needs attention—get it to a veterinarian's office or a hospital.

After an inhalation emergency (even if you've successfully administered first aid), it is best to take the pet to your veterinarian for examination and follow-up care.

SEIZURES

*A*nyone who has ever witnessed a seizure knows the terror that the sight can arouse. In my opinion, a convulsion is probably the most upsetting malady a pet owner can witness. Produced by abnormal electrical activity in the brain, they do occur more often in dogs than in cats. But felines are by no means exempt and there are numerous causes of seizures.

Causes

1. *Epilepsy:* This disease of the nervous system can be inherited, idiopathic (meaning that it is a primary condition with no known precipitating cause) or acquired (e.g., due to head trauma or cardiac/respiratory arrest, or connected with a cerebrovascular "stroke" type of incident). Epilepsy is the most common of the conditions associated with seizures.
2. *Acute encephalitis:* A disease brought on by bacterial or viral infections such as rabies, toxoplasmosis (see page 256) or feline infectious peritonitis (see pages 250–51).
3. *Toxicities:*
   a. *Exogenous* (from sources outside the body): this would include poisoning caused by ingestion of lead, strychnine or chlorinated hydrocarbons, which are found in insecticides and pesticides.
   b. *Endogenous:* toxicity resulting from liver or kidney disease in which the body poisons itself.
4. *Hydrocephalus:* a condition allowing the accumulation of excess fluid in the cranium and an enlarged head.
5. *Brain tumor*
6. *Low levels of calcium in the blood* such as sometimes occurs in a feline nursing a litter.
7. *Low levels of glucose in the blood* (caused by tumors of the pancreas or occurring in diabetic animals given an insulin overdose).
8. *Head trauma*
9. *Cardiac/respiratory arrest*

10. *Extremely high body temperature* of at least 105 degrees Fahrenheit (owing to hyperthermia or fever).
11. *Thiamine (vitamin B₁) deficiency*

SYMPTOMS

Seizures are characterized by loss of consciousness along with paroxysms of the body; complete rigidity is followed by alternating relaxation and rigidity, as well as a swimming or paddling of the legs. An episode usually lasts for one to three minutes. The cat might also salivate, defecate, urinate or vomit. Prior to convulsing, an animal is often in a state of "aura," during which it may appear to be anxious, hyperactive or strikingly quiet. Immediately following a seizure, the pet appears disoriented and uncoordinated for a period that may last only a few minutes but can extend for several hours.

FIRST AID

1. Place a light blanket or several towels completely around the cat's body to *cushion* it during the active phase of the seizure. (This is to protect the cat from the serious injuries that could result from the violent body movements accompanying a convulsion.) *Do not restrain the cat.*
2. After cushioning the cat, wait out the active phase of the seizure. (Do *not* place your fingers in the animal's mouth during the convulsion. You could sustain severe injury from a bite.) When the active phase has ceased, wipe out the cat's mouth with some gauze or your fingertips to get rid of saliva or vomitus and to ensure that the pet has an open airway for breathing. NOTE: Don't be alarmed by a small amount of blood in the saliva. This is often present because, during a convulsion, an animal may bite its tongue or the inside of its mouth.
3. Following the active phase, comfort the cat by giving it gentle, reassuring pats and by speaking to it in a soft tone. Keep the animal quiet and relaxed in a dimly lit room.
4. After 30 to 60 minutes, you can offer the cat a small amount of water. It is best to withhold food until the following day.

If your cat has a seizure, *do not panic.* You should be certain that the pet gets medical care, but the seizure in most cases will subside and you needn't get to the veterinarian immediately. When the cat is taken for veterinary care, it will be examined and tests will be performed to discover the cause so that the appropriate treatment can be administered and a prognosis offered. However, a continuous state of seizures (called "status epilepticus") is life-threatening. If the active phase of a seizure lasts longer than 5 to 10 minutes or if the cat has one seizure immediately after another, take the pet to your veterinarian at once.

SHOCK

*B*ecause of the familiarity of the word "shock" and its common everyday usage, most people don't really know what *medical* state the word is intended to describe. A cat can go into shock following a sudden trauma such as a fall or an automobile accident; shock can also occur as the result of a serious chronic illness. In either case the meaning of "shock" itself is quite specific. The cat's blood pressure is lowered and the circulation of blood to the peripheral tissues and organs is diminished to a point that can lead to life-threatening oxygen deprivation.

Causes

1. Severe injuries resulting from accidents
2. Extensive hemorrhage
3. Serious burns
4. Prolonged vomiting and/or diarrhea
5. Dehydration
6. Poisoning
7. Heatstroke
8. Respiratory and/or heart failure
9. Chronic illness

Signs

All signs of shock are attributable to the decreased blood pressure and circulatory failure.

1. Progressive weakness, collapse and loss of consciousness
2. Decreased body temperature (below 100 degrees F. as shown by rectal temperature; the cat's skin will also feel cooler than normal)
3. Pale pink or gray-white color to the gums and tongue
4. Decreased capillary refill. (You can evaluate this by applying pressure with a fingertip on the gum surface; the color will be slow to return, e.g., 3 to 4 seconds as opposed to 1 to 2 seconds, which is normal.)
5. Rapid heart rate and weak femoral pulse. (See illustration on page 118, which shows the locations where the pulse can be detected.)
6. Increased respiratory rate. (This is *not* the same as labored breathing. Rather, the respirations will be more rapid, and may be irregular.)
7. Dilation of the pupils

First Aid

1. Keep the cat as quiet as possible by wrapping it gently in a blanket or towel. This will help to preserve its body heat. You can use hot water bottles or a heating pad, but be careful that they are only warm, not hot, and be sure to place a towel between the pet and the source of heat. *Keeping the animal quiet and warm are the two most important steps to be accomplished when a pet is in shock.*
2. Maintain an open airway and administer artificial respiration or CPR if necessary (see pages 144–48).
3. Control serious bleeding and apply temporary bandages or splints if injuries are present that require these steps (see pages 196–99 and 166–69).
4. Take the cat to your veterinarian as quickly as possible. (Intravenous fluid therapy and steroids are usually administered to save the animal's life.)

SKUNKS/PORCUPINES/ ENCOUNTERS WITH NATURE

*K*eep your cat indoors and you'll never have to worry about what I refer to as unfortunate "encounters with nature." Nor, as I've said before, is the typical cat—even when given free rein out of doors—quite as bumbling as the typical dog. Nonetheless, if your cat roams in a rural setting, you had better be prepared for some unpleasant—sometimes even dangerous— surprises.

AFTER AN ENCOUNTER WITH A SKUNK
You'll have more to contend with than the revolting smell. The spray of a skunk usually goes right into the face of the cat, with some of the spray ending up in the eyes, where it can produce considerable irritation. Thus, before you bathe the cat, you must take care of its eyes. Rinse them out well with a sterile eyewash such as Dacriose and then place a small amount of ophthalmic ointment in each eye. Not only will this relieve irritation, it will protect the eyes while you give the cat a bath. (Bathing can be a formidable project, so read the instructions beginning on page 64.) *Don't forget to wear rubber gloves or you might not be welcomed in your own home!*

To get rid of the smell, use either tomato juice or a solution of vinegar and water (1 pint vinegar in 1 gallon of water). Pour the juice or the solution over the cat and rub it thoroughly into the hair coat. After letting this set for a couple of minutes, rinse the pet with clean, warm water and then bathe the animal with baby shampoo or a shampoo for cats.

AFTER AN ENCOUNTER WITH A PORCUPINE
Contrary to hearsay, porcupines do not *throw* their quills. But when a pet gets too close to the spiny creature, the porcupine slaps its tail in the approaching animal's face, a protective/aggressive action that leaves quills embedded in the mouth, throat and nostrils. On the end of those quills are tiny barbs that dig into the

surface of the skin and mucous membranes, where they create intense discomfort. When only a couple of quills are embedded, it is easy enough to remove them—providing that the animal can be restrained. Just grasp the quill with a pair of pliers or forceps and pull it straight out, being both gentle and firm while you're at it. (Be very careful not to jerk the quill or pull it out at an angle; the quill could break off, with part of it remaining to inflict further pain and cause infection.) Then disinfect the site where the quill was embedded with hydrogen peroxide. In an instance where many quills are embedded—especially if they are inside the mouth and nose—or if the cat is difficult to restrain, the whole task is best accomplished by your veterinarian. Anesthesia or tranquilization is usually required to do the job expediently and thoroughly.

Bee stings, insect bites and snake bites are the other types of "encounters with nature" that could affect your cat. For more information, refer to pages 179–81 and the following section.

Don't expect your cat to learn from experience. One tangle with a skunk or porcupine will teach it absolutely nothing!

SNAKEBITES/TOAD BITES

*T*he slithering motion of a reptile can indeed be attractive to your feline pet, though not as much as one might think. When a cat bothers with snakes at all, it usually tussles with a garter snake or some other harmless variety. Feline encounters with nastier reptiles are rare—although they have been known to occur.

Nonpoisonous Snakebites

The nonpoisonous snake does not have fangs. Produced by rows of tiny teeth, the bite wound caused by such a snake looks like a U-shaped scratch, because the punctures are so small. (See illustration on page 194 for a diagram of the teethmark patterns left by nonpoisonous snakes.) Characteristically, these reptiles have

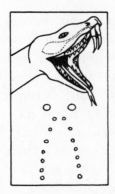 

Snakebites
(on left) poisonous
(on right) nonpoisonous

round pupils and no pits (indentations) between the eyes and nostrils, and also have what is called a double row of "plates" on the underside of the tail. To treat a nonpoisonous snakebite, cleanse the skin area with mild soap and water, then rinse with 3 percent hydrogen peroxide or rubbing alcohol to disinfect the wound. Hidden by hair covering, such a wound may not even be noticed. You will have to count on the cat's behavior—e.g., scratching, signs of discomfort—to indicate that such a bite may have occurred.

Poisonous Snakebites

While the habitat of the venomous North American snakes is generally restricted to Texas, North Carolina, Florida, Arkansas, Louisiana and Georgia, some poisonous snakes may be found in a number of other states. North American poisonous snakes include rattlesnakes, copperheads, water moccasins and coral snakes; all are equally dangerous. All but the coral snake are known as "pit vipers" because of the distinctive indentation they have on each side of the head between the eye and nostril. They also have only one row of "plates" beneath the tail. Their eyes are elliptical rather than round and in their mouths, coming from the upper jaw, are two fangs. The deep punctures they produce are accompanied by an injection of deadly venom. The illustration above shows the pattern left by the bite of a poisonous snake. That bite is terribly painful and causes rapid swelling as well as discoloration of the skin near the wound. With merciless effect, the venom acts upon the circulatory system, causing nausea, vomiting, a generalized weakness, labored breathing, shock and death.

The bite of the coral snake is not quite as painful as those of the "pit vipers" I've just described, but the result of the bite can be equally terrible. Resembling the nonpoisonous snake in that it has rounded pupils and a double row of plates, the coral snake is otherwise distinct. A small reptile, it has a black nose and a body encircled by black, red and yellow rings. Its tubular fangs carry a lethal venom that acts upon the nervous system of its victim.

When an animal is bitten by any of these dreadful creatures, you must get the pet to a veterinarian immediately. I do not believe in the use of constricting bandages and amateur methods of extracting venom. The most you can do is to keep the animal calm and quietly lying down with the affected portion of the body at or below the level of the heart. This will reduce the circulation of blood through the area of the bite and thereby delay the absorption of venom. If necessary, artifical respiration (pages 144–147) can be administered on the way to the veterinarian's office. Knowing what kind of snake has bitten the cat can be helpful in deciding what antitoxin should be used. But under no circumstances should you risk being bitten yourself.

Any pet owner who lives in an area of the country in which these deadly snakes abound would be wise to have a copy of the American Red Cross Standard First Aid and Personal Safety manual. You might also purchase a snakebite kit for your home.

Toad Bites

This is really a case of "cat bites toad," not the other way around. In the southern states and Hawaii, there lives a giant tropical toad known as *Bufo marinus.* Glands on the upper portions of its head and shoulders contain a dangerous toxin, yellow-white and thick. Woe to the playful cat that pounces on the toad, takes a bite and swallows the toxin. In Florida, the *Bufo marinus* is especially dangerous in that it secretes a more potent toxin when bitten than does its relative in other states. Signs of toad poisoning depend upon an animal's age, the amount of toxin ingested, the presence of concurrent medical conditions in the cat and the time that has passed since ingestion of the toxin. Symptoms range from minimal to excessive salivation, vomiting, depression, seizures and death. If you should see that your cat has a toad in its mouth, rinse the pet's mouth out thoroughly with water after you get it to drop the creature, and then induce vomiting (see page 185). Since other medical treatment will be needed, it is then imperative to haul the cat to your veterinarian as quickly as possible.

WOUNDS: BLEEDING AND INFECTION

*M*ost often, cats get hurt by stepping on a piece of glass, a bit of wire or metal or a thorn. Other common injuries arise when they get hit by cars, fall from trees or fight with other animals. Of course, the cat that is kept indoors in a protected environment or is allowed to roam only within the confines of an enclosed backyard will have limited opportunities to sustain any injuries.

There are two categories of wounds. *Open wounds* are those that involve the surface of the skin or mucous membrane, such as the inside of the mouth. A *closed wound*—which can range from a bruise to severe internal injury—does not involve a break in the skin or mucous membrane. Open wounds can be slight abrasions in which the outer surface of the skin is lightly scratched, possibly causing minor bleeding. They can also be more serious, leading to hemorrhage which must be stopped or controlled lest the animal die. But in the event of any open wound, you should try to stop the bleeding right away. The most effective way—and also the safest—is to apply direct pressure over the wound. *Then rush your cat to the veterinarian.*

APPLYING THE PRESSURE BANDAGE

If you notice your cat bleeding, try to stay calm and find out where the animal is cut. Then take a good look at the size and nature of the wound. When a wound is deeper or larger than a small puncture, it will probably require sutures (stitches) to close its edges. Only your veterinarian can close such a wound. But you can take the following measures to keep the wound clean and to try to stop the flow of blood:

Cleanse the wound first with mild soap and water. (Never

clean a fresh wound *vigorously* or you may aggravate the bleeding.) Then, using sterile gauze pads or a clean handkerchief,
towel or bandage, apply pressure directly over the cut for several
minutes. Should you be able to control the bleeding with this
technique, next apply a temporary bandage with gauze and tape.
This will protect the wound from further contamination. Be careful not to apply this bandage too tightly and be sure that it's clean
and dry. In most cases, putting direct pressure over a wound will
control bleeding sufficiently until you reach a veterinary facility.

In the event that blood is spurting profusely from a wound in
one of the cat's legs, don't take the time to cleanse the wound
first. Try raising the affected limb upward; this is similar to holding the bleeding hand of a person up in the air to help slow down
the flow of blood. Don't continue if the cat struggles; the bleeding
could worsen. But assuming the cat is cooperative, you should
place direct pressure over the wound at the same time that the
limb is raised. Another technique is to place pressure over the
major artery supplying the affected leg. Observe the illustration
on page 118, which shows the location of arterial "pressure
points" on the underside of the cat's body. If you can, place the
cat gently down on its side or back. Place the outer edge of your
hand down firmly over the pressure point of the affected leg as
shown in the illustration. This will limit the flow of blood through
the major artery supplying that leg. Should you be successful in
quelling the bleeding, you can then put a bandage over the
wound. Otherwise, in very extreme circumstances, you may have
to resort to a tourniquet.

THE TOURNIQUET
A tourniquet should be utilized only in a life or death situation,
when all direct pressure efforts have failed. This is because improper use of a tourniquet can impede the normal flow of blood
in the leg involved, causing permanent damage and sometimes
the loss of a limb. NOTE: This device is meant to be applied only
when a pet sustains a wound on the lower portion of a leg. Don't,
whatever you do, wrap a tourniquet around a cat's neck! In the
case of a cut of the jugular vein or carotid artery, apply direct
pressure over the vessel.

You can fashion a tourniquet by wrapping a strip of cloth (approximately 2 inches wide) or a necktie around the affected leg

Applying a tourniquet

from 1 to 2 inches above the wound. When a cut is close to a joint or below it, place the tourniquet immediately above the joint. While you should place a clean gauze dressing or handkerchief over the wound itself, do not wrap a bandage over the tourniquet. Observe the illustration above which shows the proper placement of a tourniquet.

The cleaning of wounds is extrememly important. Sometimes, when a wound is spurting blood, you may have to apply a tourniquet so quickly that using a disinfectant is impossible. This situation excepted, you should clean any open wound before applying a bandage since an open wound is a portal of entry for bacteria.

Animal bite wounds and punctures are discussed specifically on pages 150–51. Other types of which you should be aware are the more serious deep punctures, lacerations and what are known as *shearing wounds,* which occur when an animal is dragged along a rough surface (say, by a car). Although it does not bleed severely, layers of skin and muscle are sheared off right down to the bone. In such a terrible injury, layers of superficial tissues are destroyed, producing a gaping, usually jagged wound, possibly seeping blood. Cleanse this with hydrogen peroxide if the cat is not struggling too much, and then cover with a moist dressing (i.e., hand towel or gauze). If you cannot get the cat to a veterinarian in short order, apply a thin coat of antiseptic ointment over the wound and then cover with a light gauze wrap until veterinary attention can be obtained.

Bandaging a paw: A child's white sock can be placed over the paw. Tape at the top to sock and hair. Do not wrap tape too tightly.

Foot wounds indicated by blood on the pads of the foot or between the toes call for special attention; it is rare, however, for foreign material that the cat has stepped on to remain embedded in the wounds.

1. Rinse the area of injury with a fine stream of clean water; then disinfect the area either with mild soap and water or 3 percent hydrogen peroxide solution. Following this, soak the foot in warm water for 5 to 10 minutes.
2. Bandage the foot with a light dressing (see illustration above) or place a clean white child's sock over the foot. *Lightly* tape the top of the sock to the leg. If the tape is put on too tightly it could impede blood supply to the leg and cause a more serious injury. The sock will allow the air to circulate and will also keep the cat from licking the wound. A loose-fitting sock is better tolerated than a tight-fitting bandage. A clean sock should be put on daily. Observe the wound for any signs of infection (swelling, inflammation, pus); in 2 to 3 days if it doesn't seem to be healing, or if the cat is still lame, see your veterinarian.

PART SEVEN

COMMON DISORDERS AND DISEASES

FELINE ANATOMY

*T*he illustrations on page 49 show the skeletal structure and internal anatomy of the cat. The average cat, being endowed with a tail, has 230 bones (the exception is the Manx, a breed with little or no tail, which obviously would have fewer). Its rear legs are longer and more developed than its forelegs. This is the anatomical fact that makes the cat such a virtuoso of the unpredictable leap.

The lower illustration indicates the location of the feline's internal organs. The location and structure of these organs closely correspond to those of the human body. For the very reason that the cat's makeup is so similar to ours, it can and does suffer most of the same ailments that afflict members of the human race. Naturally, there are some differences. But being aware of the fundamental similarities between the feline and human anatomies ought to enable you to understand what ails your cat and to offer it aid should it become ill or injured.

CARDIOVASCULAR SYSTEM

*T*he classic coronary or heart attack that so often ends the lives of people rarely occurs in pets. Rather, cats suffer other forms of congenital or acquired heart disease, either of which can be fatal.

Congenital Heart Disease

Sometimes, felines are born with anomalies of the heart and/or major blood vessels that supply the heart and lungs. Some of these anomalies are *patent ductus arteriosus; stenosis* (constriction) of the heart valves; and defects (holes) in the walls of the chambers that form the heart. All these conditions affect the pumping action of the heart. Because they so affect the flow of blood through the heart and lungs, they can be life-threatening. Defects such as these can be inherited.

Kittens with congenital heart defects often exhibit a low tolerance for exercise and may collapse after only a few minutes of play. Frequently, too, they remain smaller in size than their littermates. Anomalies of the heart can be diagnosed quite early and are often diagnosed by a veterinarian at the time of the kitten's first vaccination. Some of these defects are correctable by surgical means; others are minor and do not progress to a life-threatening stage. Unfortunately, however, most defects are serious and carry a guarded prognosis.

Cardiomyopathy

Several types of acquired heart disease can develop in the cat, the most common being *cardiomyopathy*. A disease of the heart muscle, cardiomyopathy can occur at any age; the source is not understood although the cause is suspected to be viral. Because the early symptoms are often nonspecific—decreased appetite, vomiting and inactivity, all of which can be misleading—the disease is usually not diagnosed in its early stages. Sadly, the cat may develop heart failure or an *occlusion* (blockage) of the distal aorta (main artery to the rear legs) owing to an *embolism* (blood clot) before the condition is clearly recognized. Then, as the heart failure progresses, labored breathing (caused by an accumulation of fluid within the chest cavity) and open-mouthed breathing are noticed. In cases in which a blood clot develops in the aorta, it becomes lodged in the arteries branching off the aorta which supply the hindlimbs with blood. Because of this occlusion, a rear-end weakness and subsequent paralysis result. The onset of any and all of these signs can be very rapid and the cat's condition usually deteriorates within days if not treated. At present, the long-term prognosis is poor. Nonetheless, some cats do respond to treatment and survive for a number of months with proper follow-up care and drug therapy.

Other Acquired Heart Disease

When, owing to infection, bacteria get into the blood system, the lining of the heart and the valves that control the flow of blood into, through and out of the heart may be seriously affected. Dental disease can thus be a dangerous condition; through badly infected gums, bacteria can enter the bloodstream.

SKIN DISORDERS, INFECTIONS, DISEASES OF THE SKIN

*U*nder the clean, sleek and shiny hair coat of the healthy cat is a skin that is normally smoothly textured and pale pink. (The nose, lip margins and eyelids are often much darker.) Any disruption in the smoothness of the skin or significant change in its color is a sign that something is amiss. Moreover, in cats with disorders wherein the skin becomes dry and scaly, "dander" (dandruff) is often visible in the hair coat. This is especially noticeable when the pet's hair coat is dark or when the cat is suffering from some form of dermatitis.

Dermatitis

This is a catch-all medical term that refers to inflammation of the dermis or outer layers of the skin. Environmental extremes of temperature and humidity, various allergies, external parasites, bacterial and fungal infections and even nerves can cause such inflammation. Itchy skin is the major symptom, evident when the cat licks, bites and scratches to relieve the uncomfortable sensation. In so doing, the pet often worsens the condition, much as we do when we scratch at the bite of a mosquito until it bleeds.

In most cases of dermatitis, not only does the skin become inflamed, but small pustules ("whiteheads") surface on the skin of the cat. Larger crusty lesions sometimes appear, as well as *alopecia* (hair loss). If either of these occurs, the pet should be professionally examined. Once the cause is determined, the proper course of treatment can be undertaken, whether it be the administration of antibiotics, cortisone or cortisone-like drugs, a change of diet (appropriate when a food allergy is suspected) and/

or medicated shampoos. Allergies are frequent causes of dermatitis. The substitution of a metal or ceramic food dish for a plastic one may be recommended should your veterinarian suspect that the plastic is an irritant.

Neurodermatitis

This is symptomatically the same as any other dermatitis, but is precipitated by events that have produced anxiety or nervousness in the cat. Felines are extremely sensitive to stress. A new pet or baby in the house, clangs and bangs from nearby construction or environmental upheaval, any or all can almost unhinge the cat. Affected in this fashion, the animal will chew and lick excessively, sometimes pulling out all the hairs on its lower abdomen.

It's not uncommon for an owner to jump to the conclusion that a cat is having an "anxiety attack" that is causing it to lose its hair. Neurodermatitis is a real condition, but one must be careful to rule out other factors that can be far less dramatic. Having noticed that the hair on the animal's chest and abdomen were short, many a client has rushed into my office with a cat during the winter months. As it happened, only the owner was having an anxiety attack. The cat? In search for comfort, the animal had been keeping warm by perching above the radiator! The hair became dry and brittle from the heat, and thus was breaking off just above the surface of the skin.

Fungal and Bacterial Infections

The physical appearance of fungal and bacterial infections may be quite similar. When any sort of fungal condition is suspected, your veterinarian will order a culture to ascertain exactly what organism is involved before proceeding with treatment. Please be wary: *fungal infections can be transmitted to people.* If one is suspected and certainly if one is diagnosed, have all members of the household avoid unnecessary physical contact with the pet until it is cured. And instruct everyone that any handling of the cat should be followed by a thorough washing of hands, preferably with a soap such as Betadyne. At the sign of any skin lesions, a trip to the family physician is imperative. The most common of fungal infections is *ringworm*, which is characterized by slightly raised, circular and crusty lesions. (This condition is caused by a fungus, not a worm!)

As for bacterial infections, these are frequently induced when, as a result of dermatitis, the cat scratches its skin, thereby opening the surface to the entry of bacteria. As with fungal infections, a culture may be in order to determine the actual bacteria involved, and a sensitivity test performed to determine which antibiotic therapy should be instituted. A common bacterial infection such as *staph* is characterized by pustules and large lesions that may become sore and crusty.

Eosinophilic Granuloma

This is often referred to as *rodent ulcer*, though exposure to mice and rats is not the cause. A chronic, recurrent skin problem, this condition is manifested by raised, thickened, inflamed and clearly outlined lesions. While these lesions may be located anywhere on the cat, they most frequently turn up on the head, lips and mouth, and back of the hind legs, where they are usually aggravated by the cat's licking habits. Flare-ups of the lesions can usually be controlled quite well with cortisone and similar drugs. However, occasionally this can be very difficult to cure.

Feline Acne

Sometimes what seem to be whiteheads and blackheads appear on the underside of the chin. In all probability, they are caused by bacteria. Your veterinarian may prescribe an oral antibiotic and a topical scrub to clear up the irritation.

Dandruff

Clients spotting small white specks of dander in their pets' hair coats often become overly concerned. Even after the worries are allayed, they're not particularly happy. No one likes to see dandruff, and that's precisely what dander is. Its presence is more conspicuous in cats with darker hair coats.

Dander can be caused by skin infections, by inflammation brought on by irritants and, most frequently of all, by dry skin. Too-frequent bathing is a common cause of dry skin, as are harsh shampoo products. Even though most felines have nothing but disdain for water and rarely need a bath, their owners sometimes feel differently about the matter. I wish they'd trust the natural cleanliness of the cat. Environmental temperature changes, low humidity, and a diet with insufficient fat may also be at fault.

NOTE: The mite *cheyletiella* may be confused with dandruff (see page 210).

Pet owners sometimes use anti-dandruff products on their animal that are meant strictly for use on people. These will irritate its sensitive skin. If you must bathe your cat, use only mild baby shampoo or medicated baths approved for use on animals.

Cats allowed out of doors in winter are exposed to cold, dry air, which, alternating with dry inside heat, has a deleterious effect on the animal's skin and hair coat. A dry skin condition may sometimes be alleviated by adding ½ to 1 teaspoonful of vegetable oil to the daily meal. Other dietary supplements can be used if professionally advised. Keep in mind that daily combing and brushing removes loose, dead hairs and will contribute to keeping the animal's skin and hair coat healthy and free of dander.

Allergic Skin Conditions

Of all the causes of allergic dermatitis in the feline, the most common is the flea (see pages 208–10). But certain foods—fish, meat, milk—can induce allergic skin reactions too. By experimentally eliminating these from the diet, the source of the dermatitis may be resolved. Cats are not as susceptible as dogs to the allergic skin problems owing to inhaled allergens (pollens and grasses). On the other hand, felines do develop a contact dermatitis following exposure to certain substances (e.g., plastic, flea collars, sometimes nylon carpets).

Skin allergies give rise to intense itching that provokes the poor cat to a furious licking, biting and scratching at itself, resulting in self-inflicted wounds and *alopecia* (hair loss). Other signs of allergies are changes in the normal pale-pink color of the skin; you may notice numerous small red eruptions distributed over localized areas (these may become generalized almost everywhere on the body). Initially, these eruptions ooze serum; scab formations follow. Self-inflicted trauma aggravates the problem, until the miserable cat may be covered with sores.

NOTE: Changes in skin color can also indicate a medical disorder, e.g., liver disease or anemia when the skin and mucous membranes become yellow-orange (jaundiced).

In most cases, the dermatitis will improve with the removal of the offending allergen and the prevention of further contact. Cortisone or cortisone-like drugs used for a short period of time—as prescribed—will help to clear up the dermatitis, at least until a repeated exposure.

Stud Tail

Stud tail is a condition affecting only the Tom wherein the oil-producing (sebaceous) glands in the skin at the base of the tail produce excess oil. Dirt and dust get trapped in the hair; thus, the hair coat surrounding the tail gets greasy and discolored. These oil-producing glands can become secondarily infected. Antibiotic therapy as well as other treatment is often required; consult your veterinarian. If the greasiness becomes unsightly, the area can be shampooed.

Skin Tumors

Skin growths are most often seen with advancing age. But any growth in the skin should be checked by your veterinarian. While most are benign, the possibility of malignancy always exists. Cancerous growths usually increase in size quite dramatically within weeks or change in appearance (e.g., become ulcerated and bleed or drain). The earlier these are removed, the more likely it is that *metastasis* (spreading to other parts of the body) will be prevented. For further information about cancer, see pages 244–45.

FLEAS

A cat with fleas is an animal under siege. Because fleas have powerful, jointed legs, they have an amazing ability to hop and jump. The resultant scratching and biting are the first symptoms of flea infestation. Because fleas move so quickly, they are difficult to observe unless they are present in great numbers; they are most visible on areas where the hair is sparse. Also, since most of the flea's life cycle takes place off of the cat, for every flea on the cat there are usually many more in the house. Many animals are allergic to the flea bite. Thus, even a single flea—much less a tribe of the pests—can produce serious skin inflammation and scratching.

Some insects, including fleas, act as intermediate hosts, which means that they are carriers of parasitic or infectious diseases: fleas, in particular, can carry tapeworms. Cats, unless they are debilitated, are not as susceptible as dogs to heavy flea infestation, but they are not immune to this condition either. Note that in young kittens or sickly cats, heavy infestation can produce severe anemia. Whether the cat is allergic to a flea bite or not, it can, in trying to deal with the bites of these pests, sustain a nasty inflammation of the skin. You will not only have to treat the dermatitis, you will have to get rid of the fleas. Your veterinarian can supply you with an effective dip, spray, powder or shampoo. Please be aware that these products contain toxic ingredients and should be used with caution. *Not all can be used on cats, either— some are specifically for dogs, so read the label carefully*. In addition, do not use more than one product at any time and don't use them at all (with the exception of an approved flea powder) on cats under 3 to 4 months of age as young kittens are quite susceptible, to toxicity. After you've gotten the pests off of the pet, you will have to exterminate them from the surrounding environment or they'll come back. Your veterinarian can recommend an insect fogger (or bomb). You can also employ a professional exterminator. Be sure the cat is removed from the premises according to directions.

Fleas thrive in warm climates and warm weather. In a warm climate, always pay close attention if your cat is scratching. Study the lower portion of the animal's back, the base of the tail and the lower abdomen. Part the hairs and move your hands over these areas. Fleas are dark brown and flat. Many times, instead of the flea, only "flea dirt" is visible. This is the fecal material of the flea. It appears as small specks of dirt scattered among the hairs. Dampened with water—an excellent test—the dirt becomes reddish in color, as it contains dried blood sucked by the flea while feeding on the pet.

NOTE: In my experience, while flea collars may prove to be effective, the use of a flea powder approved for cats generally works best. A flea collar may precipitate an allergic reaction in some cats. A collar recommended by your veterinarian is best. Open the package and allow the collar to "air" for a couple of days. When you place it on, make it loose enough so that you can insert two fingers' width between the pet's neck and the collar. During the first week that the collar is worn, observe the neck every day. A local irritation around the neck would be a sign of allergy and the collar should be removed at once. If the irritation is severe and the cat uncomfortable, apply a thin coat of ½ percent hydrocortisone cream (available without a prescription) to the affected area 2 to 3 times daily, and if improvement is not noted within 2 to 3 days, see your veterinarian.

Another warning: If the cat gets wet, remove the collar until the animal is dry.

Other External Parasites

LICE

These parasites are rare in the cat and do not spread to humans. Usually they are killed by preparations effective in the control of fleas.

CHEYLETIELLA

Cats can be affected by these mites—which are actually more common in rabbits. To the naked eye they may be confused with dandruff and are only mildly irritating to the cat, but they can irritate an owner's skin. Looking at a few hairs under a microscope, I have diagnosed a number of cases in cats belonging to clients who themselves had rashes not remedied by their physicians. Flea powder effectively does away with the cheyletiella mite. Lo and behold, once the cats were treated, their owners' skin irritations disappeared.

MAGGOTS

When an animal is injured or very weak because of illness and is outside in warm weather, lying helpless, flies are attracted to its wounds and bodily discharges. They lay eggs which hatch into maggots, eating and burrowing beneath the skin and into deeper tissues. In no time at all, they produce extreme tissue damage and release a toxin that can be fatal to the animal. A cat discovered to have these nauseating parasites must be treated by a veterinarian immediately.

NOTE: Other external parasites exist but are extremely rare. Any signs of skin irritation and you can be sure that your veterinarian will consider all possibilities in arriving at a diagnosis and course of treatment.

Ticks

These ugly little creatures attach themselves securely to the surface of the skin. They are particularly attracted to the head, the neck, the insides of ears, the area under the legs, and between the toes, wherever hair covering is sparse. Like mythical vampires, ticks suck blood—and as they do so, their bodies enlarge. Thus their size is dependent on the length of time they remain attached.

To remove a tick, soak it with alcohol, mineral oil or vegetable oil, using either an eyedropper or a saturated cotton pad. After several minutes you can remove the tick with a gentle pull, firmly using your fingertips or a tweezer to force it to release its mouthparts. Then place it inside a covered jar containing rubbing alcohol, which will kill it. Never use lighter fluid, a lit cigarette or a match to burn off a tick, because you risk injuring the cat. If you can't remove it as I've instructed, take the cat to your veterinarian.

NOTE: Be sure that what you're trying to remove is a tick and not a part of the cat's anatomy. I've had clients who have tried to pull off small skin growths (see cancer, pages 244–45) or (I know it sounds crazy) the cat's nipples, thinking they were ticks.

GLANDULAR PROBLEMS/ ENDOCRINE AND METABOLIC DISORDERS

Diabetes Mellitus

*G*iven the prevalence of diabetes in the human population, one would think that pet owners would be something less than astonished at the mention of the word in the context of animal health. Yet, almost any time that I diagnose diabetes in an animal, the owner looks stunned. But these are the facts: diabetes does occur in cats; and, just as in people, a cat with the illness can lead a near-normal life as long as the owner is willing to do what is necessary.

Diabetes mellitus is probably the most common endocrine disorder occurring in cats and dogs. "Endocrine" refers to the various glands that secrete hormones; with diabetes, the affected gland is the pancreas, which fails to produce sufficient insulin to maintain normal blood sugar levels. The resultant high blood sugar throws body functions seriously out of whack. The injection of insulin restores the balance.

No one knows for sure exactly what happens to the pancreas to cause a reduction in insulin. As with people, heredity may play a role. Also it is possible that damage has occurred from previous infection or irritation of the gland. The majority of cats contracting the disease are over 5 years old and overweight at the onset of illness.

Symptoms vary. Often, affected cats don't appear ill at all during the early stages of the disease. The most frequently noticed signs are increased thirst and urinations. But these are symptoms that occur with a number of other illnesses too. When diabetes develops, there is usually a rather striking heightening of appetite coupled with a loss of weight as the disease progresses. If diabetes goes undiagnosed and thus untreated, the consequences are severe: the animal becomes weaker, vomiting and collapsing into a diabetic coma—from which it may not recover. In some cases cataracts develop because of diabetes.

Clearly, the earlier the disease is diagnosed, the better the prognosis and the chances for successful treatment. So always take your cat to your veterinarian should there be any of the above mentioned signs. Your cat's urine and blood can then be tested for the presence of *glucose* (sugar). Sometimes, high blood sugar is due to stress. But with other causes, such as stress, ruled out, diabetes may be diagnosed. After that, the veterinarian will usually start the cat on insulin in the hospital and, once the cat is regulated, give instructions for home management of the disease.

Though it may sound frightening, home treatment is not really difficult. What you must do is give a subcutaneous (under the skin) injection of insulin daily. (The veterinarian will show you how and, believe me, it won't hurt the cat as much as it hurts you. With time and experience you and the cat will tolerate this without fretting.) Each morning, a urine sample must be checked for sugar—a procedure your veterinarian will explain—and the amount of insulin adjusted accordingly. Ask your veterinarian for a chart to help you determine how much to give. Following the injection, the cat should be fed one-half its daily food with the remainder fed later in the day. Try keeping the cat's diet constant since insulin requirements will vary according to what and how much is fed. In some cases, insulin dosages will have to be split in half and given at 12-hour intervals. Your veterinarian's specific directions must be followed.

In administering insulin, it is imperative that proper syringes are utilized and that careful measurements are prepared. Fail to give enough and the blood sugar will stay too high; administer too much and there is the possibility of overdose and resultant hypoglycemia.

Hypoglycemia

This condition refers to lower than normal levels of glucose in the blood. The brain is dependent on glucose for energy. Therefore, low levels of blood sugar will bring about central nervous system dysfunction, causing the cat to appear dazed, uncoordinated and weak. The animal may become severely depressed or comatose; seizures usually occur. In felines, the condition can occur in young animals under 3 to 4 months of age because of too infrequent feeding (see page 58). As mentioned, it also happens in diabetics that receive an overdose of insulin.

All clients with kittens or with a diabetic cat should keep Karo syrup in the refrigerator. Any signs of hypoglycemia and the animal should be given ½ to 1 teaspoonful of the syrup. Most often, the animal will rapidly respond. If it doesn't or if it is unconscious or has a seizure, prompt professional care is essential.

Feline Hyperthyroidism

The thyroid glands of the feline are located on either side of the neck. When there is a tumor on one or both of these glands, excessive amounts of thyroid hormones are secreted into the blood, and *hyperthyroidism* is the result. This disease, occurring in older cats, was seldom recognized prior to the last decade but is now diagnosed quite frequently, resulting in longer lives for many felines that might otherwise not have survived.

The tumors are usually so small that they are not detectable by the owner. Nor are the early signs of hyperthyroidism always easy to discern. Increase in water consumption and urination, a voracious appetite and loss of body weight can also be confused with symptoms of diabetes or chronic kidney or liver disease. Tests are required to rule these out. Later signs include intermittent diarrhea that won't respond to conservative treatment and, most serious of all, abnormalities of the heart. A rapid heartbeat may be detected. X-rays will show that the heart is enlarged and an electrocardiogram will reveal other abnormalities. At that point, the cat will also appear emaciated, possibly exhibiting nervous twitching. While hyperactivity is sometimes evident, it happens, too, that cats can be utterly weakened by the disease. Caught in its early stages, however, this sort of decline can be prevented or certainly delayed. Surgical removal of a thyroid tumor is frequently advised, and drug therapy instituted. While the prognosis is guarded, many cats have responded well to surgical and/or medical treatment, and most veterinarians encourage their clients to let them proceed with treatment.

Since the disease has been clearly recognized only in recent years, it is possible that your veterinarian is unfamiliar with the treatment of this disorder. Should symptoms arise, you might be referred to a specialist for the testing and treatment of your cat.

PROBLEMS OF THE DIGESTIVE SYSTEM: THE MOUTH/STOMACH/ INTESTINAL TRACT

Irritations of the Mouth

HALITOSIS

No pet owner likes it when a cat gets *halitosis* (bad breath). The major cause is the accumulation of tartar on the teeth. (See page 68 for a discussion of tartar and gum inflammation or *gingivitis*.) But halitosis can be a warning of illness as well. In a cat with halitosis, watch for other signs of illness and should anything seem abnormal, have your veterinarian examine the cat. Other causes of malodorous breath may include sinusitis, lesions in the oral cavity such as an ulcer or a tooth root abscess, a stomach ulcer, diabetes or kidney failure.

TOOTH ROOT ABSCESS

Though it's more likely to occur in a dog, a tooth root abscess is seen often enough in the older cat. Usually, this abscess develops in an upper premolar or molar tooth; the evidence is a pus-draining sore on the outside of the animal's face on the affected side, just below the eye. The only remedy is to extract the diseased tooth (and administer antibiotics and other therapy when required).

RODENT ULCER

This is the term applied to lesions of *eosinophilic granuloma* (see page 206) that erupt on the lips and in the mouth of cats. As with lesions located elsewhere, rodent ulcers are treated with cortisone or cortisone-like drugs. Treatment should be completed as prescribed; however, please be aware that these lesions will frequently recur after medication is stopped.

Vomiting and Diarrhea

A full-grown cat that hasn't vomited during the course of its life would be a very strange cat indeed. The same could be said of a feline that had never endured an attack of diarrhea or, for that matter, constipation. *Anything* can cause irritation somewhere in the gastrointestinal tract and vomiting as a consequence. But owing to the innumerable causes that can bring this about, a veterinarian presented with vomiting as a symptom has to pay close attention to the esophagus, stomach, liver, pancreas, and small and large intestines, and watch for any other symptoms that could give a clue to the problem.

Occasional vomiting, say, once every week or two, ought to be taken in stride; as long as the pattern doesn't continue for too long, an owner need not worry about much more than the unpleasant task of cleaning up the floor. The host of reasons for such throwing up include hairballs, eating too rapidly (street cats are especially prone to gobbling up their food) or feeding food that's too cold (right out of the refrigerator). Parasites, however, can be a cause as well (see pages 219–21). Generally speaking, however, as long as the incidence of vomiting is infrequent, there is no reason for alarm. Try feeding smaller amounts more frequently; switch to a different brand of food; serve this at room temperature (which doesn't mean you should leave it out so long that it spoils). Should these steps fail, have your veterinarian analyze a stool specimen to rule out parasites as the cause. Stool specimens should be routinely checked 3 to 4 times each year on cats that spend time outdoors, especially if they're prone to hunting mice and birds. For information on collecting a stool sample, see pages 219–20. It is also wise to give your cat a small amount of a "hairball" preparation (—1/4 teaspoon of Vaseline will do if you run out—once or twice a week as the ingestion of hair could also be the cause. (See page 217 for a discussion of how to spot and treat a more severe incidence of hairballs.)

Repeated and persistent vomiting is another matter altogether. This is a sign of something seriously wrong, especially when associated with other symptoms such as a decreased appetite, depression, fever and dehydration. Should you observe vomiting frequently for an extended period (e.g., over 6 to 12 hours), you must act. Delaying a trip to the veterinarian could jeopardize the pet's life. Record the times the cat has vomited and the color and consistency of the vomitus. All of this will help the veterinarian make a professional determination of what is wrong.

One of the possible causes is a foreign object causing obstruction in the stomach or intestines. The period of time between the consumption of food or water and subsequent vomiting will be an indication of the location of the obstruction. An obstruction in the back of the throat or in the esophagus will induce vomiting almost immediately after the swallowing of food or water. With an obstruction in the stomach, vomiting will be delayed, often occurring 30 to 60 minutes after food or drink. An object obstructing the intestinal tract will be connected with vomiting that occurs 1 to 2 hours or more following eating or drinking. This is due not only to the location of the object but to the production of gastric secretions and bile. (See pages 156–61 for first-aid instructions regarding swallowed objects.)

The timing of the vomiting should not make you jump to the conclusion that the cat has swallowed something inappropriate. Judge the evidence. If it is unlikely that a foreign object has been swallowed, other causes must be considered, such as gastritis, enteritis, pancreatitis, liver disease, poisoning, some form of infectious disease or even cancer.

As for *diarrhea*, the causes are equally numerous. It can indicate a minor problem (see first aid for diarrhea on page 171), or could be a reaction to milk or some sort of allergy. Nonetheless, it can also—if it persists—be symptomatic of serious disease. Only the veterinarian—through a battery of tests and X-rays—can finally determine the cause.

HAIRBALLS

In the process of all its obsessive cleaning and personal grooming habits, the feline ingests enormous quantities of hair. When all that hair accumulates in the GI tract, it forms a wadded-up ball. A cat with a particularly large hairball can get quite sick as the wad creates some degree of obstruction. Persistent vomiting is the primary symptom. Following X-rays and other diagnostic tests (such as a barium enema), your veterinarian might advise surgical removal. Suffice it to say that you can best avoid this by preventing the formation of such an obstruction.

Ask your veterinarian to prescribe a laxative paste and give it routinely once or twice a week. You can place the product (such as Laxatone) on the cat's paw where it can be licked off, or slide it on to the roof of the animal's mouth with your fingertips. But don't rely on a laxative; the best preventative step is daily combing and brushing of the cat (this is especially necessary for long-haired cats, but should also be carried out regularly on shorthairs).

WARNING: Do not assume that vomiting is from hairballs. Any cat with persistent vomiting must have professional attention. Leave it to the veterinarian to decide the cause.

Constipation

As the cat ages, its digestive system may function less efficiently. While constipation can occur in a young cat, it is almost always associated with the older animal. The best treatment for this is to give your cat a laxative once or twice a week, as described above. A cat suffering extreme constipation is said to be *obstipated*, which means the stool has "backed up" in the intestinal tract in large quantities. The animal ceases to eat, becomes listless and may vomit as well. Under such circumstances your veterinarian will have to give the cat an enema or "clean it out" under anesthesia. *Never give an enema yourself.* If your cat suffers from *chronic* constipation or obstipation, your veterinarian might also advise a stool softener, which can be put in the animal's food. How much you use may be a matter of trial and error, with the error being an unfortunate case of diarrhea. This is not serious and can be eliminated by reducing the amount of the laxative product. Always follow instructions when giving laxatives or stool softeners.

REMEMBER: If you have a male cat, be sure that you don't confuse constipation with urinary obstruction (see pages 223–26 on feline urological syndrome).

NOTE: Because of their anatomy, some Manx cats have problems with fecal incontinence (inability to control bowel movements). Since this does not affect all of these cats, discuss the issue with your veterinarian if you have a Manx kitten.

Endoscopy for Diagnosis

You might be interested in knowing that there is a special diagnostic procedure, *endoscopy*, utilized by many veterinarians in the context of diagnosing and remedying gastrointestinal disorders. The animal is anesthetized and a tube passed into the mouth and down the esophagus. At the end of the tube is a movable scope with a light source. As the instrument is passed slowly through the alimentary tract, the veterinarian can see the lining of the esophagus, stomach and entrance to the small intestine. This is an excellent means of diagnosing ulcerations, foreign bodies, tumors and other causes of gastrointestinal distress. Nonetheless, it is not usually a first resort; rather, it is utilized when conservative treatment hasn't been successful, or in conjunction with initial lab tests and X-rays.

Common Internal Parasites

ROUNDWORMS

Roundworms are off-white, coiled and similar to spaghetti in appearance (admittedly, a noxious comparison), and range from 2 to 6 inches in length. Since this is a parasite that can be transmitted from the mother to the fetus, young kittens can be infected. An affected young animal will typically have a distended or "pot belly" abdomen and may exhibit vomiting, diarrhea and restlessness as well as a lusterless hair coat. As these symptoms are nonspecific, they can indicate various problems. Therefore, any kitten or cat with such symptoms should be examined. Not infrequently, a roundworm may either be vomited up or passed in the stool without the presence of any other symptoms.

To eliminate roundworms, your veterinarian will prescribe a medication that will kill the adult stage of the parasite; follow-up treatment must be administered subsequently to kill the hatching offspring. Over-the-counter preparations should be avoided. The safety of your pet is best assured by obtaining worming preparations *only* from your veterinarian. Different parasites (and their life cycles) require varied medications; follow your veterinarian's directions specifically, and give repeat dosages at the prescribed intervals. Follow up all treatments with a stool analysis 2 to 3 weeks later, to be sure the parasites have been eliminated.

Most parasites are contracted out of doors. As long as good sanitation is practiced, the indoor pet is going to have a lower incidence of infestation: another reason why the litterbox should be cleaned on a regular basis, especially in households with more than one cat. Wash your hands thoroughly whenever you handle a pet with parasites or when you clean the box of such an animal.

Routine stool analyses should be performed on all new kittens

---

WARNING:
___

Since parasites can be transmitted to humans, it is important to instruct youngsters regarding proper hygiene. Keep outdoor sandboxes covered when children aren't playing to prevent contamination of the sand by neighboring cats.

---

entering your home and on adult cats once a year (more often if the pet goes out of doors). To obtain a proper stool specimen, the stool should be fresh (taken within four hours of defecating) and formed. Remove it from the litterbox; be sure to get a sample of the stool and *not* the cat's litter. Place a small amount in a plastic bag or container and bring it to your veterinarian's office. PLEASE NOTE: Securely wrapping your pet's stool sample will further your chances that it will be properly analyzed and it will also be less offensive to the veterinary health technician.

TAPEWORMS

Sometimes a routine stool analysis fails to reveal the presence of tapeworms. Therefore, you must be alert to any symptoms. The classic symptom associated with the *tapeworm* is a ravenous appetite without any weight gain—and quite possibly with a loss of weight. Cats with tapeworms often drag or "scoot" their rear ends along the floor to relieve itching. Should you be a witness to this behavior, examine the area at the base of the tail and around the anal opening. Also, look at the stool immediately after the pet moves its bowels. What you're looking for are flat, off-white or cream-colored segments that look like grains of rice. These are the segments of a tapeworm. (Rarely is a complete tapeworm passed.) And when passed, these segments move while still alive. That's why you must search for them right away or they'll soon be out of sight, buried in the litter or deep in the grass.

Cats can pick up these parasites from eating infested prey such as rodents or by consuming raw fish or raw meat, which may contain this parasite; in addition, the examination of the cat for fleas is of the utmost importance, as the flea may transmit tapeworms. In fact, these external parasites are the most common means by which cats get an infestation of tapeworms.

Appropriate medication will be prescribed by your veterinarian.

Less Common Internal Parasites

HOOKWORMS

Similar in shape to the roundworm but only a fraction of the size, hookworms attach themselves to the intestinal wall, where they suck blood. In a young or debilitated animal, a heavy infestation of hookworms can produce anemia and even death. These parasites are more of a problem in warmer weather; animals can get them either by consuming infected stool or by licking their paws after they've walked through fecal matter, or from larvae penetrating the feline's skin and then migrating through the tissues.

COCCIDIA

Coccidia are *protozoans*, tiny one-celled parasites. The infective eggs (oocysts) are contained in the feces of afflicted dogs and cats and are spread by ingestion to healthy animals. Cats obtained from a cattery or pet store are most often infected. Coccidia cause decreased appetite, weight loss and diarrhea, and the cat may be debilitated severely by their presence and eventually die. Coccidia are diagnosed only from a fresh stool sample by careful microscopic examination. Your veterinarian will then prescribe the appropriate medication to rid this parasite.

TOXOPLASMA

This is another protozoan which may affect humans as well as animals. In most cases it produces no signs of illness in the cat and therefore often goes undiagnosed. (Usually the problem is identified only after it results in serious illness.) But it is extremely important to know that *toxoplasmosis* can affect the human fetus (see pages 256–57 for information about this very critical matter) and that the cat is the only species involved in the complete lifecycle of this parasite. In its infective stage, toxoplasma is shed in the cat's stool (only if the cat is carrying the organism, of course). Thus, outdoor cats should be periodically tested for infestation. Review pages 256–57 for a clearer understanding of the public health matters significant to this parasite.

OTHERS

Your veterinarian could diagnose the following parasites, though infestations are rare: lungworms, trichinosis, heartworms, flukes, eyeworms. Pinworms are a common problem in young children, but they *do not* come from cats.

PARASITE PREVENTION TIPS:

- Proper sanitation will prevent reinfestation. This is especially important when you have more than one pet. Frequent litterbox changing is imperative!
- Keep in mind that an indoor cat is far less likely than his outdoor counterpart to contract any parasite.
- *Do not feed a cat raw meat or fish.*

Obesity

Just like people, as cats age, they will live longer, healthier lives if they're not overweight. You are the one responsible for placing the food in front of your cat, so if the animal tips the scales (the average cat weight is 8 to 10 pounds), chances are strong that you're giving it too much to eat. If your cat is overweight and inactive (instead of running for her food she waits for you to bring it to her), I recommend reducing the daily intake by 20 percent. In a couple of weeks the cat should be a little bit thinner. Otherwise, try cutting the diet another 10 percent. Also, overweight pets often have overweight owners; it may be the case that the food portions you're giving are just too large. And more than one family member might be feeding the cat (who obviously won't turn up its nose if it has a real penchant for eating).

Obviously, it doesn't always hold that a cat is fat owing to overeating. Sometimes, a feline will become obese for other reasons, such as an underactive thyroid gland (hypothyroidism). Place a pet on a reducing diet; a lack of positive results means that a visit to the veterinarian is in order because other causes for obesity must be considered.

PROBLEMS OF THE URINARY TRACT

*L*ike the human being, the cat has two kidneys, left and right, which mark the beginning of the urinary system's path. The primary function of these critical organs is to filter fluid and toxic material from the blood and produce urine, by which the fluid and toxic material leave the body. (In addition, the kidneys regulate the chemistry of the blood and serve other purposes as discussed below.) Once formed, the urine exits the kidneys and flows into tiny tubular structures called "ureters." There is one for each kidney. From the ureters, the urine empties into the sac-like urinary bladder. More or less resembling a balloon in its swelling and shrinking motion, the bladder increases in size as it fills with urine and decreases when urination occurs. Please refer to the illustrations on page 225, which depict both the male and female genitourinary systems. Inflammations, infections, obstructions of the system and, finally, kidney disease itself, all come under the category of what we veterinarians refer to as Feline Urological Syndrome (FUS). Of the maladies that afflict the species, this is one of the most prevalent.

Medical Problems of Feline Urological Syndrome

CYSTITIS

This common inflammation of the bladder is usually traceable to a bacterial infection and can be either acute or chronic in nature. Besieged by cystitis, the cat will exhibit increased numbers of urinations (each one strikingly small), conspicuous straining to urinate and, often, blood-tinged urine. It frequently will urinate in inappropriate places, such as the bathtub. Because of pain, the cat may "cry" or "talk" a lot and generally appear out of sorts. If it is caused by bacteria, the inflammation is treated with antibiotics.

URINARY OBSTRUCTION

In order to leave the body, the urine flows from the bladder through another tubular structure known as the "urethra." In the female cat, the urine then empties into the vulva, while in the male, it passes through the penis. It is the urethra that is the site of blockages or *urinary obstruction* in male cats. Cystitis, recurrent infections, stagnation of urine and high-magnesium- and high-ash-content diets can each cause urinary salts to form crystals that congregate into small plugs or stones, the formation of which is referred to as *urolithiasis*. These obstructions are rarely a problem in female cats but are extremely common in the male. The reasons are anatomical: whereas the female cat has a wide urethra (constant in size between bladder and vulva), the male's urethra —whether the cat is intact or "fixed"—diminishes in diameter as it approaches the penis. Most obstructions occur in this narrow portion of the male's urethra.

Please understand the seriousness of urinary obstructions. Upon noticing a cat straining in the litterbox, many a pet owner mistakenly assumes that the animal is constipated. At the sight of any behavior like that (especially in a male cat), always pay close attention. If no urine is being passed in spite of the cat's efforts, there's probably an obstruction. And unless the animal is unobstructed, it may—in very short order—become *uremic* and die. To be more specific, urea nitrogen—a toxic waste normally eliminated in the urine—will build up in the bloodstream to quite literally poison the cat; symptoms accompanying the progress of the poisoning are depression, vomiting, dehydration, coma, convulsions and death. It is therefore imperative that, if you have a male cat, you know what it is doing in the litterbox. Should it be making frequent trips or standing there for lengthy intervals, watch to see whether it is urinating. If in doubt, remove the litter and place torn-up newspaper or paper towel in the box. You can relax if the paper becomes wet. But should it stay dry for more than a few hours, and the cat continues to strain, *rush to a veterinarian*. A urinary obstruction can be relieved only by catheterizing the urethral passage (the insertion of a tube into the urethra to release urine). Often, the cat will require hospitalization and treatment with intravenous fluids along with medications for several days, depending on the duration of the obstruction and the resultant uremia.

One more word of caution: catheterizing a cat is a job for a veterinarian.

Sometimes a male cat will have repeated episodes of urethral

Anatomy of the genitourinary system

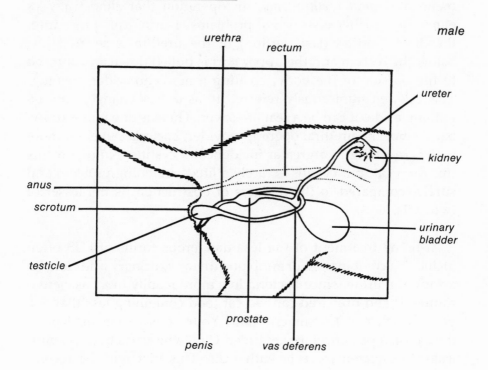

male

urethra
rectum
ureter
kidney
anus
scrotum
urinary bladder
testicle
prostate
penis
vas deferens

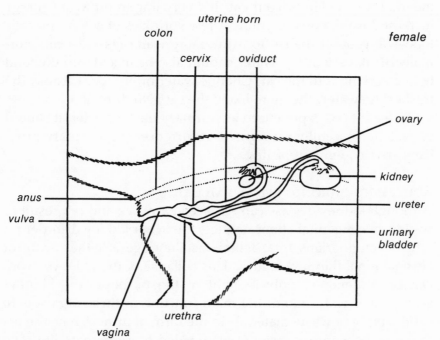

uterine horn
colon
female
cervix
oviduct
ovary
kidney
anus
ureter
vulva
urinary bladder
urethra
vagina

obstruction. In all likelihood, your veterinarian will then recommend a *perineal urethrostomy*, an operation that almost always eliminates further obstructive problems. During this procedure, the distal portion (last portion) of the urethra is severed just below the rectum and the upper part is pulled down and sutured to the outside of the body, creating a new and wider opening. This is often humorously referred to as a "sex change," but all kidding aside, it can be a real life-saver. There is one minor drawback: since the urethral opening is wider, bacteria can enter more easily, resulting in a greater incidence of cystitis. No one wants this for a cat, but cystitis is rarely a life-threatening problem and surely, compared to the dangers of obstruction, is the lesser of two evils.

At-home treatment of the less dangerous forms of FUS often includes a combination of antibiotic therapy, urinary acidifiers (to acidify the urine, since bacteria live more readily in a basic environment) and prepared canned cat food containing less than 3.5 percent ash and low magnesium. Your veterinarian may place the cat on a prescription diet called C/D, which has been scientifically formulated for cats with FUS. This diet may be recommended for the life of your cat. It's very important to encourage increased water consumption. A few sprinkles of salt in the cat's food will prompt the cat to drink more water (as most cats normally drink very little). Water should also be mixed into the food before serving it to the cat. Change water often, too, because the fresher the water, the more likely the cat is to drink it.

Once a cat has experienced any urinary tract disorder, it should be watched carefully for signs of recurrence, since urinary problems are frequently repeated.

ACUTE AND CHRONIC RENAL FAILURE

Although kidney disease can surface at any age and can result as well from congenital abnormalities, the major kidney disorder for which veterinarians treat felines as they age is either acute or chronic renal (kidney) failure. This collapse of the kidneys' work can be understood only in light of the purposes the kidneys serve. As already stated, the main function of these organs is to rid the body of waste materials in the form of urine. They also act to conserve water and chemicals needed to perpetuate life. The kidneys also play a part in the manufacturing of red blood cells by the bone marrow and aid, too, in the regulation of blood pressure.

When kidney failure occurs, the waste materials are not filtered out and, instead, build up in the circulating blood. To worsen the situation, water and electrolytes (sodium, chloride, potassium) are no longer conserved as they should be but, rather, escape in the urine. Early-stage symptoms can include increased water consumption, heightened appetite, increased urination, vomiting and dry skin. Unfortunately, by the time these symptoms are noted, the body has already been subjected to significant damage.

There are, however, cases of acute renal failure that, in and of themselves, are not especially severe. But when repeated renal episodes occur over a long period of time, the outcome is chronic kidney disease. This develops as follows: the recurrent bouts of inflammation that accompany the renal failure cause progressive scarring of renal tissue, which causes the kidneys to shrink in size and eventually deteriorate into what are termed *end-stage kidneys.* Preceding this development, for months—or even years—the animal may be in "compensated kidney failure" (i.e., increased water consumption and urinations). And the more water the animal drinks, the better off it will be. Your veterinarian might also prescribe a special diet that is composed of lower (but high-quality) protein and higher starch, as well as vitamin and mineral supplements. Periodic blood tests will determine true kidney function.

An aging cat that has undergone acute renal episodes, existing in a "compensated" state, is bound—eventually—to go into "uncompensated renal failure." The filtering mechanism simply will work no more and toxic wastes build up in the blood. This development, known as "uremia," threatens the cat's life. And not only is the cat uremic now; it also suffers an imbalance of body fluids and electrolytes. Symptoms can include increased thirst, decreased appetite, uremic (bad odor) breath, depression, listlessness, dehydration, emaciation, skin sores, ulcerations in the mouth, vomiting and anemia. Without treatment, a cat with these symptoms will progress to coma and eventually die. Now and then, episodes of uremia can be reversed (depending on the amount of damage and the degree of uremia) by the administration of intravenous fluids, antibiotics and other medications. But kidney disease is a progressive illness and the damage done is irreversible. Hard as it may be, you will have to realize that, with a cat in that state, there will come a day when it can no longer be rescued. Even the most intensive and finest veterinary care cannot accomplish the impossible.

Ruptured Bladder

Occasionally, when a cat receives a sudden, forceful blow—perhaps from being hit by a car, from being cruelly kicked or in a fall from a tree or building—it suffers a rupture of the bladder. As a result of the sheer terror from the fall, the cat usually urinates as it descends. (The bladder must be quite full to rupture. For example, if a cat has urinated right before a traumatic blow, because the bladder is emptied and not under pressure, a rupture is unlikely to occur.) Regardless of the cause, after any accident—even if there is no apparent injury—always observe the cat's ability to urinate. Should it not be able to do so or if blood is present in the urine produced, see that the cat receives immediate veterinary care; a ruptured bladder can be corrected only with surgery.

Congenital Anomalies

Every now and then, during fetal development, something goes awry that results in an abnormality in a portion of the urinary tract. Nor does it always involve both kidneys or both sides of the renal system. In such an instance the cat's life may be quite normal and the abnormality actually goes undetected. With major defects, the kitten may be stillborn or die soon after birth or within the first weeks of life.

Tumors

Cancer can affect all parts of the body, including the urinary system. As with other cancers, malignant tumors of the urinary tract are most often seen in older cats. Growths may also be benign. In many cases, surgical removal of a mass is required; when a malignancy is present, chemotherapy may be recommended. In this instance your veterinarian will refer you to a veterinary oncologist (cancer specialist).

REPRODUCTIVE DISORDERS

*R*eproductive disorders are not very common among cats, but neither are these animals immune to "female problems." It is best for an owner to be familiar with those that do crop up from time to time.

Uterine Infections

METRITIS

An acute infection of the uterus, metritis can flare up after a normal heat, mating or queening (especially when the birth process has had complications). Symptoms range from depression, decreased appetite and fever to a foul-smelling vaginal discharge. Antibiotics and fluid therapy can be effectively used, but most likely, your veterinarian will recommend prompt spaying to remove the infected uterus.

PYOMETRA

Pyometra is a condition that often follows an acute metritis that has progressed to a state of chronic metritis. What happens is that the uterus gradually fills up with pus, a phenomenon most frequently restricted to unspayed females and older female cats (though young animals can be subject to pyometra too). When the cervix is open and the pus drains out, the foul smell of the discharge is quite noticeable. But in the case of a "closed pyometra," the cervix is closed and does not allow the release of the purulent fluid (pus) and the uterus fills up with this toxic material. Many cats show little or no effects other than an enlarged abdomen. But depression, decreased appetite, increased thirst, increased urinations and fever are sometimes symptoms. The condition *can* be fatal without surgical removal of the infected uterus.

False Pregnancy

This phenomenon occurs when the hormone *progesterone* is released from an ovary even though ova have not been fertilized.

This rarely occurs in cats because their ovulation is induced by mating (thus an artificial stimulus has induced ovulation and the release of progesterone even though natural mating has not occurred). False pregnancy lasts for approximately one month and affected cats exhibit "nesting" behavior and mammary development. Your veterinarian will generally advise spaying.

BREAST CANCER
Refer to page 98 for a short discussion of breast (mammary gland) cancer.

DISORDERS OF THE NERVOUS SYSTEM

*T*he central nervous system is made up of the brain and spinal cord, while the peripheral nervous system refers to the nerves running off the spinal cord that innervate or put into motion the limbs of the cat as well as the feet and toes. Congenital anomalies, bacterial or viral infections, parasites, metabolic diseases, nutritional deficiencies, poisonings, traumatic accidents, tumors and degenerative disorders—any of these can disrupt the normal function of the feline's nervous system.

The cause of dysfunction must be assessed on the basis of the history given, observations of the animal's posture and ability to walk, the animal's mental state, neurological exams and diagnostic tests that can range from studies of the blood to X-rays. The history and symptoms can give a veterinarian a good clue as to what is wrong; tests will confirm or refute suspicions.

Head Trauma

By far the most frequent cause of nervous system dysfunction is trauma—from automobile accidents, falls from buildings and injuries sustained in animal fights (especially when a big aggressive dog takes on little cat). These traumas can be quite terrible, often making it appear that the animal is utterly beyond help. Surprisingly, though, prompt medical treatment and follow-up care can often pull the pet through, returning it to normal (or near-normal) function in short order. Should a serious accident occur, it is imperative to move the cat as little as possible to avoid aggravating the injury. *Immediate* veterinary care is imperative when trauma has affected the central nervous system. See pages 136–40 on transporting an injured animal, and pages 173–74 on first aid for trauma to the head and neck.

Seizures

These can be a result of epilepsy, trauma, poisoning and a host of infectious disorders. The violent active phase of a seizure is terribly disturbing to witness. A further discussion of seizures can be found in the first-aid section on pages 188–90.

NOTE: In some cats with heart disease, the animal may suddenly collapse for a brief interval (up to one minute) and some pet owners may confuse this with a seizure. This occurrence, known as *syncope*, lacks the violent activity usually associated with a seizure.

Vestibular Syndrome

Every once in a while a cat will suffer an acute onset of *labrynthitis*, an inflammation of the inner ear. A noticeable tilt of the head, rapid back and forth eye movements, loss of balance and difficulty with functions such as eating and standing are characteristic. When it walks, the cat drifts to the side to which the head tilts. Cats afflicted with this disorder, which occurs most often in late summer and fall, require "in-hospital" treatment for the first few days or, at least, until the intensity of the symptoms subsides. While it is believed by some authorities that this condition will be resolved without drug therapy, many veterinarians prescribe steroids and antibiotics. Restrict the cat to the house and, if necessary, confine it to a small room until it is better able to negotiate its movements. Most cases return to normal within 10 days to 2 weeks; however, it is possible that an animal will be left with a residual head tilt.

Disk Disease

This is a rare condition in cats. But sometimes a cat will indeed experience a prolapsed or ruptured disk which will cause pain, incoordination and even paralysis. This disease is fairly similar to what happens in human beings. The backbone of the cat is comprised of vertebrae, which provide a protective canal for the spinal cord, which runs from the base of the skull to the tail. As part of the normal aging process, the disks between the vertebrae degenerate, and as they do so, they become more vulnerable to rupture when subjected to trauma from accidents or falls. The ruptured disk protrudes upward into the spinal cord canal; inflammation and swelling result and this places pressure on the spinal cord. Strict rest and anti-inflammatory medications often help, but surgery is often necessary to avoid permanent spinal cord damage and permanent paralysis.

RESPIRATORY TRACT ILLNESSES AND PROBLEMS

*F*or most of us, a cold is a pain in the neck (or, more accurately, a pain in the head) and no one likes to get the flu. But unless the afflicted person is old or debilitated, a cold or even the miserable flu is not likely to turn into a truly serious condition. In the feline a respiratory illness is quite another matter. Its mildness notwithstanding—and it may not be mild at all—such an infection can sometimes carry the potential for life-threatening complications. Other respiratory disorders range from feline asthma to accumulations of fluid in the chest for a number of reasons.

Upper Respiratory Infections (URI)

The most common causes of upper respiratory infections in cats are viral. A number of viruses can be implicated; basically, the symptoms are the same: sneezing, discharge from the eyes and nose, fever, depression, decreased appetite and coughing. Affected cats may also develop ulcers in the mouth and exhibit excessive salivation. The symptoms can be mild or severe, depending upon such factors as the animal's age, physical condition, the environment it's in and the virulence of the virus involved.

The two major offending viruses are *rhinotracheitis* and *calicivirus*. Immunization against these viruses is routinely included with the feline distemper vaccine (the three-in-one vaccination discussed on page 46). You will protect your cat further by keeping it in the house. *These viruses are highly contagious* and travel easily through catteries, boarding facilities, cat shows, pet stores and even animal hospitals.

Once a cat is exposed to such a virus, it usually takes 3 to 7 days (the incubation period) for the disease to produce symptoms. Any new kitten or cat should be carefully watched during the first 1 to 2 weeks it is in your home for sneezing or signs of upper airway congestion. In the event you have other pets, you would be wise to keep a newcomer in separate quarters for the first week in order to avoid exposing your healthy pets to infection. At the first sign of so much as a sneeze, contact your veterinarian.

Just like a human cold or flu, these viruses must run their course, ordinarily lasting 5 to 10 days. The most important care you can provide is good old TLC. For example, the tip of the nose and nostrils can dry out and crack. To relieve the cat's discomfort, apply a thin coat of Vaseline or antiseptic ointment to the tip of its nose and the area around it. What the veterinarian can provide is only supportive treatment such as antibiotics, fluids and vitamins. Good nutrition is also important—and sometimes can only be guaranteed by forced feedings. This can be accomplished by feeding soft food (such as strained baby food meat) by hand. Place a little food on your index finger and then after opening the cat's mouth, slide the food off of your fingertip onto the roof of the cat's mouth. Feed small amounts frequently (e.g., ¼ jar of baby food every few hours), followed by a little water or broth (room temperature) given with a syringe (see pages 125 and 127 on administering oral medications). I know when I have a bad head cold, I usually have a lot of nasal congestion and lose my desire to eat. Similarly, the cat with a cold and upper airway congestion *can't* smell its food and is not very likely to have its usual enthusiasm for eating. Consequently, you'll have to help the animal out.

If you have a vaporizer, use it. This can be most effective in treating a cat with URI. Follow your veterinarian's directions concerning medications. Keep the cat in a warm environment and avoid stress as much as possible to hasten the cat's recovery. Above all, don't be negligent. Make sure the cat has received its yearly booster vaccinations.

An upper respiratory infection can be so mild that one barely is aware of its presence (except for an occasional sneeze). However, a particularly virulent infection or repeated incidences of URI can leave a cat with a chronic *sinusitis* (congested upper airways, noisy breathing, sneezing and nasal discharge) for life. Another possible development is pneumonia.

Pneumonia

Pneumonia is an acute or chronic inflammatory process affecting the lungs and/or bronchii. It may be a primary problem or it may be secondary to another infection. Viruses, bacteria, fungi, parasites and protozoans can all induce this condition. Cats also can contract pneumonia from improper handling; administering medications or liquids improperly or while the cat struggles against your efforts can cause it to aspirate (inhale) the substance. Please review the section on administering liquid medications to a cat (pages 125 and 127) so that you become adept at this procedure and thereby lessen the chances that your cat will ever develop "aspiration pneumonia."

The symptoms of pneumonia are similar to those described for feline asthma (below); in addition, the cat can appear more depressed, have a wet cough and a fever. Prompt professional care is essential.

Feline Asthma

Feline asthma is an allergic bronchitis, the exact cause of which is not really known. One of the irritants may be dust from the clay type of cat litter. Symptoms can develop rapidly. Initial wheezing and dry coughing progress to labored breathing and gasping for breath; the normal pink color of the mucous membranes (most noticeably in the mouth) then becomes cyanotic (gray). These life-threatening signs can arise with disorders other than asthma but, regardless of the cause, always indicate a perilous state requiring prompt veterinary care.

A diagnosis of asthma can be made from a simple X-ray of the chest. In most cases, a complete blood count is performed and a stool sample analyzed as well. These will rule out other possible causes for coughing and labored breathing. If feline asthma is diagnosed, the cat should be kept in an environment free of cat litter dust (switch to a dust-free litter), cigarette smoke and aerosol sprays as well as any other irritants. Cortisone therapy is required and, depending upon the individual case, antibiotics and bronchodilators (drugs that help to open air passages) may be employed to help the cat. The dosage of cortisone is going to vary from pet to pet in keeping with the animal's response to the drug and the frequency and severity of recurring asthmatic attacks.

Laryngitis

Inflammation of the larynx can be connected with upper respiratory or other infections, irritations from smoke or airborne chemicals and also a tumor of the larynx. One more cause: your cat *in heat* or *on the prowl* could develop laryngitis from yowling too loud and too long! Minor irritations that result will cause the cat to meow in a funny sort of way for a few days. But in a short time (less than a week) it will have its normal voice back.

Pleural Effusion and Pulmonary Edema

Fluid in the chest cavity *outside* the lungs (i.e., *pleural effusion*) can accumulate because of infections, tumors and heart disease. The chest cavity can also fill up with blood when there is internal hemorrhaging resulting from severe trauma. As a result of this trauma (such as a blow to the chest) the chest cavity can fill with air, producing what is known as *pneumothorax*. As with any severe respiratory problem, the cat will gasp for breath and have difficulty breathing. The build-up of fluid *within* the lungs is called *pulmonary edema*. This can develop following electric shock or smoke inhalation or can be an outcome of heart disease. Whatever the cause, any of these conditions impinges on the lungs' ability to fill and expand with air. If you want to save the animal's life, prompt veterinary care is necessary.

NOTE: Regardless of which respiratory problem exists, *avoid stressing the cat*, which will only worsen the problem.

THE EAR: DISORDERS AND DISEASES

*T*he outer portion of the cat's ear (see illustration, page 237) is called the *pinna*. This ear flap, which has a large supply of blood vessels, consists of a thin layer of cartilage surrounded on either side by skin. Set beneath the pinna is the ear canal itself, which is structurally similar to that of the human except that the outermost section of the external ear canal has a vertical component which predisposes the pet to infection because moisture can be trapped in this portion of the ear canal. However, dogs have many more problems than cats, especially breeds with floppy ears. (Fortunately the feline's ears are upright.) Several problems are associated with the feline ear. One of the most common is an infestation of mites.

Ear Mites

It takes magnification to see these awful mites, which live on the surface of the skin lining the ear canal. Since they pierce the skin's surface to feed, they cause considerable inflammation and discomfort. Accompanying this piercing of the skin is an accumulation within the canal of a dark brown, granular material composed of dried blood and wax.

Animals afflicted with ear mites will shake their heads and scratch at their ears with their paws, often to the point of drawing blood. Attempting to relieve the itching, the cat will also rub its head (the nasty mites have a tendency to meander) and ears up against the furniture and along the floor. Any cat that does this should be suspected of having mites; a close look into the ear is in order. (If an odor is present along with a good deal of inflammation, the problem will more likely be traced to a bacterial or yeast infection, as described below. Have the pet examined for a definite diagnosis.) Outdoor cats have a higher incidence of ear mites than do indoor felines. Young kittens, however, can get them from a mother cat, and while mites are *not* transmitted to people, they can be transferred to other family pets, the household dog, for instance.

Most of the products used to get rid of mites contain mineral oil as well as some other ingredient, e.g., a pesticide that is toxic to the pests. Unfortunately, some of the chemical additives can further irritate the animal's ear. I often recommend using mineral oil alone unless the infestation is severe, in which case, these other products must be utilized. When placed in the ear canal, mineral oil suffocates the mites. Using a small eye dropper, place 2 to 3 drops in each ear. (See pages 122–23 for instructions on how to apply topical medicines.) Then massage gently at the base of the ear so that the oil gets down into the canal. Wear old clothing and work in an area away from furniture! As surely as the cat hates a bath, it will hate the feel of anything placed in its ears and will shake its head vigorously in protest, splattering the stuff about. After the cat has stopped shaking its head, wipe the ears clean with a cotton ball. (Once again, avoid cotton-tipped applicators; the tip could jam into the ear canal and cause injury should the cat shake its head!) The morning following the first application, wipe the ear with cotton again to clean out oil and debris from the day before. Then place in fresh mineral oil, repeating the process *daily* for 3 weeks. Any sign that the ear is becoming more inflamed or that the cat is becoming more uncom-

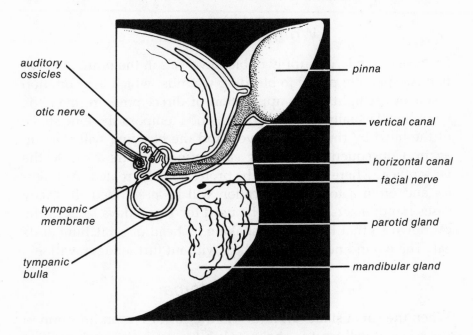

Anatomy of the inner ear

fortable calls for a quick trip to the veterinarian. Sometimes, stronger preparations than just mineral oil *must* be used. If so, use them for the prescribed length of time. All too often, an owner stops the treatment too soon, only to find that the ear mites are still crawling around in the suffering animal's ears.

NOTE: All animals in your household should be treated if an affected cat comes into close contact with them.

Infections

As you can see in the illustration on page 237 and as I mentioned earlier, the vertical component of the ear canal allows moisture to be trapped in the ear. Air circulation is poor in there too. This provides a warm, dark, moist environment in which bacteria and yeast can grow. The symptoms—shaking of the head, rubbing of the head against furniture or rug, scratching of the ear—are similar to those for ear mites. But inflammation, along with discharge and odor, are clues that infection is present. Infections can be serious and terribly painful if left unchecked. Furthermore, infections that spread to the middle and inner ear can cause permanent damage and can even be life-threatening. *Never let an infection go unattended.*

Wounds to the Ear

Because of the large supply of blood vessels in the pinna, the ear flap is especially prone to bleeding wounds, which is a common result of cat fights. The application of direct pressure over the wound will usually stop the flow of blood temporarily. One shake of the head by the cat, however, and the bleeding will start up again. Consequently, bleeding ear wounds require a trip to the vet's office, where the ear can be professionally treated. Antibiotics and often a topical medication will be prescribed. In many cases tranquilizers must also be used for 1 or 2 days to calm the cat down so that it won't be shaking its head or scratching at its ear. The wound needs time to heal without further aggravation.

Aural Hematoma

When the cat sustains an injury to the ear or has an infection or ear mites, it will tend to shake its head excessively. Such shaking can cause a blood vessel in the pinna to rupture; a *hematoma* or large pocket of blood can then develop, accompanied by a great deal of swelling and discomfort. Indeed, the swelling can be so extensive that the entire ear flap becomes thickened. Hematomas require surgical drainage and suturing to restore the normal appearance to the ear. Without such surgical correction within the first few days, the ear will contract down permanently into a deformed or what's called a "cauliflower" ear.

THE EYE: DISORDERS AND DISEASES

*T*he following section briefly describes the most frequently encountered eye problems. Refer to the illustration on page 240 to identify the different parts of the eye.

Eyelid Disorders

ABNORMAL CILIA
Cilia are eyelashes. Extra ones may be present from birth or can develop as a result of eyelid infections. Sometimes harmless enough, they can also cause corneal irritation and, in such an instance, must be removed.

ABNORMALITIES OF THE EYELID POSITION
Entropion is the condition in which the eyelid rolls inward and under, whereas with *ectropion* the eyelid rolls outward (or droops). Both of these conditions can irritate the cornea and conjunctiva and may have to be resolved surgically. They are less common in cats than in dogs. A tear of the eyelid margin, inflicted during a cat fight, is a frequent occurrence. This may cause inflammation of the conjunctiva and/or cornea in the injured eye, and requires close examination to determine the degree of injury.

LAGOPHTHALMUS
The eyelid margins of a cat with *lagophthalmus* do not close completely. The open slit allows drying of the cornea and subsequent ulceration to occur. Instilling artificial tears on a regular basis 3 or

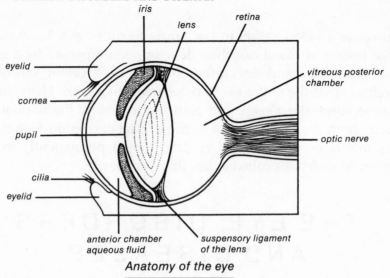

iris

lens

retina

eyelid

vitreous posterior chamber

cornea

pupil

optic nerve

cilia

eyelid

anterior chamber aqueous fluid

suspensory ligament of the lens

Anatomy of the eye

4 times a day can help (see illustration on page 123 for administering eye drops), as can corrective surgery.

BLEPHARITIS
An inflammation of the eyelid, *blepharitis* is accompanied by swelling and a purulent (puslike) discharge from the eye. A number of tiny abscesses are present in the affected lid. Draining of the abscesses, warm compresses and antiobiotics—both topical and systemic—are utilized to remedy this problem.

TUMORS OF THE LID MARGINS
In the cat these are not found very often. However, in cats with predominantly white hair coats, a malignant tumor known as a *squamous cell carcinoma* may develop. Early removal is critical to preserve the margin of the lid and prevent metastasis (spread) of the malignancy.

Diseases of the Conjunctiva

The conjunctiva is the thin membrane lining the underside of the eyelids and covering the front surface of the eyeball. See the illustration above.

CHEMOSIS
Allergy or trauma causes this swelling of the conjunctiva. The swelling can be reduced by topical ophthalmic medications containing antibiotics and/or steroids.

SUBCONJUNCTIVAL HEMORRHAGE

A traumatic blow to the head can result in hemorrhage beneath the conjunctival surface. In most cases brought on by trauma, no treatment is necessary. The subconjunctival hemorrhage looks like a bruise and will fade in 7 to 14 days. Such a hemorrhage can also become apparent when a cat suffers from a bleeding disorder (e.g., some rat poisons contain anti-coagulants such as warfarin and, when consumed by a cat, may cause the animal to bleed. See page 186 for more information on rat poisoning).

BACTERIAL CONJUNCTIVITIS

The presence of bacterial conjunctivitis (inflammation of the conjunctiva) in an eye produces a greenish-brown discharge. This can actually seal the lids shut when it collects and dries in the eye while the animal sleeps overnight. Conjunctivitis, whether mild or severe, rarely becomes a chronic problem. Nor is it always caused by bacterial infection. Conjunctivitis can also be an outcome of allergies, viruses and lid disorders. Should you notice that only one eye is affected, this may be the result of traumatic ulceration of the cornea (see page 165) or the presence of a foreign body (see page 164), both of which require prompt veterinary care. Bacterial conjunctivitis usually responds rapidly to cleaning (with sterile eyewash) and the application of topical antibiotic ophthalmic ointments or drops.

PROTRUSION OF THE NICTITATING MEMBRANE

The "third eyelid," located in the inner corner of each eye (see illustration on page 242), is normally barely visible. Sometimes it becomes raised and partially covers the eyeball. We don't always know what causes this. It can appear when the eye has been injured, or is irritated (e.g., because of an allergy); it can also accompany a systemic illness (feline leukemia virus, feline distemper or upper respiratory viruses). When it appears, the veterinarian will try to determine and treat the underlying problem. Furthermore, any abnormal protrusion of the nictitating membrane should be carefully observed since it can be the site of malignant tumors.

BLOCKED TEAR DUCTS

Epiphora, excessive tearing from the eyes, is due to blocked tear ducts that must be flushed in order to reestablish drainage. Such

Prolapsed third eyelid—nictitating membrane raised up

Normal eye—third eyelid (nictitating membrane) in normal position

blockage creates tearing which stains and discolors facial hair. It is most often a problem in breeds with "pushed in" faces, such as the Persian. The blockage can stem from an allergy, irritation (of unknown origin), upper respiratory infection, the presence of foreign material or the result of an injury. The eyes should be cleaned two or three times a day (see page 67). Your veterinarian might well provide a medication and/or recommend periodic flushing of the tear ducts.

Corneal Disorders

The cornea (see illustration on page 240) is one of the structures which helps keep the contents of the inner eye in place. If the cornea is ruptured completely through, this means that the eyeball is ruptured as well and the animal's sight in that eye may be lost even when the injury is quickly attended to. The most common corneal injury in the cat is an *ulceration* of the cornea. There are many possible causes, such as a traumatic injury resulting from an accident or animal fight, foreign body penetration, irritation as a result of other eye disorders (see above), and in conjunction with viruses. A cat with a corneal ulcer is in pain and will usually squint and keep the eye partially closed because it is very sensitive to light. The eye will usually tear more than normal, and the cat will often paw or scratch at the eye or rub its head along the floor or against furniture.

If any of these signs are noted, try to see a veterinarian as quickly as possible. If there is a delay, a superficial ulceration can worsen dramatically in 12 to 24 hours. In the event that quick veterinary care is impossible, place a liberal amount of ophthalmic ointment (in your first-aid kit) in the affected eye. Repeat this every 2 hours until the pet is examined, and then following an examination, follow your veterinarian's advice.

NOTE: If the cat is scratching at its eye, place a child's white sock on the front paw (right paw if right eye, left paw if left eye) and fasten it at the top with a piece of adhesive tape (be sure that the tape is not wrapped around too tightly). See the illustration on page 199.

Disorders of the Lens

As you can see by studying the illustration on page 240, the lens is a structure within the eye. It helps to form the image seen by your cat. Normally, it stays fixed behind the iris.

CATARACTS

When an animal (or a person) has a *cataract*, the normally transparent lens becomes opaque, forming a barrier to full vision and diminishing acuity. The degree of opaqueness depends upon the stage of cataract formation. Cataracts can be congenital or can develop at any age. They can be inherited or acquired, perhaps following a traumatic injury. Quite often, they are associated with diabetes mellitus and changes in older cats. Fortunately, in most cases the aging animal adjusts, learning through trial and error how to maneuver about without its sight. No surgical correction of cataracts should be attempted without a consultation with a board-certified veterinary ophthalmologist.

LENS LUXATION

Displacement of the lens, or *lens luxation*, can result from trauma, inflammation, glaucoma (see below), cataracts or tumors within the eye. Depending on the cause and extent of the displacement, vision may be permanently impaired.

Glaucoma

With *glaucoma*, the intraocular (within the eyeball) pressure increases so greatly that the health and function of the eye are compromised. The cat will exhibit extreme pain and be irritable and depressed because of the heightened pressure within the eye; the eyeball will start to enlarge as the glaucoma progresses. Without prompt treatment of the eye, irreversible damage is inevitable. Even immediate care may fail—the eye may not be salvageable. Often an owner will notice the problem only when the glaucoma is already well established. In cases in which medications do not provide relief and especially when the animal has lost its sight and is in pain, your veterinarian will recommend that the affected eye be removed. This surgery will not affect the cat's longevity and though you may be bothered by the thought of what a one-eyed cat will look like, please don't let this prevent you from allowing the surgery or cause you to prematurely euthanatize the pet.

CANCER

*S*urely, one of the most terrifying words in our vocabulary is *cancer*, charged as it is with implications of suffering and eventual death. We know all too well that cancer can strike at any age and that it knows no discrimination in its choice of target. Unnoticeable as it begins, insidious in its development, cancer takes many forms and ranks high on the list of killers for both people and pets.

A *neoplasm* is medically defined as "a persistent, purposeless growth composed of cells that do not respond properly to the normal mechanism that controls cell proliferation." Such growths can be *benign*, in which case they are usually harmless, or *malignant*, which means they can spread through the body and become potentially life-threatening. What causes these lethal cancers has not been established with finality. Chemical agents, certain viruses and environmental factors such as ultraviolet radiation can initiate their growth. Genetics and a failure of the immune system undoubtedly have enormous bearing on their development and progression.

The word "cancer" is almost uniformly used as a general term once a malignant neoplasm has been diagnosed. Certain animal species, however, are more or less prone to specific types. Cats can develop tumors of the skin, lymphatic system, vascular system, respiratory tract, gastrointestinal tract, muscle, bone, cartilage, liver, kidney, mammary glands, reproductive tract, thyroid glands, adrenal glands or pituitary gland or the central nervous system. This is an ominous list indeed. But the most frequently diagnosed neoplastic disease in the cat is *lymphoma*, sometimes called *lymphosarcoma*, which is often associated with the presence of the feline leukemia virus (see pages 246–49).

The prognosis for recovery from a cancerous disease varies with the type and location of the cancer, the overall health of the cat in question and the animal's response to therapy. Surgery, radiation, chemotherapy and immunotherapy are modes of treatment for malignancy. In many cases, surgical removal of a neoplastic growth is performed and a biopsy done by a pathologist to determine the exact nature of the growth. What course is followed depends on the biopsy report. Anyone familiar with cancer treatment in humans is bound to know something of the procedures. In chemotherapy, chemical agents may be used to destroy cancer cells; radiation may be used on the premise that some cancers are destroyed by X-rays. Radiation is especially employed for inoperable cancers. Immunotherapy stimulates the animal's own immune system to counter the given cancer.

Oncologists are specialists in the study of tumors, both in human and in veterinary medicine. The medical departments of most veterinary colleges have an oncology department; some of the larger veterinary hospitals have an oncologist on staff. Should your cat develop cancer, you might want to turn to an oncologist for a consultation and treatment guidance. Your veterinarian will most assuredly cooperate.

If you notice that your cat has a lump or bump that you previously had not detected, see that your veterinarian examines the pet. As animals age, they tend to develop growths, many of which are benign. Growths that rapidly increase in size, that are very firm to the touch or that ulcerate and drain, however, are quite likely to be malignant and should never be neglected. Malignant cancers that are removed early on, before they have had time to metastasize, are less likely to recur or to cause the pet's death.

INFECTIOUS DISEASES

*I*nfectious diseases—those that spread from one animal to another—may be caused by bacteria, viruses, parasites and fungi. Regardless of the infectious agent, they are most often spread by direct contact, although contact with bodily secretions alone (saliva, urine, feces) is sometimes sufficient to provoke an infection. Thus, your feline, if it stays within the safe confines of your house and yard, has a better chance of living a healthy, illness-free life than a wandering tom or queen.

Feline Leukemia Virus

The *feline leukemia virus*, or *FeLV*, belongs to a group of viruses that cause cancer in a number of species, although FeLV specifically affects only the cat. Since the occurrence of FeLV in the general cat population is relatively low (1 to 2 percent of cats are infected with the virus), the average cat owner need not be overly concerned, especially in a single-cat household. At the same time, of all the infectious disease agents affecting cats, feline leukemia virus is the most serious. A cell infected with FeLV may (though not always) be altered, allowing for the development of a malignancy and, if the cat's *immune* cells are infected, this will make it vulnerable to an onslaught of other diseases due to the immune impairment caused by the virus. The major symptom of FeLV is anemia, best indicated by the presence of pale gums. This is not specific, of course, and can be seen with many illnesses.

A colleague of mine, William D. Hardy, Jr., V.M.D., of the Memorial Sloan Kettering Cancer Center and the National Veterinary Laboratory, has been a pioneer in the detection and control of this virus. The *FeLeuk Test* he developed was the first available to the veterinary practitioner. All it requires is the examination of a small sample of blood. This isn't the only test, however; there are a number used today that detect the presence of FeLV. Yet the FeLeuk Test is still considered by leading authorities to be the most accurate. For this reason I advise that any diagnoses made of the feline leukemia virus by means of the newer tests be confirmed by running the FeLeuk.

The incubation period is up to 3 months (the time between when the infectious agent enters the body and can be first detected), but the time for disease development for FeLV is from 3 to 36 months or even longer. In addition to traveling from one grown cat to another, the virus can also be transmitted by an infected mother to her offspring, either across the placenta while the fetus is *in utero* or through the milk when the kittens nurse. Not only bodily secretions can be a vehicle for infection, so can blood: the blood that flows during cat fights, for example, can cause the virus to travel from a sick to a healthy cat. FeLV can also be transmitted through communal litter boxes and feeding bowls.

The cat's immune system is involved in the development of FeLV infection or FeLV-related diseases once exposure has occurred. Some cats produce antibodies against the virus and thereby become resistant to FeLV infection. Not all cats with an FeLV-related disease are infected with FeLV itself. Some cats are infected with FeLV but are protected from any disease development. These cats appear healthy, but because they carry the virus they act as reservoirs for infection and can spread the virus to healthy, susceptible cats.

Among the diseases proven to be associated with FeLV are lymphoma, nonregenerative anemias and reproductive disorders; other diseases are under suspicion of being related. Once a cat has been infected, *it has the virus* and, at this time, there is no way to eliminate it from its system. The animal's infected immune system is suppressed and thereby the cat becomes more susceptible to secondary infections. Some of the FeLV-caused diseases will respond to treatment (such as chemotherapy) and go into remission although no "cures" are available as yet.

Can *you* get this disease? There is no evidence to date that the feline leukemia virus can be spread to humans. My feeling is strong, however, that because infected cats—even if only carriers —are sources of infection to other cats (assuming that these other cats are FeLV negative), they should be euthanatized. Sometimes, a client will find this unacceptable. Then, at the very least, the cat should be completely restricted to the home and no new cats brought in. I am especially adamant in recommending euthanasia to a client with very young children. No, there is no evidence that FeLV is transmittable from cat to human being. I nonetheless feel that there are uncertainties with which I am unwilling to take a chance. Many veterinarians do not take this stand. I simply feel obligated to express my opinion.

Here are some general remarks regarding FeLV:

1. Before considering breeding, be sure that both cats to be used are FeLV negative.
2. If you have had a cat with FeLV, wait at least 30 days before acquiring a new one. Dispose of litter boxes and feeding/ water bowls and clean the living area with a good household cleaner.
3. If you have had a cat with FeLV and have other cats in the household, they should be given a FeLeuk test. Negative tests first time around are not good enough. Have them repeated three months later to ensure that the cats are not infected.
4. All cats should be tested for FeLV before they are allowed to enter a FeLV-free household.
5. No breed of cat is more or less susceptible than another, but kittens and older or debilitated cats are more susceptible than healthy adult cats.
6. Kittens can be tested for FeLV as young as 8 weeks of age.
7. When the FeLV is shed by an infected cat, the virus lives only a short time, approximately 3 days in a moist environment, such as in a litter box, and only a matter of minutes if allowed to dry, such as in the form of saliva in your hand. Therefore, the chance of your spreading the virus to your cat after handling a FeLV-infected feline is unlikely.

An important milestone in veterinary medicine occurred with the release of the first feline leukemia virus vaccine in February 1985. The vaccine appears to be approximately 80 percent effective in producing immunity, and has limited side effects. In approximately 5 percent of the cats vaccinated, stinging at the site of injection (this is given intramuscularly), occasional hypersensitivity reactions, fever, and/or a transient loss of appetite and inactivity (for approximately 12 to 24 hours) has been reported. Vaccinations can be started as early as 9 weeks of age. Only cats that are feline leukemia virus *negative* should be vaccinated, as this vaccine will not help FeLV *positive* cats. Three doses are required: an initial inoculation, repeated a second time 2 to 4 weeks later, and again 2 to 4 months later. Thereafter, a yearly booster is required to maintain immunity. At this time, authorities believe that this vaccine is of the most significant value for outdoor cats and cats living in multiple-cat households. If you have a single cat confined indoors, speak to your veterinarian for his or her opinion, as the preceding recommendation may change with time.

Feline Distemper (Enteritis)

The medical term is *feline panleukopenia,* but people are more familiar with names like *feline distemper* or *infectious enteritis.* All members of the cat family can be threatened by this virus as can ferrets, minks, raccoons and coatimundis. The virus is transmitted through body secretions such as feces, urine and saliva, as well as the vomitus of an infected animal. Generally speaking, the disease is easier to prevent than it is to cure. *Vaccination is the primary preventive step.* Have kittens immunized and be certain that adult cats receive their annual boosters (see page 46 on vaccinations). Although a cat can be affected at any age, kittens and younger cats are most susceptible. The incubation period is from 2 to 9 days after exposure.

Symptoms range from depression, appetite loss, vomiting and dehydration to abdominal pain, fever and, later, diarrhea. These come on suddenly and are incapacitating and severe. If supportive treatment (IV fluids, antibiotics, B-complex vitamins) is not quickly administered, death will occur within a few days. Since these symptoms can be caused by many other diseases, your veterinarian will have to perform tests to confirm a diagnosis. The most important of these tests is a white blood cell count. (*Panleukopenia* means, literally, lack of all white blood cells.)

Treating the cat can be a strain. The disease is highly contagious: if you're lucky your veterinarian will have an isolation ward in which cats with feline distemper can be placed. But instead, you may be asked to bring the cat in one or two times a day for treatment, to lessen the chance of exposing healthy animals.

Given that the distemper virus is fairly resistant to heat, cold, light and disinfectants, it can live for up to one year. Never bring an unvaccinated feline into a home where an animal with the virus lives or has recently lived. If you visit someone who has a cat with distemper, you should change your clothes and wash thoroughly before coming in contact with your own cat(s). This is especially important if your cat is not up to date on its vaccinations.

It used to be that the chances of survival for cats with distemper were slim. Fortunately, today's medications have improved the prognosis for the stricken feline. Because the vaccinations available are so very effective in preventing the disease, I find it terribly upsetting to see an animal come down with panleukopenia. There's no need for this to happen! Please, avoid unnecessary suffering; have your cat vaccinated!

Upper Respiratory Infections

For information on Upper Respiratory Infections (URI), see pages 232–35.

Feline Infectious Peritonitis

Approximately 25 percent of the general cat population in the United States has been infected by the viral disease known as *Feline Infectious Peritonitis (FIP)*, although the fatal clinical form of this disease develops only in 1 to 5 percent of the cats. It affects both domestic and wild felines and can be involved in reproductive and newborn kitten disorders. Though the virus can live only for several days in the environment, it has demonstrated strong resistance to some disinfectants.

No one is certain of the mode of infection, though bodily secretions, maternal transmission and aerosol mediums are all likely. The incubation period is generally between 2 and 6 weeks. However, the cat may not become clinically ill for several weeks to several years following exposure; sometimes, it will never contract the disease—in which case, the feline is immune. Such immunity is not clearly understood. Nor is it known why some animals develop a lethal FIP while others do not. Stress, age, environment (an overcrowded cattery, for instance), immuno-suppression, physical condition, the presence of other disease and genetics—all are influential in the course that FIP may take in a given cat.

The clinical forms of illness are as follows:

1. *Wet FIP:* Signs include chronic weight loss, fever, depression and an enlarged belly because of the development of "ascites" (fluid in the abdomen). There can also be fluid in the chest cavity or "pleural effusion," which will produce labored breathing.

2. *Dry FIP:* Weight loss, chronic and nonresponsive fever, depression and inactivity are manifest. The functions of specific organs may be impaired; the animal then shows signs of decline that can include liver failure, renal insufficiency, pancreatic disease and perhaps diseases of the central nervous system. Lesions affecting the eyes are seen in approximately 25 percent of the cats that develop this form of FIP.

As mentioned before, the FIP virus is also responsible for a number of reproductive disorders in breeding animals as well as disorders in newborn kittens.

A diagnosis of FIP can be made through various laboratory tests, but there is, as yet, no cure or vaccine for the disease. Animals with fatal FIP sometimes respond to treatment (antibiotics, cortisone, immunosuppressive drugs and general supportive care) and go into a short remission. Sadly, such remissions usually do not last for more than several months.

A new cat should not be introduced into a household in which an FIP cat has lived, for at least one week following the latter's death. New cats should be checked for FIP before being brought into a home with other cats. The study of FIP continues. Your veterinarian can supply you with up-to-date information as it becomes available.

Feline Infectious Anemia

This blood disease affects the cat's red blood cells, and is caused by the presence of the microscopic parasite *Hemobartonella felis*. In mild forms of the disease, no obvious signs of illness are present, but in severe cases symptoms include weakness, loss of appetite and weight, fever and pale mucous membranes (because of the accompanying anemia). Sometimes the animal also appears jaundiced. This disease is probably transmitted to healthy cats by the bite of fleas or other blood-sucking parasites. In its extreme form the cat will become emaciated and may die. Treatment of this disease, when diagnosed, includes antibiotic and fluid therapy as well as blood transfusions. (This disease may recur even after a cat has been treated.) It is also important to control external parasites in the environment to prevent the spread of this infection.

HEREDITARY DISORDERS/ CONGENITAL ANOMALIES

*W*hen we speak of congenital defects or anomalies, we mean that they are present at birth. It should be understood that these may be inherited but also may be acquired, the unfortunate result of exposure to infectious or toxic agents in utero.

Cerebellar Hypoplasia

This may result when the pregnant cat is infected with the feline distemper virus or vaccinated against feline distemper while pregnant. In either case, the cerebellum of the developing kitten(s) is partially destroyed. Since this portion of the brain controls muscular coordination, the damage results in varying degrees of incoordination; affected kittens appear to be drunk when they walk. While there is no cure, mildly affected kittens can lead relatively normal lives since the disease is not progressive. It may be best to euthanatize severely affected kittens.

Other Anomalies

Cleft palates, defects of the heart or kidneys, hydrocephalus (fluid-filled, enlarged head) and a myriad of other anomalies have been seen in cats but probably occur less frequently in cats than in dogs. Many of these defects are not even diagnosed, as they frequently contribute to the deaths of newborn kittens in the first few hours or days of life. Others are picked up in the course of a thorough examination when the animal is older. For instance, a cat may be born with just one functional kidney and reach adulthood, none the worse for wear. Some defects, such as umbilical hernias, are quite easy to repair. Cleft palates and heart defects are frequently surgically correctable but not with such ease.

Should you notice any abnormality in a kitten, be sure to call it to the attention of your veterinarian so that its significance can be determined.

DISEASES WITH PUBLIC HEALTH SIGNIFICANCE (ZOONOTIC DISEASES)

*D*og bites occur more often than do cat bites and I don't intend to underestimate how painful dog bites can be. However, the bite of a cat can actually cause more unfortunate consequences. Wounds from dog bites are usually tears, whereas those sustained from a cat are small but very deep punctures. Rapid surface healing does take place; in the meantime, though, bacterial infection builds up in the deeper tissues. Considerable pain and swelling can result; blood poisoning can also occur.

I advise that *all* animal bites be reported to your doctor. The law requires you to inform the public health department of dog bites; because of the threat of rabies, any dog that has delivered a bite must be quarantined until rabies is ruled out (or determined). Cat bites are not monitored as closely, so it's up to you to take them seriously—or suffer the consequences. Should you be bitten, your personal physician will instruct you regarding appropriate first-aid measures, advise on the necessity of a tetanus booster and possibly prescribe antibiotics to prevent or control infection.

NOTE: A genuine cat bite—I'm not speaking of a playful nip—is not to be expected from the normally well-behaved cat. Be sure you read the section on pages 91-93 concerning aggressive feline behavior.

Rabies

The most feared outcome associated with animal bites is *rabies*, which thoroughly deserves its terrifying reputation. This dreadful viral disease has been around for more than 2,000 years. Today there are some countries in which rabies is never seen. For the purpose of preventing the spread of the disease to "rabies-free" nations, travel and quarantine requirements for pets are strictly enforced. In countries like the United States, the goal is to keep the spread of the virus under control.

The primary reservoir of rabies infection is the wildlife population; bats, raccoons, foxes and skunks are the major carriers. The higher the incidence of rabies in your area, the more important it is that your cat be vaccinated. Immunization is legally required for all dogs, but though the edict does not extend to cats in most parts of the country, it is my conviction that a feline allowed *any* outdoor freedom whatsoever should be vaccinated every year. Although rabies is more prevalent in rural areas, bats *have* been known to inhabit urban locales. If you notice a bat in or around the home, have your cat immunized. Do the same if you take your cat to the country for weekends.

The most common method by which the rabies virus is spread is through the saliva of the infected animal when it bites another creature (be it person or pet). It can also be spread by exposure to other bodily secretions containing virus particles. Because bats live and breathe in close quarters, they spread the virus to each other primarily via the respiratory tract. The disease has a variable incubation period and can surface any time from 15 days up to several months. Skunks are outlawed as pets in many states since, although exposed, they can appear quite healthy for a rather long time before suddenly becoming symptomatic.

Once transmitted, the rabies virus travels through the nerve trunks to the spinal cord and then from there to the brain. Once symptoms are apparent, the disease is usually fatal (there have been a few recoveries recorded in man). A rabid animal should be euthanatized. Because the treatment is prolonged and painful and the prognosis for recovery poor, there is intense concern when people sustain animal bites (at least until it is known that the attacking animal is rabies-free).

The course of the disease can be divided into three different phases, which are not as distinct in the cat as they are in the dog. In the (1) *prodromal phase,* there are changes easily confused with signs of other disorders. The animal will frequently cease drinking and eating, will seek out a quiet hiding place, will urinate more frequently and may salivate excessively. Because the symptoms are so easily misinterpreted, a good number of pet owners and veterinarians have been exposed during this phase. (2) It is during the *excitative phase* that the disease has its most recognizable symptoms. The rabid animal may suddenly attack animate or even inanimate moving objects, biting, scratching wildly and usually foaming at the mouth. (3) The *paralytic phase* is characterized by muscular incoordination and seizures, with progressive paralysis ending in death.

Any person exposed to an animal suspected of having this disease must notify the health department with all due speed. Animals without a history of rabies vaccinations must be considered highly suspect, and the animal should be immediately euthanatized and laboratory tests performed to confirm infection. In the event that the animal is kept alive, it must be quarantined for at least 10 days and observed for symptoms. In the same way that a rabid animal should be euthanatized, *so should an unvaccinated pet that is bitten by an animal with rabies.* Vaccinated animals that have been bitten by a rabid animal should receive a "booster" rabies vaccination within 7 days of this exposure.

Please do not take any chances with this horrible disease.

Never handle wild animals. Call your local animal control office to report any injured or sick wildlife. Should it be necessary for you to assist, be sure to wear heavy, protective gloves.

Cat Scratch Fever

Cat scratch fever is a syndrome that affects people, not cats. It is thought to result from a gram negative bacteria that is introduced beneath the skin of a person via the wound of a scratch from a cat or another source, e.g. a thorn. Whatever the case, the lymph nodes in the area close to the scratch swell up, become painful to the touch, and the victim is stricken with a fever. In proportion to the great number of scratches cats inflict without any real trauma, instances of cat scratch fever are few. Generally speaking, if you clean the scratch thoroughly with mild soap and water, pour a liberal amount of hydrogen peroxide over the wound and then keep the scratch clean, it will rapidly heal without any complications. But if there are any scratches that are particularly deep or any symptoms of enlarged lymph nodes and fever, you should call your physician at once, because this disease can be quite serious. However, usually the symptoms are mild and will disappear in short order without any treatment.

Toxoplasmosis and the Pregnant Woman

There's nothing new about toxoplasmosis itself, but owing to greater concern about issues of public health, it is a disease that is receiving increasing attention, for it can do tremendous harm to the developing fetus. The disease is specifically caused by the organism *Toxoplasma gondii*, which is a single-celled parasite (or protozoan). Although the organism can be found in many species of mammals and birds, which act as "intermediate" hosts, the cat is the only "definitive" host—the only species that ingests this parasite (usually by eating raw meat or unwashed vegetables) and then spreads it via its feces when the parasite is in an infectious stage.

Obviously, this organism must be avoided by pregnant women. Please understand that many more people are exposed to the parasite by ingesting raw or undercooked meats; *steak tartare* is more likely to get you than the cat, and cooking meat thoroughly is a better way to avoid the disease than steering clear of felines. However, the pregnant woman owes it to herself and the fetus she is bearing to take unusual precautions when handling any cats.

Your veterinarian can perform fecal analyses and blood tests to determine if your cat is infected. Following the tests, keep the cat indoors; if you allow your cat to roam outdoors, it could subsequently pick up the parasite from the birds and small animals it preys upon.

Since it takes 1 to 5 days following defecation for the infectious stage of the *Toxoplasma gondii* to develop, if you empty and disinfect the litter box daily you should not be exposed to infection. However, pregnant women should follow these precautions:

1. Do not eat any raw or undercooked meats.

2. Have your cat tested by your veterinarian to be sure it's free of infection. Then, keep it indoors so that it won't eat infected prey. Also, do not feed it any raw meats.

3. If you can, let someone else change the litter box daily. If

this is not possible, wear rubber gloves and wash your hands thoroughly following this daily task.

4. Avoid contact with cats other than your own and stay away from sand boxes and gardening soil in which fecal contamination may exist.

5. Also discuss toxoplasmosis with your personal physician, who will probably recommend performing a toxoplasmosis titer (a simple blood test that indicates previous or existing exposure to toxoplasmosis).

Other Zoonotics

Roundworms (see pages 219–20) and *ringworm* (see pages 205–6) also have public health significance and caution should be exercised when handling infected animals, especially when there are young children in the household.

PART EIGHT

THE GERIATRIC CAT

*T*o face the facts of life is to face the nature of aging, whether it be in people or in pets. "You're only as old as you feel" may be a terrific motto for a human to subscribe to, but despite its reflective appearance, the cat is no philosopher (a thinker perhaps, but not a philosopher), and we have no way of knowing what it feels in regard to its aging faculties. We can only observe that the aging cat is decidedly a creature slowing down. We also know that the aging feline is subject to unfortunate afflictions. As with people, however, some cats are more fortunate than others.

The life of the average cat is short when measured in human terms. But by the measurements applied to animal life, it takes a good while to reach senior feline status. When I was growing up, we used to calculate the human equivalent to the age of cats and dogs as follows: one human year was approximately equal to seven years of a cat or dog. In the past decade or two, this assessment has been changed. The first year in the life of a cat is thought to be the equivalent of 15 to 20 human years. By the time a cat reaches middle age (5 to 12 years), then old age, each year is lessened to 3 or 4 human years.

There's tremendous variance to the life span of the cat, depending on its living situation. The average life expectancy of an indoor cat (14 to 15 years) is far greater than that of the free-roaming stray, who may not last beyond 3 years. The reason is obvious: the indoor cat is not exposed to the same dangers as the outdoor animal. If your cat is neutered, receives proper veterinary care and lives in the comfort and safety of your home (without exposure to a lot of other felines), it might even live for as long as 20 to 25 years.

I'm sure you know people who start to age earlier than others, and those in whom the process seems to proceed with amazing rapidity. Cats are like that too. In other words, each one is different, and no solid criteria hold for every cat. No one really knows why this is so. But genetics and environment play a part in human aging and scientists assume this is also true with felines. The biggest differences between humans and pets when it comes to the business of getting old have to do with life-style. Animals are far more accustomed to regular patterns of eating and sleeping than people. Nor do they subject themselves to social hazards such as alcohol, tobacco and drugs.

Early signs of aging in the feline can begin when the pet is 6 to 8 years old. It's then in its middle years, and it might become more sedentary, sleeping more and playing less. Gray hairs may appear and are usually restricted to the face, around the mouth and nose. The feline's intense obsession with grooming may decrease and the glossiness of its hair coat fade. (This is a sign for you to be especially conscientious about combing and brushing the cat.) If the cat overeats and also becomes less active, it might become overweight, but this is rare. More often, the geriatric cat begins to lose weight, the evidence showing in the prominence of the skeletal points along the backbone and hips. Skin sagging from the cat's lower abdomen is another sign that it is becoming thin.

Quite commonly, the aging cat also becomes less fastidious in its elimination habits. Your tolerance is required as the cat seems to get lax about eliminating directly into the box. It's not that the cat doesn't "care"; rather, its sense of place and balance may be slipping. The pet may even become senile. Try not to get angry at the elderly cat when you find its droppings right near the box. Clearly, the pet has tried. You may also notice that it's hard for the cat to defecate. Even with the help of a stool softener or laxative, the old feline may have trouble in the way it moves its bowels. Incontinence is another problem that may arise in elderly felines. This may be difficult to tolerate; discuss this problem with your veterinarian.

With the approach of old age (13 years and up), the cat might start to lose some of its hearing and sight. *You* may find this terribly sad and depressing. I assure you, though, that the cat adjusts. Generally, loss of hearing and sight is an extremely gradual process; the animal has time to cope with the change. As long as the physical appearance of the household is maintained as the cat has always known it, the animal will get around surprisingly well. (This is not the time to rearrange the furniture!)

The aging of the cat requires your special patience and understanding. An old animal is not going to feel as well as a spry young creature; it's entitled to get persnickety now and then. As long as you don't expect it to perform with the playfulness of its younger years, the cat should not be noticeably irritable. It may, in fact, become even more affectionate, in special need of love. And a cat that has always been "nice" will not—believe me— suddenly turn into a monster. No responsible owner should reject or desert the aging animal, or fail to understand and appreciate the reasons behind subtle changes in behavior. So put up with whatever are your aging feline's foibles; through all those years, the animal has put up with yours.

THE GERIATRIC CAT AND ILLNESS

*I*f only all creatures great and small could enjoy old age and skip deterioration. We should be grateful, though, that our pets—barring conditions that produce extreme discomfort—are able to adjust. Decline is usually gradual, so in spite of the fact that old age is settling in, the animal—at first—may show no visible signs that its body is degenerating.

In cats that live to be very old, renal (kidney) failure is one of the most common causes of death. The kidneys act as filters for waste products in the blood. Aging that occurs in the kidney tissues slowly destroys the tiny filtering systems. Once the decline has begun, the process continues to progress at varying speed. It is when the filtering systems cease to function that the cat begins to show signs of renal failure (pages 226–28). Before those signs are clearly evident, the cat may appear fine, so extraordinary is the ability of the body to compensate for the diminishing workings of its organs. For example, older cats will generally consume more water than younger ones—a natural attempt by the body to make up for the deteriorating renal function. To cope as best you can and perhaps to forestall the inevitable, you should be sure that your older cat is examined once a year and preferably every six months. Your veterinarian will be able to assess the cat's overall physical condition and to evaluate, by a simple blood test, the animal's kidney function.

Cancer is more common in older pets. Many types can occur and I suggest you read the material on pages 244–45 to familiarize yourself with the varieties of this dreadful disease. Some malignancies, of course, are more serious and life-threatening than others. Older animals are also prone to developing lots of lumps and bumps that are benign. In most cases, these are of no real consequence, and your veterinarian will advise you as to whether removal is appropriate.

Another frequent problem in geriatric cats is dental disease. Refer to pages 68–69 on dental care.

Any owner who has an aging cat should keep a scrupulous record of the animal's weight, recording it on a regular basis.

With a cat, this is easy. Just stand on the bathroom scale and weigh yourself. Do it again, holding the cat; its weight is the difference between the two. Dramatic weight loss (2 pounds, for instance, or in a small cat, even 1 pound) in a relatively short period of time (2 to 4 weeks) is almost always an indication of a serious problem. In an elderly cat, one of the causes of weight loss is hyperthyroidism (see page 214).

Since constipation is a frequent occurrence in many older cats, your veterinarian might advise a stool softener or laxative to be used periodically. Any product of this sort should be given only when professionally advised, as their long-term use—or misuse—could be deleterious to the animal's health.

Arthritis, a typical affliction of older age, is not as common a problem in cats as it is in dogs. When it does occur, it is probably the result of prior injuries that have precipitated arthritic changes. Obese felines, however, are more prone to the condition than cats of normal weight. But generally, because cats are small creatures, they don't show significant symptoms even when arthritic changes are present.

Organs such as the heart, lungs and liver often show the effects of age. But even so, it is far more typical that the kidneys start failing first. When the animal does not fall victim to kidney failure, the decline of these other organs may then be the ultimate cause of death . . . unless, as I am about to discuss, you decide to intervene.

EUTHANASIA

*T*he first time I was required to euthanatize an animal, I was in my first year of veterinary school. Never before had I been in the position of deciding that an animal's life was to end and that *I* was to end it. In the years I have been in practice, I have euthanatized a great many pets; a part of me resists each time.

Nonetheless, I take comfort in knowing that I am preventing further suffering in a creature that is sick and beyond my help. The euphemistic term for euthanasia—"putting to sleep"—is a true approximation of what occurs.

The drugs used by most veterinarians to end an animal's life are similiar to those employed in anesthesia. It's only that the concentrations are stronger. I myself generally give a dosage of an intravenous anesthetic, such as sodium pentothal or pentobarbital, to anesthetize the animal first and then follow this with an appropriate dosage of euthanasia solution. It is peaceful and painless and over in a matter of seconds. But I cannot remember a time when I've done this lightly. Many of my clients have wished to be present when their pet is euthanatized. This is something you should discuss with your veterinarian.

Ultimately, the decision to euthanatize a pet has to be the owner's. Sometimes, however, a veterinarian has to exert some influence—and that influence is not always on the side of performing the act. I have had clients request that I euthanatize an animal when my evaluation of the pet's medical condition did not warrant such a course. People choose to euthanatize the animal, rather than to find it a new home. They discover quickly, when talking to *me*, that they'll also have to choose another veterinarian. I refuse to be accommodating in such an instance. But the reverse also occurs. When an animal is suffering and cannot be restored to health, ending the animal's pain is the most humane option. It is my stand that an owner should be fully informed that the suffering cannot be relieved except by the termination of life. In the face of the owner's profound unhappiness, I will still encourage taking that step. I know that in every instance where an animal has truly been loved, euthanasia is an indescribably painful choice. But the perpetuation of life commingled with unrelieved suffering is worse.

Beyond the act of euthanasia itself is a problem that concerns a lot of people. If the subject of disposal of the body seems indelicate, it is still a matter that must be dealt with. When I was growing up, I had a pet cemetery in my backyard. Each time I lost a pet—and it happened several times—I would hold a little service attended by members of my family, who were, after all, the animal's family too. People who live in the country are able to do the same. But it may be against a local city ordinance or public health department regulation to bury animals in the backyard. For people living in urban areas, cremation is the most logical choice for disposition of the animal's body. The procedure is relatively inexpensive unless the owner requests a return of ashes. If an owner really prefers, he or she can choose a pet cemetery that might offer a whole host of arrangements for deceased animals. But I ask you to beware: I have found some of these places to be extremely expensive and exploitative of human vulnerability at the time of a pet's loss. I advise alternative courses. In many cities, humane organizations such as the ASPCA will take care of euthanasia and cremation of pets for little or no fee (although donations are always welcomed).

Once again, let me repeat that the animal feels no pain when humanely euthanatized. Indeed, I feel fortunate that as a veterinarian I have the legal right to perform euthanasia. Once the quality of life has diminished below a certain level, when suffering and pain are intolerable, I can find no reason to perpetuate an animal's miserable existence. Then euthanasia seems an honorable act and, in fact, an act of charity.

PET LOSS

"*E*veryone can master a grief but he who has it," said the Bard. Indeed, nothing I—or anyone else—can say or do will fully help a pet owner cope with the supreme and terrible sorrow that has to accompany the end of a loved and loving animal's life. The loss of a pet can be every bit as devastating for many people as the loss of a relative or close friend; such a sense of loss is entirely valid, and failure to appreciate its depths is both insensitive and unkind. The death of a pet can be infinitely sad, and all we can offer in the face of it is the age-old phrase that time heals —which it does.

Today we—the human community—are given over to a sincere attempt at understanding all the components that can contribute to grief and mourning, whether it be over human beings or pets. In fact, it would be utterly heartless not to recognize the intensity of love that can result—particularly for the lonely— from the human-animal bond. There are several books that address the many issues connected with the death of an animal. *Pet Loss and Human Bereavement*, edited by William J. Kay, Herbert A. Neiburg, Austin H. Kutscher, Ross M. Grey and Carole E. Fudin

(Iowa State University Press); *Pet Loss: A Thoughtful Guide for Adults & Children*, by Herbert A. Nieburg and Arlene Fischer (Harper & Row); and *When Your Pet Dies*, by Jamie Quackenbush and Denise Graveline (Simon and Schuster) all cover the subject of pet loss with admirable thoroughness, and I recommend them highly.

It is my belief that discussing the death of a pet before one is faced with its reality can make it less difficult to deal with. Obviously, I mean this to be taken most seriously when an animal is aging and when the inevitable is starting to loom. If you do lose a pet, your veterinarian ought to be someone to whom you can talk. An individual who has been involved in the medical care of the very animal you've lost is not likely to be insensitive to your unhappiness.

The suppression of feelings and emotional pain that occurs when an animal dies is not healthy; we know that discussing the loneliness, sorrow and guilt that may be involved in the grieving process serves a useful purpose.

There are two additional points I want to make about pet loss:

1. One has to be particularly sensitive to the feelings of young children when a pet dies. Never dismiss the secret terror and hurt they may be feeling. It often happens that an adult's own inability to deal with the subject of death is an obstacle to discussing it with a youngster. Please do whatever you can and make the effort to broach the subject, no matter how hard it may seem. You must never underestimate how deeply the experience of death can affect a child.

2. Come the death of a pet, the subject of replacing the animal will inevitably arise. Some clients eagerly want to know how soon they should do it; others categorically refuse to consider having another pet. Having seen this situation countless times, it has always struck me that a person should get a new pet only when (and if) he or she is ready. A formula to determine just the right time would make life easy, but it doesn't work. The heart of the owner has to be the guide. Nothing is more natural than that a person should feel that no other pet can possibly replace the one that is gone. Moreover, it's true; it can't be done. A new pet is going to be different, but that animal, too, will be very special in its own particular way.

APPENDIXES

1. Plants Potentially Dangerous to Cats—Toxic Effects and Early Symptoms*

COMMON NAME	SCIENTIFIC NAME	EARLY SYMPTOMS
I. Oral, Pharyngeal and Esophageal Irritants		
Alocasia	*Alocasia spp.*	Salivation and
Caladium	*Caladium spp.*	edema
Calla lily	*Zantedeschia acthiopica*	(swelling)
Dumbcane	*Dieffenbachia spp.*	
Elephant's-ear	*Colocasia spp.*	
Green dragon, Oregon root	*Arisaema dracontium*	
Jack-in-the-pulpit, Indian turnip	*Arisaema triphyllum*	
Malanga	*Xanthosoma spp.*	
Philodendron	*Philodendron spp.*	
Skunk cabbage	*Symplocarpus foetidus*	
II. Gastric Irritants		
Amaryllis	*Amaryllis spp.*	Immediate vomiting
Daffodil	*Narcissus spp.*	
Wisteria	*Wisteria spp.*	
III. Intestinal Irritants		
Balsam pear	*Momordica charantia*	Salivation,
English ivy	*Hedera helix*	immediate
Horse chestnut, buckeye	*Aesculus spp.*	vomiting, abdominal pain
Mock orange	*Poncirus spp.*	and diarrhea
Pongam	*Pongamia pinnata*	
Rain tree, monkey pod	*Samonia samen*	
Soapberry	*Sapindus saponaria*	
Yam bean	*Pachyrhizus erosus*	
Bloodberry, baby-pepper	*Rivina humilis*	Immediate vomiting, abdominal pain
Daphne, spurge laurel	*Daphne spp.*	and diarrhea
Iris, flag	*Iris spp.*	
Lords-and-ladies	*Arum spp.*	
Pokeweed	*Phytolacca americana*	

*Reprinted from *First Aid for Pets*, by Robert W. Kirk, DVM, E. P. Dutton & Co., New York, 1978. Adapted from *Plant Toxicity and Dermatitis* by K. F. Lampe and R. Fagerstrom (Baltimore: Williams & Wilkins).

American yew	*Taxus canadensis*	Immediate vomiting,
English yew	*Taxus baccata*	abdominal pain,
Japanese yew	*Taxus cuspidata*	pupil dilation and
Western yew	*Taxus breviflora*	irregular heartbeat
Baneberry	*Actaea spp.*	Immediate vomiting,
Clematis	*Clematis spp.*	diarrhea and rash

IV. Miscellaneous Gastrointestinal Irritants and Cathartics

Bird-of-paradise		Immediate vomiting,
bush	*Poinciana gilliesi*	abdominal pain
Buckthorn	*Rhamnus spp.*	and diarrhea;
Candlenut	*Aleurites spp.*	nervous or kidney
Christmas candle	*Pedilanthus*	involvement
	tithymaloides	follows with some
Clusia	*Clusia rosea*	plants in this
Common box	*Buxus sempervirens*	group
English holly	*Ilex aquifolium*	
Euonymus	*Euonymus spp.*	
Honeysuckle	*Lonicera tatarica*	
Poinsettia	*Euphorbia*	
	pulcherrima	
Privet	*Ligustrum spp.*	
Yellow allamanda	*Allamanda cathartica*	

V. Delayed Gastrointestinal Effects

Black locust	*Robinia pseudoacacia*	Delayed vomiting,
Castor bean	*Ricinus communis*	abdominal pain,
Coral plant	*Jatropha multifida*	diarrhea (followed
Rosary pea,		by constipation with
precatory bean	*Abrus precatorius*	Robinia), depression
Sandbox tree,		or coma and low
monkey pistol	*Hura crepitans*	blood pressure
Bittersweet, woody		Delayed vomiting,
nightshade	*Solanum dulcamara*	abdominal pain,
Chalice vine	*Solandra spp.*	diarrhea and dry
Ground Cherry	*Physalis spp.*	oral mucous
Jerusalem cherry	*Solanum*	membranes in
	pseudocapsicum	Cestrum; cardiac
Jessamine	*Cestrum spp.*	activity with
Potato	*Solanum tuberosum*	Jerusalem cherry
Garden sorrel	*Rumex acetosa*	Delayed vomiting,
Rhubarb	*Rheum rhaponticum*	abdominal pain,
Virginia creeper	*Psedera quinquefolia*	diarrhea, depression
		or coma
Autumn crocus	*Colchicum spp.*	Delayed vomiting,
Glory lily	*Gloriosa spp.*	abdominal pain and
		diarrhea

COMMON NAME	SCIENTIFIC NAME	EARLY SYMPTOMS
VI. Cardiovascular Disturbances		
Foxglove	*Digitalis purpurea*	Immediate nausea
Lily of the valley	*Convallaria majalis*	and vomiting,
Oleander	*Nerium spp.*	abdominal pain,
Yellow oleander	*Thevetia peruviana*	slow and irregular heartbeat
Aconite, monkshood	*Aconitum napeilus*	Immediate nausea, tremors and
Larkspur	*Delphinium spp.*	convulsion, slow
Western monkshood	*Aconitum columbianum*	and irregular heartbeat and difficult breathing
VII. Nicotine-like Action		
Cardinal flower, Indian tobacco	*Lobelia spp.*	Salivation, immediate nausea
Golden chain	*Laburnum anagyroides*	and vomiting, and rapid heartbeat
Kentucky coffee tree	*Gymnocladus dioica*	
Mescal bean	*Sophora spp.*	
Poison hemlock	*Conium maculatum*	
Tobacco	*Nicotiana spp.*	
VIII. Atropine Action		
Angel's-trumpet	*Datura arborea*	Dilated pupils, dry
Belladonna, deadly nightshade	*Atropa belladonna*	mouth, difficult breathing, fever
Henbane	*Hyoscyamus niger*	and rapid
Jessamine	*Cestrum spp.*	heartbeat
Jimson weed, thorn apple	*Datura spp.*	
Matrimony vine	*Lycium halimifolium*	
IX. Convulsants		
Chinaberry	*Melia azedarach*	Convulsions
Coriaria	*Coriaria spp.*	
Moonseed	*Menispermum canadense*	
Nux vomica	*Strychnos nux-vomica*	
Water hemlock	*Cicuta maculata*	
X. Behavioral Alterants, Hallucinogens		
Marijuana	*Cannabis sativa*	Abnormal emotional
Morning-glory	*Ipomoea spp.*	or dispositional
Nutmeg	*Myristica fragrans*	effects
Periwinkle	*Vinca rosea*	
Peyote, mescal	*Lophophora williamsii*	

COMMON NAME	SCIENTIFIC NAME	EARLY SYMPTOMS

XI. Cyanogenetic Action

Apricot, almond, peach, cherry, chokecherry, wild cherry	*Prunus spp.*	Vomiting, stupor, difficult breathing and coma; bright red venous blood
Hydrangea	*Hydrangea macrophylla*	
Japanese plum	*Eriobotrya japonica*	

XII. Contact Irritants or Mechanical Injury

Nettle	*Urtica chamaedryoides*	Salivation, vomiting,
Nettle	*Laportea canadensis*	slow and irregular
Nettle spurge	*Cnidoscolus stimulosus*	heartbeat, difficult breathing
Stinging nettle, bull nettle	*Urtica dioica*	
Blackberry	*Rubus spp.*	Inflamed mouth,
Burdock	*Arctium lappa*	conjunctivitis,
Cacti	Numerous genera	abscesses,
Carolina nightshade	*Solanum carolinense*	fistulous tracts,
Foxtail	*Setaria spp.*	reduced
Goathead	*Tribulus terrestris*	performance,
Honey locust	*Gleditsia triacanthos*	hemorrhage or
Needlegrass	*Stipa spp.*	lameness
Sandbur	*Cenchrus pauciflorus*	
Tripleawn	*Aristida spp.*	
Wild barley	*Hordeum spp.*	
Wild brome	*Bromus spp.*	

2. Some Chemical Products Hazardous to Cats*

ARTS AND CRAFTS SUPPLIES

Antiquing Agents
Methyl ethyl ketone
Turpentine

Pencils, Indelible
Crystal violet

Oil Paints and Tempera Paints
Pigment salts of lead, arsenic, copper, and cadmium

---

*Reprinted from Kirk, *First Aid for Pets*. Adapted from "Some Chemical Products Hazardous to Pets," by Gary D. Osweiler, DVM, in *Current Veterinary Therapy 6*, Robert Kirk, ed., W. B. Saunders Co., Philadelphia, 1977.

PHOTOGRAPHIC SUPPLIES

Developers
Borates
Bromides
Iodides
Thiocyanates

Fixatives
Sodium thiosulfate

Hardeners
Aluminum chloride
Formaldehyde

AUTOMOTIVE AND MACHINERY PRODUCTS

Antifreeze, Fuel System De-icer
Ethylene glycol
Isopropyl alcohol
Methanol
Rust inhibitors
  a. Borates
  b. Chromates
  c. Zinc chloride

Brake Fluids
Butyl ethers of ethylene glycol and
  related glycols
Ethyl ethers of ethylene glycol and
  related glycols
Methyl ethers of ethylene glycol
  and related glycols

Carburetor Cleaners
Cresol
Ethylene dichloride

Corrosion inhibitors
Borates
Sodium chromate
Sodium nitrate

Engine and Motor Cleaners
Cresol
Ethylene dichloride
Methylene chloride

Frost Removers
Ethylene glycol
Isopropyl alcohol

Lubricants
Barium compounds
Isopropyl alcohol
Kerosene
Lead compounds
Stoddard solvent

Motor Fuel
Gasoline
Kerosene
Tetraethyl lead

Radiator Cleaners
Boric acid
Oxalic acid
Sodium chromate

Shock Absorber Fluids
Petroleum ether

Tire Repair
Benzene

Windshield Washer Fluids
Ethylene glycol
Isopropyl alcohol
Methyl alcohol

CLEANERS, DISINFECTANTS, SANITIZERS

Cleaners, Bleaches, Polishes
Ammonium hydroxide
Benzene
Carbon tetrachloride
Hydrochloric acid

Disinfectants, Sanitizers
Acids
Alkalies
Hypochlorites
Iodophors

Cleaners, Bleaches, Polishes cont.
Methyl alcohol
Naphtha
Nitrobenzene
Oxalic acid
Phosphoric acid
Sodium fluoride
Sodium or potassium hydroxide
Sodium hypochlorite
Sodium perborate
Sulfuric acid
Trichloroethane
Turpentine

Disinfectants, Sanitizers cont.
Paradichlorobenzene
Phenol, Cresols
Phenyl mercuric acetate
Pine oil
Quaternary ammonium

HEALTH AND BEAUTY AIDS

Athlete's Foot
Caprylic acid
Copper
Propionic acid
Sodium
Undecylenic acid
Zinc salts

Bath Preparations
Bath oils
Perfume
Sodium lauryl sulfate
Trisodium phosphate

Corn Removers
Phenoxyacetic acid
Salicylic acid

Deodorants and Antiperspirants
Alcohol
Aluminum chloride

Diet Pills
Amphetamines
Diuretics
Thyroid hormone

Eye Makeup
Boric acid
Peach kernel oil

Hair Preparations
Cadmium chloride
Cupric chloride
Dyes, tints
Ferric chloride
Lead acetate

Permanent wave lotions
Pyrogallol
Silver nitrate
Thioglycolic acid

Headache
Aspirin
Phenacetin

Laxatives
Irritant or Stimulant Laxatives
 Aloes
 Aloin
 Cascara sagrada

Liniments
Camphor
Chloroform
Oil of wintergreen (methyl
 salicylate)
Pine oil
Turpentine

Nailetics
Acetone
Alcohol
Benzene
Ethyl acetate
Nail enamel
Nail polish
Nail polish remover
Toluene
Tricresyl phosphate

Ointments
Benzoic acid
Borates
Caprylic acid
Menthol
Mercury compounds
Oil of wintergreen (methyl
  salicylate)
Phenols
Salicylic acid

*Perfumes, Toilet Waters, and
  Colognes*
Alcohol
Essential oils
Floral oils
Perfume essence

Shampoos
Sodium lauryl sulfate
Triethanolamine dodecyl sulfate

Shaving Lotions
Alcohol
Boric acid

Somnolents (Sleeping Pills)
Barbiturates
Bromides

Stimulants
Amphetamine
Caffeine

Suntan Lotions
Alcohol
Tannic acid and derivatives

PAINTS AND RELATED PRODUCTS

Caulking Compounds
Barium
Chlorinated biphenyl
Chromium
Lead
Mineral spirits
Petroleum distillate
Xylene

Driers
Cobalt compounds
Iron compounds
Manganese compounds
Vanadium compounds
Zinc compounds

Lacquer Thinners
Aliphatic hydrocarbons
Butyl acetate
Butyl alcohol
Toluene

Paint
Arsenic oxide
Coal tar
Cuprous oxide
Lead chromate
Petroleum ether
Pine oil

Red lead oxide
Zinc chromate

Paint Brush Cleaners
Benzene
Kerosene
Napathas

Paint and Varnish Cleaners
Ethylene dichloride
Kerosene
Naphthalene
Trisodium phosphate

Paint and Varnish Removers
Flammable
  Benzene
  Cresols
  Phenols
  Toluene
Nonflammable
  Methylene chloride
  Toluene

Preservatives
Brush
  Kerosene
  Turpentine
Canvas
  2-Chlorophenylphenol
  Pentachlorophenol

Floor
  Magnesium fluorosilicate
Wood
  Copper naphthenate
  Copper oleate
  Mineral spirits
  Pentachlorophenol
  Zinc naphthenate

PEST CONTROL

Birds
Endrin
Toluidine

Fungicides
Captan
Copper compounds
Maneb
Mercurials
Pentachlorophenol
Thiram
Zineb

Insects and Spiders
Baygon
Carbaryl
Chlordane
Diazinon
Dichlorvos
Kelthane
Mirex
Paradichlorobenzene
Pyrethrins

Rotenone
Toxaphene

Lawn and Garden Weeds
Arsenic
Chlordane
Dacthal
Pentachlorophenol
Trifluralin
2,4-D

Rats, Mice, Gophers, Moles
Arsenic
Barium carbonate
Dicoumarol
Phosphorus
Sodium fluoroacetate
Strychnine
Thallium (rare)
Warfarin
Zinc phosphide

Snails, Slugs
Metaldehyde

SAFETY PRODUCTS

Fire Extinguishers
Liquid Fire Extinguishers
  Carbon tetrachloride
Miscellaneous Fire Extinguishers
  Methylbromide

Powder Extinguishers
  Borax compounds

Nonskid Products
Stoddard solvent
Methyl ethyl ketone

SOLVENTS

Alcohols

Chlorinated Solvents
Carbon tetrachloride
Methylene chloride
Orthodichlorobenzene
Trichloroethylene

Esters
Amyl acetate
Ethyl acetate
Isopropyl acetate
Methyl acetate

Hydrocarbons
Aromatics, chiefly benzene,
   toluene, and xylene
Naphthenes

Ketones
Acetone
Methyl ethyl ketone

Other Common Solvents
Aniline
Carbon disulphide
Cresylic acid
Kerosene
Mineral spirits
Phenols
Turpentine

3. Directory of Animal Behavior Consultants

This is a listing of animal behavior consultants with demonstrated expertise in the diagnosis and treatment of animal behavior problems, and includes only those practitioners/researchers with terminal degrees (or Ph.D. in progress) in animal behavior or other behavioral science. If no consultants are listed for your state, consult your veterinarian or local chapter of the Veterinary Medical Association for a referral. I have not listed those individuals with a preference for treating dogs, and I apologize for the omission of any individuals who feel that they should have been included.

CALIFORNIA:

Ian Dunbar, Ph.D.
San Francisco SPCA
Animal Behavior Clinic
2500 16th Street
San Francisco, CA 94103
(415) 621-1700 Ext. 6

Affiliated with the Department of Psychology, University of California at Berkeley. Serves the San Francisco Bay and Northern California areas.

Benjamin C. Hart, D.V.M., Ph.D.
Lynette A. Hart, Ph.D.
Behavioral Science Veterinary Medical Teaching Hospital
University of California
Davis, CA 95616
(916) 752-1418

Both are affiliated with the Department of Physiological Sciences, School of Veterinary Medicine, at the University of California at Davis, and serve the area of Northern California.

Richard H. Polsky, Ph.D.
Animal Behavior Counseling Service
11251 Greenlawn Avenue
Culver City, CA 90230
(213) 398-2556

Serves the area of Beverly Hills and Malibu.

COLORADO:

Philip N. Lehner, Ph.D.
Suzanne Arguello, M.S.

Animal Behavior Assoc., Inc.
P.O. Box 8473
Fort Collins, CO 80525
(303) 493-0415

Dr. Lehner is affiliated with the Zoology Department of Colorado State University, Fort Collins, CO 80525, (303) 491-7011. Both practitioners serve the area of Colorado and southern Wyoming.

Jack C. Hunsberger, Ph.D.
Animal Behavior Consultants
5034 S. Youngfield Court
Morrison, CO 80465

Stephen W. Horn, Ph.D.
Consultants in Animal Behavior
55 Hoyt Street
Lakewood, CO 80226
(303) 237-6683

Dr. Horn serves the Denver area.

FLORIDA:

Walter F. Burghardt, Jr., D.V.M., Ph.D.
10010 N.W. 11th Manor
Coral Springs, FL 33065
(305) 753-8759

Serves the area from Miami to West Palm Beach.

GEORGIA:

Sharon Crowell-Davis, D.V.M., Ph.D.
Teaching Hospital
College of Veterinary Medicine
University of Georgia
Athens, GA 30602
(404) 542-3221 ext. 303

Serves areas in Georgia and the Southeastern U.S.A.

John C. Wright, Ph.D.
Animal Behavior Therapist
P.O. Box 180 MU
Macon, GA 31207
(404) 524-5500 (Atlanta)
(912) 742-2538 (Macon)

Affiliated with the Psychology Department, College of Liberal Arts, Mercer University, Macon, Georgia 31207, (912) 744-2973. Serves the area of central Georgia and Atlanta.

INDIANA:

Eric Klinghammer, Ph.D.
Animal Behavior Advisory Service
Battle Ground, IN 47920
(317) 567-2098

Affiliated with Purdue University Department of Psychological Services, Laboratory of Zoology, West Lafayette, Indiana 47907, (317) 494-6279. Serves the Midwest.

MARYLAND:

Ginger Hamilton, Ph.D.
Consultants in Animal Psychology
1508 Vivian Court
Silver Springs, MD 20902
(301) 649-6337

Serves the Washington, D.C., area, Maryland, Virginia, Southern Pennsylvania and southern West Virginia.

MICHIGAN:

Eli Barlia, Ph.D.
Hunters Creek Animal Behavior Clinic
P.O. Box 10
Metamora, MI 48455
(313) 664-9399

Affiliated with the Department of Psychology, Wayne State University, Detroit, MI 48202, (313) 577-2800. Serves the area of Detroit and Flint.

New York:

Peter L. Borchelt, Ph.D.
Animal Behavior Consultants, Inc.
108–25 63rd Road
Forest Hills, NY 11375
(212) 275-9505

Affiliated with The Animal Medical Center, 510 E. 62nd Street, New York, New York 10021 (212) 838-8100. Serves the New York City area.

Kathryn A. Houpt, V.M.D., Ph.D.
Animal Behavior Clinic
Department of Physiology
New York School of Veterinary Medicine
Cornell University
Ithaca, NY 14853
(607) 256-5454 ext. 2450

Serves the area of upstate New York, Maryland and Ottawa, Canada.

North Carolina:

Margaret Sery Young, Ph.D.
Donna S. Brown, Ph.D.
North Carolina State University
School of Veterinary Medicine
4700 Hillsborough Street
Raleigh, NC 27606
(919) 829-4200 ext. 439

Both serve the Raleigh, Durham and Chapel Hill areas.

Ohio:

David Hothersall, Ph.D.
Animal Behavior Associates
1853 H. Kenny Road
Columbus, OH 43220
(614) 486-2242

Affiliated with the Department of Psychology, Ohio State University, Columbus, Ohio 43210, (614) 422-5114. Serves the Columbus area.

David Tuber, Ph.D.
Animal Behavior Associates
1853 H. Kenney Road
Columbus, OH 43220
(614) 486-2242

Affiliated with the Department of Psychology, Ohio State University, Columbus, Ohio 43210, (614) 422-6512. Serves the Columbus, Dayton and central Ohio areas.

PENNSYLVANIA:

Victoria L. Voith, D.V.M., Ph.D.
Animal Behavior Clinic
Department of Clinical Studies
School of Veterinary Medicine
University of Pennsylvania
Philadelphia, PA 19104
(215) 898-4515

Serves Pennsylvania.

VIRGINIA:

Suzanne B. Johnson, M.S., Ph.D. (ip)
Route 2, Box 66
Beaverdam, VA 23015
(804) 270-9310

Serves Virginia, Washington, D.C., and Maryland.

Please understand that this list was up to date at the time this book went to press, and that changes in address and additions or deletions are not predictable. Dr. John C. Wright, whose name is included on this list, can be contacted should you have any difficulty reaching one of these Animal Behavior Consultants.

Your veterinarian may suggest a consultation with someone not on this list. There are a number of individuals throughout the country who are in this category, and who may be very helpful to you with a behavior problem. My choice in not listing some of them is in no way meant to be interpreted as a personal judgment that they are not capable of aiding in the solution and treatment of some animal behavior problems. However, as stated at the top of this list, I felt it best to limit the list herein to only those individuals with terminal degrees (or Ph.D. in progress) actively involved in animal behavior practice/research.

INDEX

lice, 180, 210
liquid medications, 125–27
litter boxes, 22–23
  design of, 40–41
  kittens' use of, 107
  location of, 41
  odor control for, 41
  toxoplasmosis and, 256–57
  for travel, 78
litter materials:
  changing of, 41, 91
  disliked by cat, 88–89
  types of, 41
liver, examination of, 50
liver disease, 208
lungs, punctured, 149
lungworms, 222
lymph nodes, examination of, 48
lymphoma, 245, 247
lymphosarcoma, 245

maggots, 210–11
Manx, 218
marijuana, 186
mastitis, 109
mating, 96–97
  competition created by, 150
  ovulation induced by, 96
medical records, 51, 113
Memorial Sloan Kettering Cancer
    Center, 246
metastasis, 208, 245
metritis, 229
milk, mother's:
  discolored, 109
  insufficient, 105, 108
  shunning of, 109
  substitutes for, 57, 108, 109
mineral oil, 125, 172
mineral supplements, 53
mites, *Cheyletiella*, 207, 210
mosquito bites, 180
mouth:
  burns on, 162, 183
  examination of, 35, 48
mouth-to-nose resuscitation, 146–47

National Veterinary Laboratory, 246
neck traumas, 172–74
neoplasms, 244
nervous system disorders, 230–32
neurodermatitis, 205
neutering, 34, 99–100
  aggressive behavior decreased by,
    93, 100
  importance of, 72–74, 101

optimum age for, 99
postoperative care for, 120
spraying decreased by, 87, 100
weight gain and, 74
nictitating membrane, 116, 163, 165
  protrusion of, 241
nose:
  discharge from, 35
  solar dermatitis on, 179
nursing:
  from bottles, 57–58
  after delivery, 105–6
nutrition, 53

obesity, 222
obstipation, 172, 218
occlusion, of distal artery, 203
ophthalmoscopes, 48
ovarian cancer, 98
ovariohysterectomy (OHE),
    see spaying
ovulation, induced, 96

pancreas, 212
parasites:
  external, 208–11
  internal, 219–22
  intestinal, 35, 51, 171
patent ductus arteriosis, 202
pentobarbital, 264
perineal urethrostomy, 224–26
Persians, 67, 111, 163, 175, 242
pet cemeteries, 265
Pet Loss and Human Bereavement, 265
*Pet Loss: A Thoughtful Guide for Adults
    and Children* (Nieburg and
    Fischer), 266
petroleum products, poisoning by,
    184–85
pets, as health assets, 22
pet stores, 30
phosphate enemas, 126
pills, 123–25
pilo erection, 93
pinworms, 222
placenta (afterbirth), 104
plants:
  eating of, 61–62, 83, 170
  poisonous, 61–62, 129, 186, 268–71
pleural effusion, 235, 251
pneumonia, 234
pneumothorax, 149, 235
Poison Control Centers, 184
poisoning, 183–96
  by drugs, 186
  by ingestion, 183–85

before cat shows, 79
against feline distemper, 46–47,
233, 249–50, 252
against feline leukemia virus, 248–
249
for kittens, 107
during pregnancy, 102
against rabies, 47, 74, 254
three-in-one, 47, 233
Valium, 186
vestibular syndrome, 231
veterinarians, 44–46
emergency facilities of, 45–
46
interviewing of, 45
veterinary examinations, 48–
52
vitamin K, 187
vitamin supplements, 53
for nursing mothers, 106
during pregnancy, 102
Voith, Victoria L., 90
vomiting, 115, 169–70, 215–18
dehydration and, 170
first aid for, 170
induced, 135, 185

warfarin, 186, 241
wasp stings, 179–80
water, 53, 56
changes in consumption of, 113,
115
dishes for, 40, 77
heatstroke and, 175
weight, 50, 113, 262–63
When Your Pet Dies (Quackenbush
and Graveline), 266
whiskers, 67
windows:
falls from, 141
open, 60–61
wounds, 196–99
closed, 196
disinfection of, 135
to ears, 238
on feet, 199
open, 196
puncture, *see* puncture wounds
shearing, 198

X-rays (radiographs), 50

yellow jacket stings, 179–80